Listening to Children and Young People with Speech, Language and Communication Needs

D1211861

© 2011 J&R Press Ltd

All rights reserved. No part of this publication may be reproduced, stored in a retrieval system or transmitted in any form or by any means, electronic, mechanical, photocopying, recording, scanning or otherwise, except under the terms of the Copyright Designs and Patents Act 1988 or under the terms of a licence issued by the Copyright Licensing Agency Ltd, without the permission in writing of the Publisher. Requests to the Publisher should be addressed to J&R Press Ltd, Farley Heath Cottage, Albury, Guildford GU5 9EW, or emailed to rachael_jrpress@btinternet.com.

The use of general descriptive names, registered names, trademarks, etc. in this publication does not imply, even in the absence of a specific statement, that such names are exempt from the relevant protective laws and regulations and therefore free for general use.

Library of Congress Cataloguing in Publication Data

British Library Cataloguing in Publication Data

A catalogue record for this book is available from the British Library

Cover design: Abigail Beverly and Jim Wilkie

Copy-editing: Nikky Twyman; nikky.twyman@talktalk.net

Project management, typesetting and design: J&R Publishing Services Ltd, Guildford, Surrey, UK; www.jr-publishingservices.co.uk

Printed and bound by CPI Group (UK) Ltd, Croydon, CR0 4YY

Listening to Children and Young People with Speech, Language and Communication Needs

Sue Roulstone and Sharynne McLeod
(Editors)

J&R Press Ltd

Contents

Part III: Examples   153

About the Editors

Professor Sue Roulstone leads a team of researchers at the Speech & Language Therapy Research Unit, North Bristol NHS Trust, and the University of West of England, Bristol, UK. She is an elected fellow of the Royal College of Speech and Language Therapists and was Chair of the RCSLT (2004–2006). Professor Roulstone contributes regularly to national clinical and policy debates and has contributed to a number of national consultations with parents and children, including the *Bercow Report*.

Professor Sharynne McLeod, of Charles Sturt University, Australia, is an elected fellow of Speech Pathology Australia and the American Speech-Language-Hearing Association. She is the editor of the *International Journal of Speech-Language Pathology* and vice president of the International Clinical Phonetics and Linguistics Association. She provided advice on the World Health Organization's *International Classification of Functioning, Disability and Health – Children and Youth* and her research foregrounds strategies for enabling children to communicate and participate.

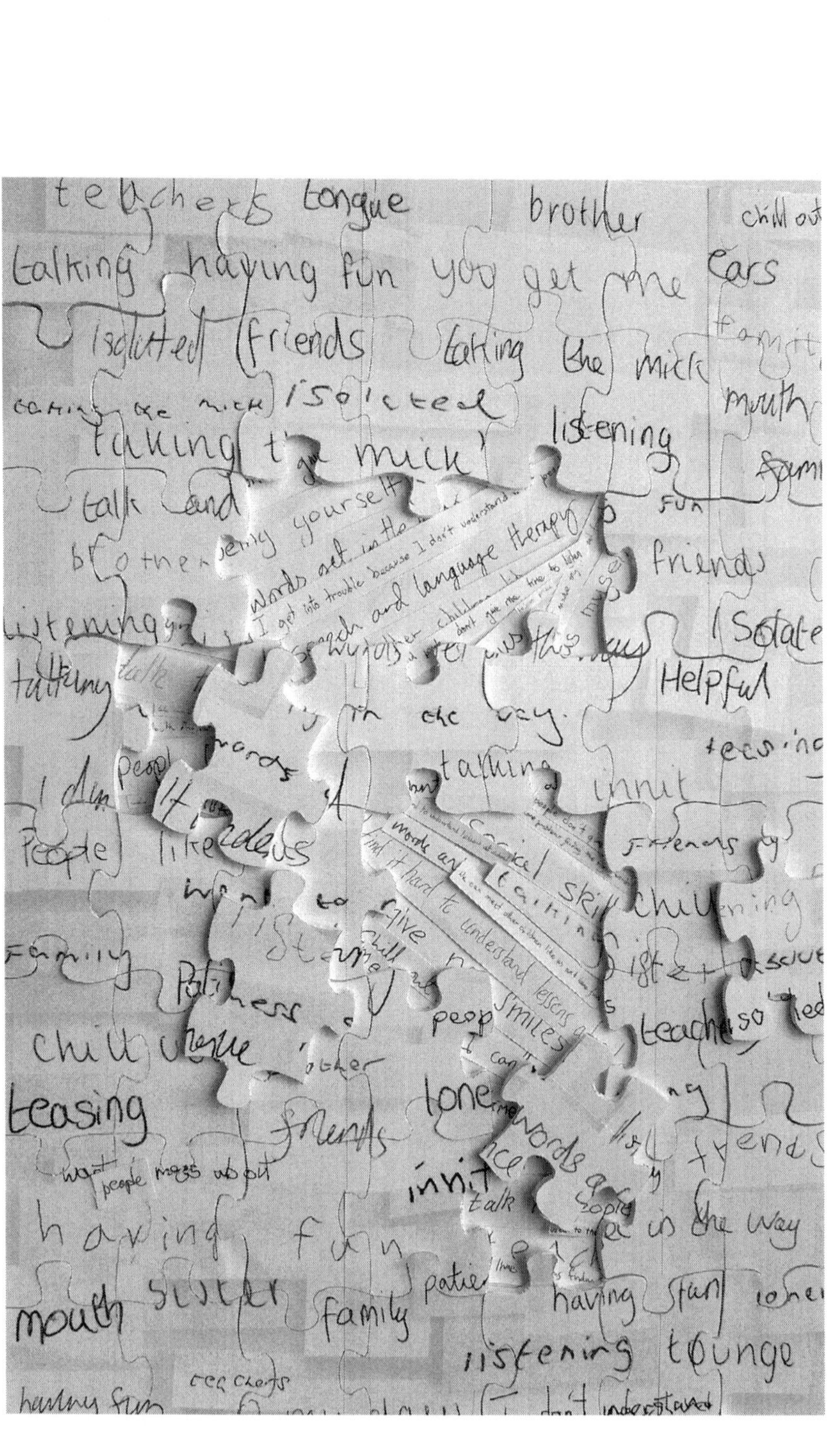

tongue
brother
chill out
talking
having fun
you get me
cars
friends
talking the mick
mouth
listening
speech and language therapy
I get into trouble because I don't understand
friends
Helpful
talking
innit
People
social skills
Family
teasing
friends
innit
having fun
mouth
sister
family
having fun
listening
tounge
I don't understand

About the Cover

Sue Roulstone and Sharynne McLeod invited me to design the illustration for the book cover. I wanted to develop some of the ideas behind my *Making Sense of the Puzzle* artwork, where I tried to convey what it is like for someone who has a speech and language difficulty when they are confronted with lots of 'words'. For the design I wanted to capture actual words that might come from children and young people of different ages, so I asked a group of 6- to 19-year-olds to write out different words of their choice. We then took these words and made a collage of them on to a jigsaw puzzle, which we then cut up to give a 3D effect. I like the physical nature of this puzzle. You get a sense of what it is actually like to use words, as if they were jigsaw pieces, to try to construct a sentence. It is like handling the words – playing around with them to try to get them to fit together to make sense.

Abigail Beverly
London

Acknowledgements

First, we acknowledge those children, young people, and their families, who participated in the research that is summarized in this volume. It is our sincere hope that we have listened to you respectfully, and have gained insights that will enable us to provide more responsive speech and language therapy services and to conduct more sensitive research in order to enhance the lives of all children and young people with speech, language and communication needs.

Second, we are grateful to all of the authors for their enthusiastic participation in this book. Many of them also presented the initial ideas for their chapters at a seminar held in July 2010 at the University of the West of England in Bristol. Those initial discussions played a significant role in shaping the book and determining its content; the quality that was evident made us certain this would be an exciting project.

Next, we thank Rachael and Jim Wilkie at J&R Press for their enthusiasm for the project, and for breaking new ground by publishing this comprehensive book. We also thank Hannah Wilkin for her editorial assistance.

Sue acknowledges support from the Underwood Trust and from the Centre for Health and Clinical Research at the University of the West of England, Bristol. She is indebted to colleagues at the Speech & Language Therapy Research Unit, Frenchay Hospital for their ongoing support and to her family for their stimulating discussions and unconditional support.

Sharynne acknowledges support from the Australian Research Council Future Fellowship (FT0990588) and the Research Institute for Professional Practice, Learning and Education (RIPPLE) at Charles Sturt University, Australia. She also acknowledges the support, encouragement and insights gained from listening to her family: David, Brendon and Jessica.

About the Contributors

Jacqueline Barr is a PhD student in the School of Teacher Education at Charles Sturt University, a primary school teacher, and a disability services client consultant. Her PhD studies investigate the needs of siblings of children with disabilities within school settings. Email: jbarr@csu.edu.au

Rt Hon John Bercow is the Member of Parliament for Buckingham and Speaker of the House of Commons. In 2007, he was appointed by the Secretary of State for Children, Schools and Families to lead a review of services for children and young people with speech, language and communication needs. The report was published in 2008. He is President of Afasic, a UK charity working to support parents, children and young people with communication impairments.

Ali Berquez has worked as a specialist speech and language therapist at the Michael Palin Centre since 2000. She completed a Post Graduate Diploma in Cognitive Behavioural Therapy from Oxford University in 2005. Her current role involves clinical work with children, teenagers and adults, teaching and contributing to research projects. She currently coordinates the Centre's national teaching programe about stammering and was joint project lead for the Stammering Information Programme, funded by the Department for Education. Email: ali.berquez@nhs.net

Abigail Beverly is a graduate of Central St Martin's, London, UK, and gained a distinction in her thesis 'How we understand words', which was based on having grown up with a speech and language disorder. She is a volunteer with Afasic Youth Project, specializing in art workshops designed to encourage members to develop their language skills via creative activities. Email: abigailrbeverly@aol.com

Ben S. Bradley, PhD is professor of psychology at Charles Sturt University, Australia. His book *Visions of Infancy* (Polity Press, 1989) argues that infancy research too easily becomes a screen for theorists' own preoccupations, rather than examining infants' experience. With Jane Selby he is pioneering a group-psychological paradigm for the study of early sociability. Email: bbradley@csu.edu.au

Bonnie Brinton, PhD is professor of communication disorders at Brigham Young University, Utah, USA. She served as dean of graduate studies from 1999 to 2009 and is a fellow of the American Speech-Language-Hearing

Association. Her research focuses on the social and emotional competence of children with language impairment. Email: bonnie_brinton@byu.edu

Karen Bryan is Head of the Division of Health and Social Care, University of Surrey, UK. She developed and evaluated a speech-language therapy service for young offenders in two prisons, and recently evaluated this within a Youth Offending Team. She is a consultant speech and language therapist in forensic mental health. Email: k.bryan@surrey.ac.uk

Catherine Carroll is senior lecturer in special and inclusive education at Roehampton University, UK. She has previously taught in secondary mainstream and special schools. Email: Catherine.Carroll@roehampton.ac.uk

Jane Coad, PhD is a professor in children and family nursing at Coventry University, leading a programme of research around children, young people and families who have long-term, complex and palliative care needs. Jane has a background in both art and children's nursing, with an extensive portfolio in undertaking arts-based participatory research with children and families including consultation, collaborative and user-led projects. Her work has also included several projects with children and young people who have a range of speech, language and communication needs. Email: jane.coad@coventry.ac.uk

Frances Cook is a specialist speech and language therapist and the Head of Service at the Michael Palin Centre, London, UK. She has extensive experience in the field of stammering in children and adults. She has studied speech and language therapy to master's level and has a certificate in Cognitive Behaviour Therapy. She has contributed to the development of therapy programmes and has written manuals, books, chapters and articles in peer-reviewed publications. Frances has participated in the training of speech and language therapists at the Centre, as well as around the UK and internationally. She has also presented at international conferences in the field of stammering and contributes to the research programme at the Centre. Email: frances.cook@islingtonpct.nhs.uk

Tillie Curran, PhD is a senior lecturer in social work at the University of the West of England, Bristol, UK. Her research is around social work with disabled children and research use in children's services. Her teaching interests include understandings of disabled children's childhoods, and children and families' participation in education and practice. Email: tillie.curran@uwe.ac.uk

Michael Curtin, EdD, is associate professor of occupational therapy at Charles Sturt University, Australia. His research interests primarily have an interpretative phenomenological focus and broadly explore the interaction of health professionals working with people with disabilities, particularly in regional and rural Australia. Email: mcurtin@csu.edu.au

Jane Dalrymple, PhD is a senior lecturer at the University of the West of England, Bristol, UK. She worked as a social worker in children's services for over 20 years and was director of a national children's advocacy service for five years. Her research and writing primarily focus on advocacy and children's rights. Email: Jane.dalrymple@uwe.ac.uk

Graham Daniel, PhD is a lecturer in child development and educational psychology at Charles Sturt University, Australia. His research focuses on the role of family–school partnerships in supporting students' schooling experiences and learning. Email: gdaniel@csu.edu.au

Clare Davies-Jones has been a Development Officer with Afasic (London, UK) since 1996 and set up the Afasic Youth Project in 1999. She has a background in developing services for children and young people – including user consultation both with the children and young people and their families – in statutory and voluntary sectors. Email: claredj@afasicengland.org.uk

Julie E. Dockrell, PhD is professor of psychology and special needs at the Institute of Education, London, UK. A central theme of her research is the application of evidence-based practice and evaluating interventions to support children with speech, language and communication needs in educational settings. Email: jdockrell@ioe.ac.uk

Sheena Elwick is a full-time doctoral student with Charles Sturt University, Australia. Her background includes working as an early childhood teacher in long day care and mobile settings throughout regional and rural New South Wales and Victoria, and also as a primary school teacher in regional Victoria. Email: selwick@csu.edu.au

Martin Fujiki, PhD is professor of communication disorders at Brigham Young University, Utah, USA. He is a fellow of the American Speech-Language-Hearing Association, and currently serves as associate editor for the journal *Language, Speech, and Hearing Services in Schools*. His research focuses on the social interactions of children with language impairment. Email: martin_fujiki@byu.edu

Juliet Goldbart, PhD lectures in developmental psychology at Manchester Metropolitan University, UK. Her research interests include communication and intellectual disability, augmentative and alternative communication (AAC), working with families, and service delivery models in the UK and India. Her report *Communication and People with the Most Complex Needs: What Works and Why This is Essential* was published in December 2010 (http://www.mencap.org.uk/page.asp?id=1539). Email: j.goldbart@mmu.ac.uk

Joy Goodfellow, PhD has had extensive experience in the field of early childhood as a researcher, academic, early childhood consultant, mentor and practitioner. She is currently involved in the Infants' Lives in Child Care project at Charles Sturt University, Australia, where she is particularly interested in methodologies that enable researchers to 'listen' to pre-linguistic infants. Email: jgoodfellow@bigpond.com

Helen Hambly, MSc is a health psychologist with an interest in improving support and outcomes for children with speech, language and communication needs. She is studying for a PhD at the University of the West of England, Bristol, UK, examining experiences and aspirations of children with primary language impairment, their families' aspirations for their child and the aspirations of the professionals who support them. Email: helen.hambly@speech-therapy.org.uk

Linda J. Harrison, PhD is Associate Professor of Early Childhood Education at Charles Sturt University, Australia. Her research has investigated infant, toddler and preschoolers' experiences of child care/early education, quality in centre-based child care, and the broad determinants of socio-emotional, cognitive and speech-language development. She is a founding member of the Research Consortium that is responsible for the design of the Longitudinal Study of Australian Children (LSAC). Email: lharrison@csu.edu.au

Erin Holliday is a schoolteacher who completed her BEd (Primary) at Charles Sturt University, Australia, in 2008 with Class 1 Honours. Her Honours project incorporated the analysis of drawings completed by 4- to 5-year-old children with speech impairment. Email: erin.laura.holliday@gmail.com

Elaine Kelman is a specialist speech and language therapist at the Michael Palin Centre, London, UK, and has extensive experience in the field of stammering in children and adults. She has studied speech and language therapy to master's level and has an additional qualification in Cognitive Behaviour Therapy. Elaine has contributed to the development of therapy programmes and has written manuals, books, chapters and articles. She has participated in the training of speech and language therapists at the Centre, as well as around the UK and internationally, and has presented at international conferences in the field of stammering and contributes to the research programme at the Centre. Email: elaine.kelman@islingtonpct.nhs.uk

Linda Lascelles is the Chief Executive Officer of Afasic, London, UK, an organization that supports children with speech and language difficulties and their families. Linda has been involved with the special educational needs (SEN) voluntary sector for the past 20 years. She received an Honorary Fellowship of the Royal College of Speech and Language Therapy (RCSLT) for her role in a number of important RCSLT and government projects to improve services for children and young people with speech, language and communication needs. Email: lindal@afasic.org.uk

Wendy Lee is a speech and language therapist, and has worked predominantly in educational contexts during her 25-year career, with some time working as a senior lecturer training speech and language therapists. Since 2007, she has worked in the third sector, currently with The Communication Trust, London, UK, as professional director. Email: wlee@thecommunicationtrust.org.uk

Ann Lewis, PhD is emeritus professor at the University of Birmingham, UK, where she was research leader for a unique, 35-strong academic group focusing on children with special needs or disabilities. She is also honorary professor at the University of Warwick, and has a longstanding interest in the 'voice' of disabled children. Email: a.lewis@bham.ac.uk

Geoff Lindsay, PhD is director of the Centre for Educational Development, Appraisal and Research (CEDAR), University of Warwick, UK, and professor of special needs education and educational psychology. He was previously principal educational psychologist for Sheffield. Email: Geoff.Lindsay@warwick.ac.uk

Rena Lyons is a senior lecturer in the discipline of speech and language therapy in National University of Ireland Galway (NUI Galway). She has a particular interest in listening to the perspectives of children with speech, language and communication needs and this is the topic of her PhD studies in University of the West of England, Bristol. Email: rena.lyons@nuigalway.ie

Lindy McAllister, PhD is professor and associate dean in the Faculty of Health Sciences, The University of Sydney. She was previously deputy head (teaching and learning) of the School of Medicine at The University of Queensland and prior to that was head of the speech pathology programme at Charles Sturt University, Australia. She researches service delivery issues, clinical education and applications of qualitative research to practice development. Email: Lindy.McAllister@sydney.edu.au

Jane McCormack, PhD is a lecturer at Charles Sturt University, Australia. Her research has investigated the experiences of individuals with speech impairment and their families, and the impact of speech impairment on participation throughout the lifespan. Email: jmccormack@csu.edu.au

Sharynne McLeod, PhD is professor of speech and language acquisition at Charles Sturt University, Australia. She is a Fellow of Speech Pathology Australia and of the American Speech-Language-Hearing Association. She provided advice on the World Health Organization's *International Classification of Functioning, Disability and Health – Children and Youth* and her research foregrounds strategies for enabling children to communicate and participate. Email: smcleod@csu.edu.au

Chris Markham, PhD is a senior lecturer in speech and language therapy at the University of Portsmouth, UK, where he carries out teaching and research in children's speech, language and communication needs. Email: chris.markham@port.ac.uk

Julie Marshall, PhD lectures in speech and language therapy at Manchester Metropolitan University, UK. Her research interests include cultural influences in speech, language and communication needs, family perspectives, service provision in countries with limited or no speech and language therapy, and augmentative and alternative communication (AAC). Email: j.e.marshall@mmu.ac.uk

Rosalind Merrick PhD has worked as a children's speech and language therapist in schools and health clinics, and has published articles on the subject. She has also interviewed children about their experiences, and her recent doctorate explored children's views of communication. Email: Rosalind.Merrick@uwe.ac.uk

Clodagh Miskelly, PhD is an independent researcher and workshop facilitator who specializes in participatory research and participatory media methods. She facilitates, researches, evaluates and manages projects that use these methods for social change in projects with children, young people and adults in a range of contexts in the UK and internationally. Email: miskellaneous@hotmail.com

Sandra Neumann, PhD is postdoctoral research fellow at the University of Cologne and at the Institute of Neuroscience and Medicine (INM-3), Cognitive Neurology Section, at the Research Centre Juelic in Germany. Her main research focuses on children with cleft palate speech. She developed the first speech assessment for clients with cleft palate speech in German-speaking countries (*LKGSF komplex*, Neumann, 2011). Email: sandra.neumann@uni-koeln.de

Barry Percy-Smith, PhD is reader in childhood and participatory practice at the University of the West of England, Bristol, UK. He has extensive experience of using participatory action inquiry approaches in research, evaluation and development projects with children, young people and professionals to develop children's participation and improve services across the public sector. He is co-editor of *A Handbook of Children's Participation* (Routledge). Email: Barry.percy-smith@uwe.ac.uk

Frances Press, PhD is senior lecturer at Charles Sturt University, Australia. She has a longstanding interest in early childhood education policy and its influence on the experiences of children and families in early education settings. Email: fpress@csu.edu.au

David John Ramsbotham, Baron Ramsbotham, GCB, CBE, served in the British Army from 1952 to 1993, retiring in the rank of general. He was Her Majesty's Chief Inspector of Prisons from 1995 to 2001. He sits as a crossbench member of the House of Lords, where he concentrates on penal reform, and chairs the All Party Group on Speech and Language Difficulties.

Hazel Roddam, PhD is Chair of Council (2010–2012) at the Royal College of Speech and Language Therapists (RCSLT). She is a speech and language therapist with extensive experience of working within the UK National Health Service and local authority contexts with children who have special educational needs. Hazel currently works as a researcher at the University of Central Lancashire. Email: HRoddam@uclan.ac.uk

Sue Roulstone, PhD is the Underwood Trust Professor of Language and Communication Impairment at the University of the West of England, Bristol, UK. She also leads the research programme at the Speech &

Language Therapy Research Unit at Frenchay Hospital, Bristol. Email: susan.roulstone@uwe.ac.uk

Dixie D. Sanger, PhD is a professor of speech-language pathology at the University of Nebraska-Lincoln, USA. Her areas of interest include: exploring the communication behaviours of adolescents residing in correctional facilities, addressing the needs of struggling learners through Response To Intervention, and working with children and adolescents with language and literacy problems. Email: dsanger1@unl.edu

Lucie Shanahan is the speech and language therapist with the Kids' Team at the South West Brain Injury Rehabilitation Service in Albury, Australia. Lucie is also completing a Doctor of Health Science with Charles Sturt University, and her research has investigated adolescents' perception of their executive functioning skills following traumatic brain injury. Email: lucie.shanahan@gsahs.health.nsw.gov.au

Robbie Simons is a student with Asperger's Syndrome who was a participant in the *Speech and Language Therapy Research Project*. He is currently studying on a health and social care course at a college of further education.

Pamela C. Snow, PhD is an associate professor at Monash University, Australia, and both a psychologist and a speech pathologist. Her research concerns the role of oral language competence and risk in early life. She has published extensively on language difficulties in high-risk children and youth, in particular on young offenders, and also on children undergoing investigative interviews. Email: pamela.snow@monash.edu

Tina Stratigos is a full-time doctoral student with Charles Sturt University, Australia. Her background includes working as an early childhood teacher in preschool and primary-school settings in Sydney, New South Wales. Email: tstratigos@csu.edu.au

Jennifer Sumsion, PhD is foundation professor of early childhood education in the School of Teacher Education at Charles Sturt University, Australia. Her research interests lie in the use of innovative theoretical, methodological, pedagogical and collaborative approaches to address enduring challenges within early childhood education research, policy and practice. Email: jsumsion@csu.edu.au

Andrea Wershof is a psychotherapist and the mother of a teenage daughter with Asperger's Syndrome. She speaks publicly, to many audiences, about what it is like to be the parent of a child with special needs, and runs workshops for other parents in how to manage difficult feelings so that they can be effective advocates for their children.

Mary Wickenden, PhD worked as a speech and language therapist, mainly with preschool children with severe and complex disabilities, before moving into academia to teach speech and language therapy students. Work in Asia precipitated her change of discipline and PhD training in anthropology. She currently teaches and researches about children, disability, culture and health in global contexts at University College London, UK. Email: m.wickenden@ich.ucl.ac.uk

Foreword

I am really delighted to be able to offer an introduction to this very important volume. This book explores new territory and with a depth that has not been attempted so far in the academic literature. However, it is more than an exercise in theory (as important as ideas in the abstract are) but is also a practical handbook for professionals. It deserves the widest possible audience.

The fundamental principle behind all of these essays is that children and young people with speech, language and communications needs have, potentially, within them many of the answers to the questions which others are posing about them. Despite this, they tend to be ignored, as if in some sense they are silent victims rather than active participants in their own situation. I became aware of the challenges in this field during my time leading the Bercow Review into many of these issues, an experience which was among the most rewarding of my professional life. My assessment here is reinforced by my experience as a parent of a child who faces communication challenges. We have to bring children and young people into this debate, rather than treat them as outsiders from it.

It is for this reason that I am so pleased to be able to associate my name with the pioneering thoughts that are set out here. It is especially appropriate that this book is to be published during the National Year of Speech, Language and Communication. Although more attention has been paid to this sphere in recent years, it remains the case that much of what children and young people endure and the efforts made by professionals on their behalf are a complete mystery to the majority of the public. This is still a cause which has not fully entered the mainstream of our public discourse, and I have been determined to do all that I can from the position of Speaker of the House of Commons to draw attention to it and, wherever possible, to allow others within the professional community a platform to make their case. Parliament, of all places, should be at the heart of efforts to ensure that all can communicate.

If that noble end is to be realized, then the children themselves have to be centre stage of our discussions. Professors Sue Roulstone and Sharynne McLeod are absolutely determined to achieve this, and the evidence assembled here will be invaluable to that endeavour. In years to come I suspect it will, rightly, seem strange that it took so long to produce a book in which children and young people with communication difficulties were to the fore rather than being under the microscope. The material that can be found here will surely make the case for repeating this exercise many times over. There is so much more that we could, and should, be doing to improve the lives of these individuals. I am completely confident that this book will be a seminal contribution to that crucial cause.

Rt Hon John Bercow MP
Speaker of the House of Commons
2011

Preface

In 1989 the *United Nations Convention on the Rights of the Child* was published. Two articles in this convention challenged adults to listen to the views of children and young people.

Article 12

Parties shall assure to the child who is capable of forming his or her own views the right to express those views freely in all matters affecting the child, the views of the child being given due weight in accordance with the age and maturity of the child (UNICEF, 1989, p. 4).

Article 13

The child shall have the right to freedom of expression; this right shall include freedom to seek, receive and impart information and ideas of all kinds, regardless of frontiers, either orally, in writing or in print, in the form of art, or through any other media of the child's choice (UNICEF, 1989, p. 4).

Since 1989, the importance of listening to children and young people has received considerable attention in the literature, but little has been written about the particular challenges of listening to those with speech, language and communication needs.

This book profiles the voice of the children and young people with speech, language and communication needs. Throughout the book, many examples of children's opinions and thoughts are included, delivered via a range of frontiers, including art, photographs and quotes. Fifty people have contributed chapters to this book, providing insights from speech and language therapists, social workers, psychologists, teachers, researchers, advocates, parents and young people with speech, language and communication needs.

Part I provides views about the importance of listening to children written by advocates for children with speech, language and communication needs.

Part II unpacks the complexities and issues, providing theoretical perspectives about the listening process.

Part III contains real-life examples of listening to children and young people through structured reports of research and clinical projects. One of the aims of this part is to document a range of creative techniques and solutions for listening to children and young people. Additionally, Part III includes key messages from children and young people with speech, language and communication needs about their lives, and their insights into how services can be improved to better accommodate their needs.

It is our hope that this book will provide direction for health, education and social care services to enhance the lives of children and young people with speech, language and communication needs.

Sue Roulstone, Bristol, UK
Sharynne McLeod, Bathurst, Australia

Reference

UNICEF (1989) *United Nations Convention on the Rights of the Child (UNCRC)*. Retrieved 7 April 2011, from http://www2.ohchr.org/english/law/crc.htm

Part I Advocates' Views

1 A Duty to Listen

General Sir David John Ramsbotham, Baron Ramsbotham GCB CBE
HM Chief Inspector of Prisons 1995–2001

In 1997, I visited Her Majesty's Young Offender Institution (YOI) Polmont, in Scotland, whose excellent governor suddenly said to me, 'If I had to get rid of all my staff, the last one out would be my speech and language therapist' (SLT). Never having come across an SLT in any YOI before, I asked him why. 'Because these young people cannot communicate, either with each other or with us, and, until and unless they can, we do not know what it is that has prevented them from living useful and law-abiding lives, or how to begin helping them to do so in future.' His admirable therapist then told me how her assessments picked up all manner of problems that others did not, thus enabling education, health and disciplinary staffs to determine, and tackle, the needs of every individual prisoner.

She also told me the name of the best SLT in England, who joined me on a YOI inspection, proving exactly the same. Armed with this, I tried – and failed – to convince Jack Straw, then Home Secretary, to put an SLT in every YOI. Later, Lady Helen Hamlyn funded a two-year trial, during which, within a month, the governors of the two institutions involved said that they could not imagine how they coped before their therapists came. This foundered, too, because the Department of Health, the Ministry of Justice (under Jack Straw) and the Department of Education could not agree on who should fund them. My campaign continues!

What this experience proved to me was that age 15, when young people enter YOIs, is far too late in their lives for such an assessment to be made. If carried out before a child enters primary school, timely remedial treatment could enable him or her to engage with their teacher, and so with education. Based on the evidence that I have seen, and heard, I firmly believe that the inability to communicate is one of the principal reasons for truancy, eviction and exclusion, because the frustration and boredom that it engenders are behind much of the subsequent attitudes to education as a whole.

This belief was endorsed by talking to those whose problems had been identified, and who were undergoing remedial work. The stories that they told of their lives before assessment are an indictment of society in the 21st century: virtually no communication at (what passes for) home between parents and children, other than violence or criticism; no praise or encouragement for potential or achievement; personal relationships so nonexistent that, as one 19-year-old said to me, 'The first time that anyone took any interest in me as a person was when a prison officer made my sentence plan with me.'

What all this says to me is that, if children are assessed and listened to, as early as possible in their lives, there is every likelihood that potential problems, including lack of communication skills, can be identified, and treated, so preventing their ending up in prison. It is our duty to listen!

2 Listen Up!

Abigail Beverly
London, UK

My name is Abigail Beverly. I'm 27 years old and I graduated from Central Saint Martins in 2006 with a degree in Textile Design. I'm a young person with a speech and language difficulty.

Having a speech and language disorder means that communication and understanding of words and language can be more difficult for me than others. I have problems understanding complex language and also in using language to organize and express my ideas, particularly in written form.

This has affected many aspects of my life and meant that I have to find different ways to convey my thoughts, feelings and ideas to others. Problems with 'words' have changed how I look at the world and make sense of it.

If you have a speech and language difficulty, you have to work extra hard to get through all the barriers. There is a lot of negativity around. For example, when I was looking at A level courses there were a lot of people who just made an assumption that I would be doing resits and not bothering to look at my predicted grades – they just assumed that I would fail.

When they hear you have a disability, some people treat you differently – usually in a very patronizing way – which is my pet hate! Those people never looked at the whole person, and what were my strengths.

Now that I'm a grownup, my speech and language difficulty has not gone away. It's part of who I am. So, for example, although my language has improved and I've grown in confidence, I still really struggle with email responses and texting. I have to work hard to get them right, so it takes me longer and I have to check and recheck that I've used the right words. It is more difficult with text: you can't hear my voice or tone, can't see me or my body language.

I still don't feel very confident in situations that I'm not prepared for – spontaneous comment isn't ever going to be my thing. So, although people say that I come across as confident and self-assured, what these people forget is that I am now 27 and, although I've had plenty of practice at putting words together, it still involves a lot of thought and preparation to get the words right. I'd just like to say that when I was in my teens I'd have never dreamed of writing anything like this – it was difficult enough communicating on a one-to-one basis.

It was because of all the help that I got – finding out what suited me best, and playing to my strengths – that gave me this confidence. So, it didn't just happen overnight. It all depends on people finding out what works for the individual; being willing to try new things and adapt to specific needs. That's why I think it is important that researchers and practitioners should listen to the views of children with speech, language and communication needs.

3 The Bridge between the World of the Disabled and the World of the Fully Functioning

Andrea Kaye
London, UK

I wish I could be one of those mothers who could bestow a beatific smile and tell the world that I love my daughter's disability, and that I wouldn't want to change it for a second because it's part of what makes her who she is. My daughter, P, is 15, and has both Asperger's Syndrome and a disability that affects her muscles. One of the results of this disability is that the muscles in her tongue and mouth don't work properly, so there's an impairment in the development and quality of her speech. This, together with the communication difficulties presented by Asperger's Syndrome, means that life is difficult for P. Social interaction in particular is a very tricky business for her.

But I can't claim to be at peace with it all. Her disability is cruel, and means that almost always she is marginalized from society, on the outside, looking in, knowing she's different, wanting to get involved but just not in possession of the skills to do so. Life is – and will continue to be – so very hard for P, and if you were to say to me, 'We can make it better, but for payment we'll have to chop your arms off,' I'd roll up my sleeves and tell you to cut where you like.

Like many children with autistic spectrum difficulties, P is intellectually a very bright girl. For a long time it wasn't completely apparent what her difficulties actually *were*, as they are the kinds of things that only really become clear once a child has grown up a little, and then it's noticeable that he or she isn't behaving in the same way as their peers.

And so it is, then, that many families like mine one day find themselves in a situation where they have a mainstream life, a mainstream school, mainstream aspirations and expectations, and a child who may have certain mainstream capabilities but is anything *but* mainstream.

Then there comes the sticky question: inclusion or exclusion?

What would *you* do if you had a child whose difficulties were not profound enough to label them 'disabled' and yet who clearly did not fit into the fully functioning world? Where would they belong?

None of the options is that enticing, or that satisfactory.

Perhaps you decide to ignore your child's differences, and resolutely decide that your square-peg child *will* fit into the round hole that is the world in which we live. Some might call this denial; others, merely practical.

Or you can embrace your child's problems, use their diagnosis as both a weapon and a shield, and vow to change the world to make it a better, less hostile place for your child. You seek out specialist disability groups – and, if there isn't one, you start one yourself – and somehow you find your voice.

Or you can attempt to live on some kind of bridge between those two worlds – the world of the disabled and the world of the fully functioning.

In my own experience, this bridge is a very densely populated place, and it's also an extremely lonely and isolated one. You try to get some support and at the same time you hold on to the belief that, with the right strategies, your child might *just* be OK. In fact, you cling on to the able end of that bridge with all your might. Once your arms start to ache from all that hopeful hanging-on, you perhaps take a few baby steps into the world of the disabled and shrink away, not quite ready to face the fact that you hover on the brink of this world, relieved that your own child's special needs aren't quite 'special' enough, yet frustrated at the lack of any relevant support. The help and facilities available are limited and very often inappropriate for young people like P – not needy enough to be involved in disabled activities, yet unable to cope without support in the 'real' world.

And when you live on this bridge that spans the no-man's land between the world of the disabled and the world of the fully functioning, you come to realize that the notion of 'inclusion' is, in fact, a fallacy. There *is* no such thing. The very things that provided P with the help and support she needed to attend her mainstream school, for example, were the very things that contributed to meaning she was not fully included in the life of the school, such as feeling so unsafe that she would spend all her time shut in the special needs room.

So the whole inclusion/exclusion debate becomes a huge, personal dichotomy when the person involved hovers on the cusp between ability and disability. Nowhere feels like home.

P was just not coping at her mainstream school, which meant that remaining there was no longer an option… and so, for the past 18 months, she has been attending a special needs school.

The impact on our family has been huge – not least because her school is *residential*; it would be hard enough sending any child away to boarding school, let alone one as needy and vulnerable as P. While the adjustments have been very hard to make, the progress and improvements we are witnessing in terms of P's behaviour and capabilities make it all worthwhile. And one of the key things a boarding school provides is sustained opportunities for supported socializing, which, for young people with speech, language and communication problems, is so often such a harrowing experience.

Most charities and organizations set up to help disabled young people focus on more profound and obvious needs, such as Downs syndrome or cerebral palsy, and ignore this less apparent (but every bit as vital) area of speech and communication difficulties, which impacts so hugely upon the lives of adolescents and which the Afasic Youth Project so brilliantly accommodates.

At the Afasic Youth Project, P felt she fitted in – a feeling which, for her at that time, was unique. There are plenty of activities, and yet there is also plenty of free time (done with sensitivity and support), something which in mainstream clubs is usually such a frightening challenge for a person like P. But at Afasic, just 'hanging out with your mates' is what makes it special. P was able, for the first time ever, to make friends with people just like herself.

For people like P, whose communication capabilities are impaired, it's as if the world moves too fast. Crucially, what they manage to do at the Afasic Youth Project is slow the world down, giving these young people somewhere they can – for a couple of hours each week, at least – feel normal.

4 Working in Partnership
Therapists, Children and Families

Hazel Roddam
Royal College of Speech and Language Therapists, UK

When I finished my first job as a speech and language therapist in a residential school to move to another part of the country, the staff and pupils presented with me with a photo album filled with smiling faces and special messages so that I wouldn't forget them. I never have done. I very often find myself thinking about some of those children I worked with as a new graduate. And it's not only a select few: I can recall names and faces from almost all the clinics and schools where I have worked. That's a fair number of children over 30 years of practice. I wonder how many of them – and their families – feel that those early experiences still impact on how they feel about themselves today? That isn't indulgent sentimentality. As speech and language therapists, we are aware of the uniqueness of every family we work with. We invest our art and skills to form a bond with every child; to motivate them with the things that interest them most, to make their therapy as relevant and fun as we can. And we strive to build a strong relationship with their parents and carers; to gain their trust and to understand their anxieties and priorities. Our ultimate goal is to help each child to maximize their potential as an independent and successful communicator, but we can only achieve this by working in close partnership with them and their families.

Across the country there are children who need expert help with speaking and understanding. Their families need to be able to call on the distinctive skills and experience of a speech and language therapist. Speech and language therapists draw on their specialist training and expertise to make an accurate and informed assessment and to give appropriate advice to the child and their family. The therapy management plan includes speech, language and communication skills that will support the child's self-esteem, emotional development, social confidence and behaviour, as well as their progress in learning and access to the curriculum. Without this help, these children risk lower levels of literacy, poorer educational attainment and less employability. We also know that these factors can lead to later problems in mental health and wellbeing. It is urgent that we protect key services for timely access to specialist speech and language therapy services for the future.

Evidence-based practice (EBP) is the current mantra of our health services, with its three pillars of research evidence, the professional's experience and the patient's perspectives (Sackett, Rosenberg, Gray, Haynes & Richardson, 1998). For over a decade the predominant focus has been on the research evidence base – or on the limitations of this in some areas of our practice. Well-designed and well-conducted research is essential to demonstrate the effectiveness of our therapy, to assure the highest-quality standards of care and to help to secure these services into the future. But the ongoing drive for relevant high-quality research has to be balanced by our commitment to recognize the perceptions and expectations of the individuals and families who need our services, in line with Sackett et al.'s original vision of EBP. This book is unique in its emphasis on listening to the experiences of the children and young people themselves – it will inspire and challenge us all.

Reference

Sackett, D., Rosenberg, W., Gray, J., Haynes, R. & Richardson, W. (1998) Evidence-based medicine: What it is and what it isn't. *British Medical Journal, 312*, 71–72.

5 Tuning into Children with Speech and Language Impairment

Linda Lascelles
Chief Executive Officer, Afasic, UK

It only takes a moment's thought to realize why listening to children is so important. It is the only way we can know if they are hungry or thirsty, upset or confused. Those of us who are parents know that when our children are babies and cannot talk to us we quickly learn to 'tune into' them, and can tell what's wrong when they start crying. We carry on doing this as they get older, sensing whether anything is troubling them or noticing if there is any activity they particularly enjoy or seem good at. Other adults, especially those who spend a lot of time with young children, such as childminders and nursery staff, often do this too.

As children get older still and become fluent talkers, they learn to communicate effectively with a wider range of people, without their parents or someone else who knows them well having to mediate. At least, that applies to most children. Children with speech and language impairments will have a limited ability to do this – in some cases, very limited. They need adults, and others, to continue 'tuning into' their needs for much longer.

Parents automatically do this, of course – as do good speech and language therapists. They would not be able to do their job properly, otherwise!

Many adults, however, seem to find it really difficult to 'tune into' children of school age and beyond. This is partly due to lack of time. A busy teacher trying to deliver a packed curriculum to a class of 30 children cannot develop the same sort of relationship as a parent, or a therapist who only ever sees children one-to-one or in a very small group. But it is more complicated than this. We seem to be 'hard-wired' to know how best to communicate with typically developing children and expect to be able to use speech and language. If this does not work, we are thrown.

The solution is not rocket science, though. 'Tuning in' at this stage means modifying the way we communicate with young people appropriately. This does not mean 'talking down' to them – addressing a 14-year-old as though they were about 6 – but using language clearly, and checking that you have understood them and they have understood you. Consulting the young person's parents or speech and language therapist is always advisable. As experts in listening to and understanding the young person, their experience and insights will be invaluable.

This whole subject can perhaps be summarized as 'No decision about me, without me'. This has been a mantra within health-related circles for some time, and even appears in the recent health White Paper (Department of Health, 2010). It also neatly encapsulates Articles 12 and 13 of the *United Nations Convention on the Rights of the Child*. Professionals owe it to children to make this a reality for all young people, including those with speech and language impairments.

Reference

Department of Health (2010) *Equity and Excellence: Liberating the NHS*. London: Crown Copyright.

6 Social Work and Communication with Children with Speech, Language and Communication Needs

Tillie Curran

University of the West of England, Bristol, UK

Working with children with speech, language and communication needs involves the children's workforce as a whole. Its success depends not simply on the communication skills of children, but on the attitudes and communication skills of practitioners and members of the wider community. In the UK the children's workforce is expected to work together to improve the lives of children and young people and to ensure specialist and universal support is made available with minimum delay (Children Acts 1989 and 2004 – Department of Health, 1991; Every Child Matters (ECM) – Department of Education and Skills, 2003). Disabled children continue to have a greater likelihood of experiencing poverty, a higher risk of being bullied or abused and to experience segregated, distant and marginalized patterns of service provision than non-disabled children (Read, Clements & Ruebain, 2006). The children's workforce is supported by the Equality Act 2010 to address discrimination and to actively promote equality (Government Equalities Office, 2010). Opportunities for sharing and developing knowledge and skills to improve communication with children and to support children with speech, language and communication needs are strengthened in current reviews of children's services (Munro, 2011; Support and Aspiration – Department for Education, 2011). These documents set out the UK Government's aims to ensure early identification of children's needs and to form effective professional relationships with children and families by reducing bureaucracy and giving greater control of resources to parents of disabled children.

Social workers comprise one of the professions that work with children with speech, language and communication needs. It is suggested here that working together with speech and language professionals is important in the following areas:

- teaching of skilled communication in social work education

- facilitation of children's involvement in assessment of their needs

- assessment of children's communication needs

- intervention to protect and safeguard children's wellbeing

- promotion of inclusion in all aspects of community life

- research and policy development.

Skilled communication with children is a core requirement in social work education: 'Good communication, both oral and written, is at the heart of best practice in social work. It is also essential for establishing effective and respectful relationships with children' (Luckock et al., 2006, p. 1). In their review of qualifying social work programmes, Luckock et al. found a need for courses in communication at a more advanced level and called for more systematic assessment. Working together with speech and language departments in higher education is a valuable opportunity to make further improvement.

In the assessment process social workers need to have skilled communication to promote the involvement of children in decision-making. This is expected in legislation (at least in the UK) and this must apply to all children: 'Disabled children cannot be assumed to be incapable of sharing in decision making and arrangements must be made in order to establish their views' (Franklin & Sloper, 2009, p. 3). In their research into disabled children's involvement, Franklin and Sloper stress the time needed to build purposeful relationships and state that further development is needed especially in practice with children who do not use speech for communication. Working together with communication experts and people with frequent contact with children was seen as central to social workers' learning: 'social workers and parents/carers were often not aware of techniques and systems being used within schools or skilled in using the child's communication method' (Franklin & Sloper, 2009, p. 11).

Communication is a key area of a child's assessment of needs necessary for the achievement of other key outcomes (Department for Education, 2011). In the research by Sloper, Beresford and Rabiee (2009) into disabled children's views of the *Every Child Matters* outcomes, children and young people shared the aspirations but added 'fundamental' outcomes: 'being able to communicate was seen as fundamental to meeting desired outcomes in other areas of life for all groups' (Sloper et al., 2009, p. 271). For the children and young people and their parents, this meant being able to communicate and having a system to communicate that is sensitive and responsive to them as individuals. Recognition of all dimensions of a child's identity, including ethnicity, range of languages used and cultural life, is necessary for support to be made relevant and readily accessible (Ali, Fazil, Bywaters, Wallace & Singh, 2001).

When social workers are working to protect and safeguard children and young people, involvement can be at an intense level. Children who are in situations of crisis, major uncertainty and change need to have their own methods for communication *and* safe, supported opportunities to communicate to people about their experiences and to express their wishes. Practitioners in all professions need to be aware of existing myths around disability and recognize when practices have been accepted that are in fact abuses of human rights (Murray & Osbourne, 2009). Oliver and Sapey (1999) recognize the need for parents to have emotional support, but suggest that parents will not necessarily experience adverse emotional reactions to their baby or child's diagnosis or have difficulty with family relationships. Parents may experience distress due to a lack of practical support or due to negative responses from others around them, and this can have a significant impact on their child's sense of identity. According to Howe (2006), children with speech and language needs are particularly vulnerable to neglect, but not as a result of disability per se. Secure family attachments, he suggests, depend on the confidence and skills of parents and on their having sufficient relevant support. Both social workers and speech and language experts recognize the long-term significance of support for children and young people that needs to continue into adulthood.

Social workers and speech and language professionals have an important part to play in promoting community inclusion and addressing discrimination and bullying. This inclusive emphasis is advanced in children's rights and disability rights campaigns (Oliver, 1990; *United Nations Convention on the Rights of the Child* – United Nations High Commissioner for Human Rights, 1991). Ordinary aspects of childhood can be dominated by professionals' ideas of normal development and their associated practices. Goodley and Runswick-Cole point to the negative view of disabled children produced in developmental psychology and challenge the Western economic myths of 'autonomy' and 'independent' adulthood: 'Developmental psychology itself constructs both "the child" and "development"' (2010, p. 508). The authors point out that disabled children are more likely to experience play as a 'tool' for assessment or learning and as part of adult-controlled agendas and have limited opportunity to play for its intrinsic, child-led value. Sharing and developing working definitions of 'inclusion' is a vital starting place (Beresford, Clark & Borthwick, 2010).

Alongside direct practice and community development, members of social work and speech and language departments can share skills in research with children with speech, language and communication needs. Research activities can include postgraduate projects, doctoral supervision, the evaluation of outcomes to inform policy development, and conferences towards the development of concepts of disabled children's childhoods that recognize diversity and complexity.

References

Ali, Z., Fazil, Q., Bywaters, P., Wallace, L. & Singh, G. (2001) Disability, ethnicity and childhood: A critical review of research. *Disability and Society, 16:7*, 949–968.

Beresford, B., Clarke, S. & Borthwick, R. (2010) Improving the wellbeing of disabled children and young people through improving access to positive and inclusive activities. *Disability Knowledge Review*. London: C4EO.

Department for Education (2011) *Support and aspiration: A new approach to special educational needs and disability. A consultation.* Retrieved from http://www.education.gov. uk/publications/eOrderingDownload/Green-Paper-SEN.pdf

Department for Education and Skills (2003) *Every child matters.* Retrieved from www. everychildmatters.gov.uk

Department of Health (1991) *The Children Act 1989.* London: HMSO.

Franklin, A. & Sloper, P. (2009) Supporting the participation of disabled children and young people in decision-making, *Children and Society, 23*, 3–15.

Goodley, D. & Runswick-Cole, K. (2010) Emancipating play: Dis/abled children, development and deconstruction, *Disability and Society, 25*, 499–512.

Government Equalities Office (2010) *Equality Act 2010.* Retrieved from http://www. equalities.gov.uk/equality_act_2010.aspx

Howe, D. (2006) Disabled children, maltreatment and attachment, *British Journal of Social Work, 36*, 743–760.

Luckock, B., Lefevre, M., Orr, D., Jones, M., Marchant, R. & Tanner, K. (2006) *SCIE Knowledge review 12: Teaching, learning and assessing communication skills with children and young people in social work education.* Retrieved from http://www.scie.org.uk/publications/knowledgereviews/kr12.asp

Munro, E. (2011) *The Munro Review of Child Protection interim report: The child's journey.* Retrieved from www.education.gov.uk/publications/standard/publicationDetail/Page1/DFE-00010-2011

Murray, M. & Osbourne, C. (2009). *Safeguarding disabled children: Practice and guidance.* London: HM Government DCSF.

Oliver, M. (1990) *The politics of disablement.* London: Macmillan.

Oliver, M. & Sapey, B. (1999) *Social work with disabled people.* London: Macmillan.

Read, J., Clements, L.J. & Ruebain, D. (2006) *Disabled xhildren and the law: Research and good practice,* 2nd edition. London: Jessica Kingsley Publishers.

Sloper, P., Beresford, B. & Rabiee, P. (2009) Every Child Matters outcomes: What do they mean for disabled children and young people? *Children and Society, 23:4,* 265–278.

United Nations High Commissioner for Human Rights (1989) *United Nations Convention on the Rights of the Child.* Switzerland: Office for United Nations High Commissioner for Human Rights.

Part II Issues

7 Listening to Children and Young People with Speech, Language and Communication Needs

Who, Why and How?

Sharynne McLeod

Abstract

This chapter commences with an overview of the historical perceptions of childhood, and of listening to children. Next, children with speech, language and communication needs are identified, and described as an important group to listen to. Historical, present and future techniques of listening to children and young people with speech, language and communication needs are outlined. The chapter concludes with insights gained from listening to children, and an exhortation to use our 'listening ears' (see Figure 7.1).

Figure 7.1 Talking to someone with listening ears.
Reprinted with permission from Speech Pathology Australia. Published in McLeod, Daniel and Barr (2006)

Why listen to children and young people?

Children represent both the present and the future of the world, since everyone either currently is, or once was, a child. Children should have the right to *be* children, *belong* in the world as children, as well as to *become* adults of the future (Australian Government Department of Education, Employment and Workplace Relations (DEEWR), 2009; Sumsion & Wong, 2011). Children need to feel safe and supported and have a sense of wellbeing that fosters their sense of autonomy and purpose. Childhood is a time of learning and exploration as children become confident and creative problem-solvers, communicators and contributors to their worlds (DEEWR, 2009). Children's interactions with others should be reciprocally respectful and supportive within the communities in which they live and interact.

Children have been viewed differently in different countries and cultures at different times. Throughout history children have been viewed along a continuum from being 'agents and inheritors of their own development' to 'objects to be shaped for defined purposes' (Ritter, 2007, p. 73). In some cultures and at some times, children are 'trusted… agents of their own destiny' and are given independence and a voice in their lives; whereas, in other cultures and at other times children are seen as 'mistrusted agents' where parents and society work to shape children into future adults (Ritter, 2007, p. 73). Within the Western world, perceptions of childhood are changing. Traditionally, the dominant view of childhood was as an apprenticeship to learn to become successful adults. This view was upheld within education, health and research practices, where children were treated as passive recipients of information and knowledge. For example, much of Western research has been *on* the child, not *with* or *for* them. As Dockett and Perry (2005, p. 508) stated, 'In schools, rarely are young children recognised as holders of expert knowledge, or even experts on their own experience'. More recently, health and education researchers have begun to incorporate children as participants rather than as passive objects. Children's own perspectives have been seen as genuine and valid.

A major factor that facilitated this shift in the view of children in Western contexts was the publication of the *United Nations Convention on the Rights of the Child* (UNCRC) (UNICEF, 1989). This landmark document contained two articles that have been quoted extensively, changing international policy and practice with respect to children's rights. These two articles have challenged adults to listen to the views of children and young people in areas that are important to them:

Article 12

Parties shall assure to the child who is capable of forming his or her own views the right to express those views freely in all matters affecting the child, the views of the child being given due weight in accordance with the age and maturity of the child. (UNICEF, 1989, p. 4).

Article 13

The child shall have the right to freedom of expression; this right shall include freedom to seek, receive and impart information and ideas of all kinds, regardless of frontiers, either orally, in writing or in print, in the form of art, or through any other media of the child's choice. (UNICEF, 1989, p. 4).

In its interpretation of Article 12, UNICEF identified the need to:

create spaces and promote processes designed to enable and empower children to express views, to be consulted and to influence decisions... the child's evolving capacity represents just one side of the equation: the other involves adults' evolving capacity and willingness to listen to and learn from their children, to understand and consider the child's point of view, to be willing to re-examine their own opinions and attitudes and to envisage solutions that address children's views. (www.unicef. org/crc)

The UNCRC came into effect in September 1990 and has been ratified by 193 countries, exceptions being the USA and Somalia (who are signatories, but not ratified). The UNCRC has profiled the importance of children's perspectives and has meant that, throughout the world, people have begun to listen seriously to children. For example, in Denmark, where the majority of children attend childcare, Danish law (Dagtilbudsloven, LOV nr. 501; 06.06.2007. Velfaerdsministeriet (Law on Child Care in Denmark, Ministry of Welfare, 06.06.2007)) requires that children's views of their own childcare must be collected annually and posted on the internet for parents and others to use when making decisions about childcare centres to attend (Kragh-Müller & Isbell, 2011). In the UK, the government has instigated many initiatives to include the voices of children in policy and practice. For example, the National Health Service White Paper (Department of Health, 2010, p. 13) states: 'We want the principle of 'shared decision-making' to become the norm: *no decision about me without me*' and, while this quote does not mention listening to children, related documents show the Department's commitment to listening to children:

> Children and young people are patients and members of the public too... Involvement is not a cosmetic exercise or an end in itself, but the fundamental way by which we can ensure our policies and services are relevant to what our young people need. Ultimately, this will produce better outcomes for children and young people as well as stronger communities, as we draw on children and young people's contributions to shape and develop services. Only by doing this can we understand children's needs and make sure our policies meet their needs. (Department of Health, 2003, p. iii)

While many other governments have not embraced listening to children and young people to the extent of the UK government, young people's views have been sought in New Zealand's Youth Parliament (Ministry of Youth Development, 2010), and children's views have been sought in Australian government initiatives such as selection of a commissioner for children and young people (Vardon Report Implementation Team, 2005), and recommending initiatives within the Australian capital territory (MacNaughton, Smith & Lawrence, 2004). There is limited information regarding listening to children and young people outside of Western contexts.

Who are children and young people with speech, language and communication needs?

Children and young people with speech, language and communication needs (SLCN) are first and foremost children. They have needs, likes and dislikes similar to any other children and young people. They live in families and communities like any other children and young people. They have aspirations and hopes as any other children and young people do. They are citizens of the world: children and young people now, who are becoming adults of the future.

The phrase 'speech and language and communication needs' was coined in the UK and promoted within *The Bercow Report* (Bercow, 2008). The definition from this report is that 'The term speech, language and communication needs (SLCN) encompasses a wide range of difficulties related to all aspects of communication in children and young people. These can include difficulties with fluency, forming sounds and words, formulating sentences, understanding what others say, and using language socially' (Bercow, 2008, p. 13). This all-inclusive definition captures aspects of an impairment-based model. That is, children and young people with speech, language and communication needs may have difficulties with communicating, speech (articulation, phonology), language (expressive, receptive), stuttering/stammering, voice production and/or hearing. For the majority of children with speech, language and communication needs, the cause of their difficulties is typically unknown; however, for some children, their communication difficulties are associated with hearing loss, cleft lip and palate, cerebral palsy, developmental disability or other known causes. Table 7.1 provides some associated terminology that is used throughout the world to classify these areas of difficulty for children and young people using an impairment framework.

Table 7.1 Examples of terminology used to describe specific areas of need for children and young people with speech language and communication needs.

Overarching area	Terminology relating to delay, disorder, difficulty, impairment and/or need in children	Affiliated terminology
Speech	speech sound disorder, speech impairment, phonological impairment, childhood apraxia of speech (CAS), developmental (verbal) dyspraxia, dysarthria, lisp	articulation, phonetics, phonology, prosody, intelligibility, phoniatrics
Language	Specific language impairment (SLI), expressive language delay/disorder, receptive language delay/disorder, aphasia (previously used for children, now typically reserved for use to describe the speech of adults after a stroke)	vocabulary (semantics), grammar (morphology), syntax, discourse, linguistics, pragmatics, logopedica
Voice	dysphonia, voice disorder, vocal nodules, vocal pathology, psychogenic voice disorders	phonation
Fluency	stuttering, stammering, cluttering, dysfluency	fluency
Hearing	deaf, hearing loss, hearing impairment, hard-of-hearing	
Communication	alternative and augmentative communication (AAC), complex communication needs	

The biopsychosocial framework of health and wellness from the World Health Organization is also relevant when we consider children with speech, language and communication needs (McLeod & Threats, 2008). Specifically, the *International Classification of Functioning Disability and Health: Children and Youth Version* (ICF-CY, WHO, 2007) defines several domains for considering the health and wellness of children with the goal of full participation in society. Traditionally, most speech and language therapists have considered the domains of Body Structures (e.g. tongue, ears) and Body Functions (e.g. articulation of sounds) within a medical (impairment) model for working with children with speech, language and communication needs (McLeod, 2004). However, the views of children, young people and their parents must be consulted to incorporate the domains of Activities and Participation, Environmental and Personal Factors within speech and language therapy practice.

Why listen to children and young people with speech, language and communication needs ?

Listening to children enables us to respect children both as present and future citizens of the world. As Kragh-Müller and Isbell (2011, p. 27) stated:

> growing up is not only about what children are to become once in the future. It is also about having a good childhood in itself. Interviewing children provides us as adults with information of how it feels to be a small child here and now, in the present. The interviews remind us that we have an obligation to give the children we care for happy childhoods, so that they can grow up to become both well educated and healthy adults.

Since the publication of the UNCRC, there have been many books, journal articles and reports that have been written about listening to children and young people's views (e.g. Clark & Moss, 2001; Hallet & Prout, 2003; Harcourt, Perry & Waller, 2011; Lewis & Lindsay, 2000; Percy-Smith & Thomas, 2010). However, few of these have included the voice of children and young people with speech, language and communication needs.

Children with speech, language and communication needs are often excluded from having a say in their lives because: (a) they are children, (b) they (may) have a disability and (c) they have difficulty communicating. However, there are at least two reasons why it is important to listen to these children and young people. Firstly, the prevalence and incidence of children and young people with speech, language and communication needs, and secondly the impact of speech, language and communication needs on children's lives.

Prevalence of children and young people with speech, language and communication needs

Speech and language delay is a 'high prevalence condition' (Law, Boyle, Harris, Harkness & Nye, 2000, p. 179), particularly in comparison with other learning needs. A study of over 14,500 Australian school-aged children (aged 5–18 years) demonstrated that communication impairment was the second most prevalent area of learning need after specific learning difficulties (McLeod & McKinnon, 2007). During the two waves of data collection, there were 13.0% (in one year) and 12.4% (two years later) of children identified with communication disorders, whereas fewer children were identified with the following learning needs: behavioural/emotional difficulty (9.2% and 6.1%), English as second/other language (8.2% and 5.8%), early achievers/advanced learners (7.3% and 5.5%), physical/medical disability (1.5% and 1.4%), intellectual disability (1.4% and 1.2%), hearing impairment (1.0% and 0.8%), and visual impairment (0.2% and 0.3%).

It is difficult to quantify the exact prevalence of speech, language and communication needs in childhood, due to differing methodologies, definitions and age groups that have been studied around the world. However, a population study of 4983 Australian children showed that 25.2% of parents had concerns about how their 4- to 5-year-old child talked and made speech sounds and 22.3% of teachers reported that children were considered to be less competent than others in their expressive language ability (McLeod & Harrison, 2009). Identified risk factors were 'being male, having ongoing hearing problems, and a more reactive temperament', while protective factors were 'having a more persistent and more sociable temperament, and higher levels of maternal wellbeing' (Harrison & McLeod, 2010, p. 508). When these children were 6 to 7 years, their teachers and parents reported that they had more difficulty with literacy, numeracy and approaches to learning than their peers (Harrison, McLeod, Berthelsen & Walker, 2009). At 7 to 9 years, the children themselves reported 'more bullying, poorer peer relationships, and less enjoyment of school' than their peers, and their parents and teachers reported 'slower progression in reading, writing, and overall school achievement' (McCormack, Harrison, McLeod & McAllister, 2011, p. 1328).

Impact of speech, language and communication needs on the lives of children and young people

Law, Boyle, Harris, Harkness and Nye (1998, p. 2) summed up the impact of speech, language and communication needs on children's lives by indicating that 'speech and language development is intimately related to all aspects of educational and social development'. Childhood speech, language and communication needs has both short- and long-term impacts on children's lives. The broad-reaching effects of speech and language impairment were highlighted in a systematic review and extended to 'learning to read/reading, learning to write/writing, focusing attention and thinking, calculating, communication, mobility, self-care, relating to persons in authority, informal relationships with friends/peers, parent-child relationships, sibling relationships, school education, and acquiring, keeping and terminating a job' (McCormack, McLeod, McAllister & Harrison, 2009, p. 155). Children who do not receive intervention, or who begin intervention in the school years, can continue to have difficulties for at least 28 years (Law et al., 1998).

How to listen to children and young people with speech, language and communication needs?

Listening respectfully to any child can present a challenge. However, listening to children and young people with speech, language and communication needs can present an even greater challenge, since effectively communicating is what they have difficulty doing. One major facilitator for listening to children is to use creative methods, and to triangulate these so that a broad picture can be gained. The need for a breadth of techniques for listening to children is poignantly articulated in the following poem titled *The hundred languages of children*, originally written in Italian and used to describe the philosophy of the Reggio Emilia approach to early childhood education:

> The child
> is made of one hundred.
> The child has
> a hundred languages
> a hundred hands
> a hundred thoughts
> a hundred ways of thinking
> of playing, of speaking...

The child has
a hundred languages
(and a hundred hundred hundred more)
But they steal ninety nine...
And thus they tell the child
that the hundred is not there. The child says:
No way.
The hundred is there. (Malaguzzi, 1998, p. 3)

How have we listened to children and young people with speech, langauge and communication needs in the past?

There are a number of early examples of listening to the views of children with speech, language and communication needs. For example, Van Riper (1963) wrote some of the earliest and most influential textbooks in the field of SLT and within them included children's pictures and quotes. At the end of his chapter titled 'The emotional problems of the speech handicapped' Van Riper (1963, p. 72) included a number of anecdotes, illustrations and case presentations, including quotes from children with speech, language and communication needs. One quote that he included was:

> The most wonderful thing about being able to pronounce my sounds now is that people aren't always saying 'What? What's that?' I bet I've heard that fifty thousand times. Often they'd shout at me as though I were deaf and that usually made me talk worse. Or they'd answer 'Yes' when that just didn't make sense. I still occasionally find myself getting set for these reactions and steeling myself against them and being surprised when other people just listen. (Van Riper, 1963, p. 72)

Van Riper also included pictures drawn by children, including some drawn by a child with a cleft palate, showing enlarged ears in one picture, and an enlarged nose and teeth in another. Accentuated mouths and ears have also been noted as features within drawings of children with speech, language and communication needs in more recent research (Holliday, Harrison & McLeod, 2009). Similarly, Sheehan, Cortese and Hadley (1962) studied the drawings of 48 people who stuttered (aged from 11 to 44 years) to demonstrate 'guilt, shame and tension in graphic projections of stuttering' (p. 129).

Within the intervening years between Van Riper's work and now, the profession of speech and language therapy has moved between craft-based and science-based approaches to practice (Justice, 2010). The UNCRC, as well as the broader adoption of qualitative research methods, has reignited interest in listening to the perspectives of children and young people with speech, language and communication needs. Since the publication of the UNCRC in 1989, the early examples of listening to young people with possible speech, language and communication needs were written by Donaghue (1997) and Costley (2000), who described insights from children with learning difficulties. Since then, there has been renewed interest in listening to children and young people with speech, language and communication needs, and to relying on their perspectives for informing policy and practice relevant not only to speech and language therapy but the broader contexts in which children inhabit.

How have we listened to children and young people with speech, language and communication needs more recently?

Many respectful and creative ways have been used to listen to children and young people with speech, language and communication needs and are profiled in the third part of this book. Some of the previously published techniques that have been used to listen to children and young people with speech, language and communication needs have included the use of:

Interviews

- individual interviews (McCormack, McAllister, McLeod & Harrison, 2011; Owen, Hayett & Roulstone, 2004; Palikara, Lindsay & Dockrell, 2009; Simkin & Conti-Ramsden, 2009; Spencer, Clegg & Stackhouse, 2010)

- individual interviews with Talking Mats (Rabiee, Sloper & Beresford, 2005)

- focus groups (Markam, van Laar, Gibbard & Dean, 2009)

- consultation groups (Ayre & Roulstone, 2008)

Questionnaires

- *Marsh Self-Description Questionnaire* (Marsh, 1992)

- *Strengths and Difficulties Questionnaire* (SDQ, Goodman, 1997)

- *Pictorial Scale of Perceived Competence and Acceptance* (used in Rannard & Glenn, 2009)

- *Kiddy Communication Attitude Test* (KiddyCAT, Vanryckeghem & Brutten, 2007)

- *Speech Participation and Activity Assessment of Children* (SPAA-C, McLeod, 2004)

Arts-based approaches

- children's drawings (Holliday et al., 2009; McCormack, McLeod, Harrison, McAllister & Holliday, 2010; McLeod, Daniel & Barr, 2006)

Observations

- direct observations supplemented by fieldnotes (Wickenden, 2011)

- videography (including babycam) (Sumsion, Harrison, Press, McLeod, Goodfellow & Bradley, 2011)

- internet chat sites (Barr & McLeod, 2010)

- and combinations of approaches (Merrick & Roulstone, 2011).

The examples in this list pertain to previously published research; however, the chapters in Part III of this book contain many more examples of the application of these techniques, as well as additional techniques such as filmmaking (Roulstone, Miskelly & Simons, 2011, Chapter 32 in this volume) and mixed arts-based methods (Hambly, Coad, Lindsay & Roulstone, 2011, Chapter 30 in this volume).

Most of these approaches also have been used in research with children and young people who do not have speech, language and communication needs; however, adjustments are often applied for children with speech, language and communication needs. For example, the inclusion of more non-verbal ways of listening to children may diminish the impact of the speech, language and communication needs. For example, as Malchiodi (1998, p. 1) suggested, drawing can allow children to 'express themselves in ways that language cannot'. Other adjustments include spending longer time with children on undertaking tasks, listening, and reflecting and giving a greater emphasis to checking that the intended message has been received. Children's choice to be silent has been advocated as important during all research focused on listening to children (Lewis, 2010); however, acknowledging children's silence may be even more important when considering children with speech, language and communication needs, who may be unable to coherently express their views. The importance of 'recognising, noting, responding to, interpreting and reporting silence from children' (Lewis, 2010, p. 14) is of great importance when working with children with speech, language and communication needs.

Research that aims to listen to children and young people can be undertaken within both quantitative and qualitative paradigms. During qualitative research, data analysis includes immersion in the data, constant comparative analysis, triangulation of data sources and methods, and participant validation. One method of triangulation is the Mosaic approach (Clark & Moss, 2001), which promotes joint exploration of an issue by interpreting multiple sources of data from multiple perspectives. Taking time to listen and understand each unique perspective is key to this approach. Some of the analytical frameworks that have been employed or used as guiding principles in research with children and young people with speech, language and communication needs have included:

- ethnography (Wickenden, 2011)
- grounded theory (Markham et al., 2009; Merrick & Roulstone, 2011)
- framework analysis (Markham et al., 2009)
- inductive thematic analysis (Barr & McLeod, 2010)
- phenomenology (McCormack, McAllister, McLeod & Harrison, 2011, in press).

How can we listen to children and young people with speech, language and communication needs in the future?

Listening to children and young people with speech, language and communication needs is only in its infancy if we consider the five levels of participation proposed by Shier (2001, p. 107):

1. Children are listened to.
2. Children are supported in expressing their views.

3. Children's views are taken into account.
4. Children are involved in decision-making processes.
5. Children share power and responsibility for decision-making.

Currently, most research with children and young people with speech, language and communication needs has included them as research participants, and occasionally co-researchers. To date, these children have been listened to (level 1) and their views have been taken into account (level 3), but rarely have they been involved in decision-making processes (level 4) about research questions, methods and outcomes. Research topics and processes mostly have been generated by adults. The future of our research with children and young people with speech, language and communication needs will facilitate the sharing of power and responsibility (level 5), ideally in ways that will be conducive to them having a voice in their own lives. Participatory research is discussed in greater depth in Chapter 11 (Miskelly, 2011, Chapter 11 in this volume).

What are children and young people with speech, language and communication needs telling us?

Many adults, including those who are parents, teachers, psychologists and speech and language therapists, have been paying attention to the views of individual children for a long time. Individual children have provided insights that have shaped their own goal-setting and decisions that have been made about their own lives. However, since the UNCRC, collectively people have been paying more attention to the voice of children and young people. This collective listening has begun to shape policy and practice.

A few examples of unexpected insights gained from listening to children include:

- Chocolate makes children hyperactive, and gives them autism (Kelly, 2005). This led the researcher to consider the need for talking with children about their interpretation of impairment and disability.

- Communication is three different things: a disability requiring intervention, a behaviour under children's control where children can decide whether or not to change it, and a skill (that is a worthwhile, but difficult challenge) to be practised and learned (Merrick & Roulstone, 2011). This led the researchers to compare the discourse of impairment with the discourse of empowerment within the intervention process.

- Children don't have speech problems – others have problems with their ears (McCormack, McLeod, McAllister & Harrison, 2010). This led the authors to recommend the development of interventions to support people to understand unintelligible children's speech.

- Friendships are central to enjoyment and quality of life for children and young people (Markham et al., 2009; Palikara et al., 2009). The role of making and maintaining friends could be included as a goal and measured outcome of intervention.

- Having a language impairment is like driving through life on a tricycle, when everyone else is driving a racing car (Brinton, Fujiki & Robinson, 2005). Intervention should be targeting broad-ranging goals and consider children's quality of life.

By listening to children and young people with speech, language and communication needs, our professional practice will be enhanced, challenged and will become more targeted to the actual needs and life experiences of the children and young people we are working with. We need to increase the size of our 'listening ears' (Figure 7.1).

Acknowledgements

This work is supported by Australian Research Council Future Fellowship (FT0990588). In preparing this chapter, I have benefited from conversations and collaborations with Sue Roulstone, Jane McCormack, Linda J. Harrison, Erin Holliday, Lindy McAllister, Graham Daniel, Jennifer Sumsion and Diane Jacobs.

References

Australian Government Department of Education, Employment and Workplace Relations (2009) *Belonging, being and becoming: The early years learning framework for Australia.* Canberra: Commonwealth of Australia. Retrieved from http://www.deewr.gov.au/ Earlychildhood/Policy_Agenda/Quality/Documents/Final%20EYLF%20Framework%20 Report%20-%20WEB.pdf

Ayre, A. & Roulstone, S. (2008) *Services for children with speech, language and communication needs: Evidence from parents and children.* Bristol: Frenchay Speech and Language Therapy Research Unit.

Barr, J. & McLeod, S. (2010) They never see how hard it is to be me: Siblings' observations of strangers, peers and family. *International Journal of Speech-Language Pathology, 12:2,* 162–171.

Bercow, J. (2008) *The Bercow report: A review of services for children and young people (0–19) with speech, language and communication needs.* London: Department for Children, Schools and Families. Retrieved from www.dcsf.gov.uk/bercowreview

Brinton, B., Fujiki, M. & Robinson, L. (2005) Life on a tricycle: A case study of language impairment from 4 to 19 years. *Topics in Language Disorders, 25:4,* 338–352.

Clark, A. & Moss, P. (2001) *Listening to young children: The Mosaic approach.* London: National Children's Bureau.

Costley, D. (2000) Collecting the views of young people with moderate learning difficulties. In A. Lewis & G. Lindsay (Eds), *Researching children's perspectives* (pp. 163–172, 214–216). Buckingham: Open University Press.

Department of Health (2003) *Listening, hearing and responding: Department of Health involving children and young people.* London: Crown Copyright.

Department of Health (2010) *Equity and excellence: Liberating the NHS.* London: Crown Copyright.

Dockett, S. & Perry, B. (2005) Researching with children: Insights from the starting school research project. *Early Child Development and Care, 175:6,* 507–521.

Donahue, M.L. (1997) Beliefs about listening in students with learning disabilities: Is the listener always right? *Topics in Language Disorders, 17:3,* 41–61.

Goodman, R. (1997) The Strengths and Difficulties Questionnaire: A research note. *Journal of Child Psychology and Psychiatry, 38:5,* 581–586.

Hallet, C. & Prout, A. (Eds) (2003). *Hearing the voices of children: Social policy for a new century.* New York: RoutledgeFalmer.

Hambly, H., Coad, J., Lindsay, G. & Roulstone, S. (2011) Listening to children talk about their desired outcomes. In S. Roulstone & S. McLeod (Eds), *Listening to children and young people with speech language and communication needs.* London: J&R Press.

Harcourt, D., Perry, B. & Waller, T. (Eds) (2011) *Researching young children's perspectives: Debating the ethics and dilemmas of educational research with children.* London: Routledge.

Harrison, L.J. & McLeod, S. (2010) Risk and protective factors associated with speech and language impairment in a nationally representative sample of 4- to 5-year-old children. *Journal of Speech, Language, and Hearing Research, 53:2,* 508–529.

Harrison, L.J., McLeod, S., Berthelsen, D. & Walker, S. (2009) Literacy, numeracy and learning in school-aged children identified as having speech and language impairment in early childhood. *International Journal of Speech-Language Pathology, 11:5,* 392–403.

Holliday, E.L., Harrison, L.J. & McLeod, S. (2009) Listening to children with communication impairment talking through their drawings. *Journal of Early Childhood Research, 7:3,* 244–263.

Justice, L.M. (2010) When craft and science collide: Improving therapeutic practices through evidence-based innovations. *International Journal of Speech-Language Pathology, 12:2,* 79–86.

Kelly, B. (2005) 'Chocolate… makes you autism': Impairment, disability and childhood identities. *Disability and Society, 20:3,* 261–275.

Kragh-Müller, G. & Isbell, R. (2011) Children's perspectives on their everyday lives in child care in two cultures: Denmark and the United States. *Early Childhood Education Journal, 39:1,* 17–27.

Law, J., Boyle, J., Harris, F., Harkness, A. & Nye, C. (1998) Screening for speech and language delay: A systematic review of the literature. *Health Technology and Assessment, 2:9,* 1–183.

Law, J., Boyle, J., Harris, F., Harkness, A. & Nye, C. (2000) Prevalence and natural history of primary speech and language delay: Findings from a systematic review of the literature. *International Journal of Language and Communication Disorders, 35:2,* 165–188.

Lewis, A. (2010) Silence in the context of child 'voice'. *Children and Society, 24,* 14–23.

Lewis, A. & Lindsay, G. (2000). *Researching children's perspectives.* Buckingham: Open University Press.

MacNaughton, G., Smith, K. & Lawrence, H. (2004) *Hearing young children's voices: ACT children's strategy. Consulting with children birth to eight years of age.* Canberra: Children's Services Branch, ACT Department of Education, Youth and Family Services.

Malaguzzi, L. (1998) No way. The hundred is there. In C. Edwards, L. Gandinin & G. Forman (Eds), *The hundred languages of children: The Reggio Emilia Approach – Advanced reflections* (p. 3). Greenwich: Ablex Publishing.

Malchiodi, C.A. (1998) *Understanding children's drawings.* New York: The Guilford Press.

Markham, C., van Laar, D., Gibbard, D. & Dean, T. (2009) Children with speech, language and communication needs: Their perceptions of their quality of life. *International Journal of Language and Communication Disorders, 44:5,* 748–768.

Marsh, H.W. (1992) *Self-Description Questionnaire III: Manual.* Sydney, Australia: University of Western Sydney.

McCormack, J., Harrison, L.J., McLeod, S. & McAllister, L. (2011) A nationally representative study of parents', teachers', and children's perceptions of the impact of early childhood communication impairment at school-age. *Journal of Speech, Language, and Hearing Research, 54:5,* 1328–1348.

McCormack, J., McAllister, L. McLeod, S. & Harrison, L.J. (2011, in press) Knowing, having, doing: The battles of childhood speech impairment. *Child Language Teaching and Therapy.*

McCormack , J., McLeod, S., Harrison, L.J., McAllister, L. & Holliday, E.L. (2010) A different view of talking: How children with speech impairment picture their speech. *ACQuiring Knowledge in Speech, Language and Hearing, 12:1*, 10–15.

McCormack, J., McLeod, S., McAllister, L. & Harrison, L. J. (2009) A systematic review of the association between childhood speech impairment and participation across the lifespan. *International Journal of Speech-Language Pathology, 11:2*, 155–170.

McCormack, J., McLeod, S., McAllister, L. & Harrison, L.J. (2010) My speech problem, your listening problem, and my frustration: The experience of living with childhood speech impairment. *Language, Speech, and Hearing Services in Schools, 41:4*, 379–392.

McLeod, S. (2004) Speech pathologists' application of the ICF to children with speech impairment. *Iinternational Journal of Speech-Language Pathology, 6:1*, 75–81.

McLeod, S. & Harrison, L.J. (2009) Epidemiology of speech and language impairment in a nationally representative sample of 4- to 5-year-old children. *Journal of Speech, Language, and Hearing Research, 52:5*, 1213–1229.

McLeod, S. & McKinnon, D.H. (2007) The prevalence of communication disorders compared with other learning needs in 14,500 primary and secondary school students. *International Journal of Language and Communication Disorders, 42:S1*, 37–59.

McLeod, S. & Threats, T.T. (2008) The ICF-CY and children with communication disabilities. *International Journal of Speech-Language Pathology, 10:1*, 92–109.

McLeod, S., Daniel, G. & Barr, J. (2006) Using children's drawings to listen to how children feel about their speech. In C. Heine & L. Brown (Eds), *Proceedings of the 2006 Speech Pathology Australia National Conference* (pp. 38–45). Melbourne: Speech Pathology Australia.

Merrick, R. & Roulstone, S. (2011) Children's views of communication and speech-language pathology. *International Journal of Speech-Language Pathology, 13:6*, 281–290.

Ministry of Youth Development (2010) *Youth parliament 2010*. Retrieved from http://www.myd.govt.nz/have-your-say/youth-parliament/index.html

Miskelly, C. (2011) Issues and assumptions of participatory research with children with speech, language and communication needs. In S. Roulstone & S. McLeod (Eds), *Listening to children and young people with speech language and communication needs*. London: J&R Press.

Owen, R., Hayett, L. & Roulstone, S. (2004) Children's views of speech and language therapy in school: Consulting children with communication difficulties. *Child Language Teaching and Therapy, 20:1*, 55–73.

Palikara, O., Lindsay, G. & Dockrell, J. E. (2009) Voices of young people with a history of specific language impairment (SLI) in the first year of post-16 education. *International Journal of Language and Communication Disorders, 44:1*, 56–78.

Percy-Smith, B. & Thomas, N. (Eds) (2010) *A handbook of children and young people's participation: Perspectives from theory and practice*. London: Routledge.

Rabiee, P., Sloper, P. & Beresford, B. (2005) Doing research with children and young people who do not use speech for communication, *Children and Society, 19:5*, 385–396.

Rannard, A. & Glenn, S. (2009) Self-esteem in children with speech and language impairment: An exploratory study of transition from language units to mainstream school. *Early Child Development and Care, 179*:3, 369–380.

Ritter, L. (2007) Historical and international perspectives of childhood. In S. McLeod (Ed.), *The international guide to speech acquisition* (pp. 73–77). Clifton Park, NY: Thomson Delmar Learning.

Roulstone, S., Miskelly, C. & Simons, R. (2011) Making a film as a means of listening to young people. In S. Roulstone & S. McLeod (Eds), *Listening to children and young people with speech language and communication needs.* London: J&R Press.

Sheehan, J.G., Cortese, P.A. and Hadley, R.G. (1962) Guilt, shame and tension in graphic projections of stuttering. *Journal of Speech and Hearing Disorders, 27*, 129–139.

Shier, H. (2001) Pathways to participation: Openings, opportunities and obligations. *Children and Society, 15*, 107–117.

Simkin, Z. & Conti-Ramsden, G. (2009) 'I went to a language unit': Adolescents' views on specialist educational provision and their language difficulties. *Child Language Teaching and Therapy, 25*:1, 103–122.

Spencer, S., Clegg, J. & Stackhouse, J. (2010) 'I don't come out with big words like other people': Interviewing adolescents as part of communication profiling. *Child Language Teaching and Therapy, 26*:2, 144–162.

Sumsion, J., Harrison, L.J., Press, F., McLeod, S., Goodfellow, J. & Bradley, B.S. (2011) Researching infants' experiences of early childhood education and care. In D. Harcourt, B. Perry & T. Waller (Eds), *Researching young children's perspectives: Debating the ethics and dilemmas of educational research with children* (pp. 113–127). London: Routledge.

Sumsion, J. & Wong, S. (2011) Interrogating 'belonging' in belonging, being and becoming: The Early Years Learning Framework for Australia. *Contemporary Issues in Early Childhood, 12*:1, 28–45.

UNICEF (1989) *The United Nations Convention on the Rights of the Child (UNCRC).* Retrieved from http://www2.ohchr.org/english/law/crc.htm

Van Riper, C. (1963) *Speech correction principles and methods* (4th ed.). New York: Prentice Hall.

Vanryckeghem, M. & Brutten, G.J. (2007) *KiddyCAT: Communication Attitude Test for Preschool and Kindergarten Children who Stutter.* San Diego, CA: Plural Publishing.

Vardon Report Implementation Team (2005) *Listening to kids: Emerging themes from children's responses to a commissioner for children and young people.* Canberra: ACT Department of Disability, Housing and Community Services.

Wickenden, M. (2011) Talking to teenagers: Using anthropological methods to explore identity and the lifeworlds of young people who use AAC. *Communication Disorders Quarterly, 32*, 151–163.

World Health Organization (2007) *ICF-CY: International Classification of Functioning, Disability and Health: Children and Youth Version.* Geneva: author.

8 Children's Voice and Perspectives

The Struggle for Recognition, Meaning and Effectiveness

Barry Percy-Smith

Abstract

This chapter critically reflects on the way in which 'listening to the perspectives' of children is understood and the complexities at play when ideas about children's participation unfold in practice. Drawing on children's participation literature across the world as well as wider theories of participatory practice, the chapter uses *space, audience* and *influence* to discuss how listening to children with speech, language and communication needs becomes a struggle for recognition within public sector systems which are themselves not participatory. The chapter outlines the importance of understanding children's participation as a relational concept in the context of everyday lived realities.

> *At the meeting we were told what was proposed and we put our views across about it. No one wanted the merger [of special needs schools]... Mine's the only school for disabled that still does GCSEs. If I am put into a special school with young people with mental or behavioural difficulties my chances of succeeding would be affected. But they did it anyway. They were just ticking boxes, because it looks like they are just listening to us even if they are not. The decision then went to the young people's scrutiny committee but the decision is going through anyway.*
> (Young person, 16, with special needs)

Introduction

As a result of the *United Nations Convention on the Rights of the Child* (UNCRC) and, in the UK, legislation such as the Children Act (2004), the imperative for children to 'have their say in all matters that affect them' is now embedded in mainstream social and public policy and practice in the UK. The sociology of childhood, in turn, acknowledges the active agency of children as *competent social actors* in their own right (James & Prout, 1990) and in anthropology as *active cultural producers* (Wulff, 1995). Article 12 of the UNCRC states that:

> Children have a right to express their views freely in all matters affecting the child, the views of the child being given due weight in accordance with the age and maturity of the child.

The significance of this article for decision-making is that children should have a chance to express their wishes, feelings and needs about the individual education, health and care they receive and have their contributions taken seriously.[1] To that extent there is an onus on services to 'involve' children in decision-making and ensure practice reflects children's needs. This in turn necessitates adults fully understanding the reality of children's everyday experiences, but also to do so from the child's perspective.

Article 12 is seen as one of the most powerful and symbolic rights for children in that it provides the conduit for children to access power and decision-making and for children to realize their other rights. 'Having a say', 'listening to children's perspectives' and 'involving children' have all become synonymous with the notion of children's participation. Children's participation is especially important for children who are vulnerable, 'excluded', have specific needs, and whose needs and circumstances might otherwise go unrecognized or misunderstood. The value of listening to children in these situations is not just to ensure their needs are met through 'effective' service delivery, but also to challenge professional assumptions and stereotypes about the lives of children with particular needs. In addition, children derive immense benefits and sense of inclusion from being involved in a decision, regardless of the outcome. This is especially important for children who have particular

---

1   The United Nations Committee on the Rights of the Child (2009) has made it clear that Article 12 is to be read as applying not only to the child as an individual, but to groups of children and children in general.

difficulties with communicating their everyday realities such as children with speech, language and communication needs.

In the UK, as elsewhere, there has been significant progress in developing children's participation in decisions about service provision. Participation is now high on policy and programme agenda and the language of participation commonplace for many practitioners. For the most part 'listening to children' has focused attention on the use of 'appropriate', often creative, methods and techniques (Clark & Moss, 2001; Coad & Hambly, 2012, Chapter 16 in this volume). However, attention has also been directed to establishing structures for hearing the voice of the child such as children in care forums, youth councils and student councils and a readiness to consult with children when decision-making requires. Young people's advisory groups are a common feature, particularly in health and social care settings and there has been a rapid increase in initiatives promoting children as researchers (Christensen, 2004; Kellett, 2005[2]). Christensen argues that 'in order to hear the voices of children... it is important to employ research practices such as reflexivity and dialogue [to] enable researchers to enter into children's *cultures of communication*' (2004, p. 165). To a large extent there is much to celebrate in hearing the perspectives of children. But critics are increasingly asking what the impacts and benefits are when children participate and share their perspectives and for whose benefit. Specifically:

- To what extent does listening to children/children's participation really influence decisions, and how far are benefits realized in children's lives?

- What constitutes meaningful participation, and whose agenda is children's participation working to?

- What are the implications for relationships with adults when children participate?

- To what extent are children able to articulate their perspectives in everyday life contexts?

Using these questions as a focus, this chapter critically reflects on the way in which listening to children is understood and operationalized with a particular focus on some of the complexities at play when theories of children's participation unfold in practice. The chapter draws on the wider children's participation

---

2   See also the Young Researchers Network at the National Youth Agency in the UK.

literature and in turn wider theories of participatory practice, but focuses the discussion on children with speech, language and communication needs.

Children's perspectives: A concept struggling for recognition?

The explosion in development of children's participation in public sector settings at the turn of the century has given rise to a widespread array of practice. What commonly passes for participation is, in effect, consultation, wherein children's involvement is restricted to a one-off articulation of a viewpoint on issues and decisions taken elsewhere. However, professionals are becoming increasingly aware that, to have impact, children's perspectives need to inform all phases of the decision-making or development cycle – including inquiry (developing a better understanding of the issues at hand), being involved with others in deciding on actions, taking actions and evaluating the outcome.[3] By focusing on 'children's perspectives', we are in essence saying we want to understand the world through children's eyes. But for what purpose? If we seek children's views and ideas for the purpose of organizational change and service development (as is so often the case), then we need to think about how effectively children's perspectives inform decision-making beyond simply voicing issues.

The state of children's participation seems to be characterized at present by a hiatus between the imperative of capturing children's views and producing tangible outcomes. Whilst practitioners and managers are becoming increasingly adept at hearing children's views, they are now confronting the challenge of 'embedding' children's participation within their systems and practices. This has given rise to a growing number of critical voices seeking to reflect on and develop a more focused theory of practice in a bid to more effectively realize the aspirations of the UNCRC (Fielding, 2007; Lundy, 2007; Percy-Smith 2010a; Thomas, 2007[4]). Lundy, for example, argues that voice is not enough; instead we need to pay attention to:

- the **spaces** for children to express a view

---

3   For those involved in commissioning services, this may be better known in terms of a commissioning cycle – assess, plan, do, review.

4   See also special issues of *International Journal of Children's Rights*, 16 (2008) and *Children, Youth and Environments*, 16 and 17 (2006)

- that there should be an **audience** to listen to that view

- and that the voice should exert an **influence.**

By bringing *audience* and *influence* into the picture, we are in effect deepening and widening our understanding of children's perspectives as occurring in relation to others (Cockburn, 1998; Fielding, 2007; Mannion, 2010; Percy-Smith, 2006). But what happens when children's perspectives collide with those of adults? Who decides which perspectives should prevail and influence, and what types of spaces are most appropriate for children to participate? The remainder of this chapter will use Lundy's framework to explore further these three key issues in children's participation.

Impact and *influence*: From 'perspectives' to 'power' in decision-making

A key question running through many of the discussions about children's participation is whether it has any impact on policy and practice (Tisdall & Davis, 2004). In essence, are children's perspectives really heard? At the level of practitioner intervention there is considerable scope for the 'individual' child to influence proceedings about the services and care they receive. This is dependent on the nature of the relationship the professional strikes with the child, as will be discussed later. For children with speech, language and communication needs, this necessitates developing a quality of engagement which allows two-way exchange involving effective communication, learning and joint decision-making.

However, evidence suggests that, at a policy level, influencing change is more difficult. Part of the problem here is that local public sector service systems are hierarchical rather than participative, which means that ultimately adults retain control over decisions. Decision-makers may be keen to take account of children's views but children rarely have an input into final decision-making (Percy-Smith, 2009; Thomas & Percy-Smith, 2011). Children are often consulted, but then don't hear what happens after they have had a say. In the worst cases children may be consulted on decisions already made. In contrast to prevailing approaches wherein children's perspectives are sought in a relatively instrumental and often detached way, in a participatory system children are involved as active participants in all phases of the decision-making or commissioning cycle – identifying and making sense of the issues at hand, developing solutions and evaluating outcomes. Within this latter articulation of praxis, children are part of the decision-making process rather than inputting into it. The more comprehensive the involvement of children in all phases of decision-making, the more likely it is that the outcome decisions will reflect the needs and realities of the children taking part and the more likely children will realize a positive experience from their participation. Yet, the more children are involved, the more power they have, which for many decision-making adults can be seen as a threat and a challenge to their identity as knowledgeable professionals (Lansdown, 2006). Learning how to work collaboratively with children with speech, language and communication is central to the development needed in public service systems for children's perspectives to have an impact (see Figure 8.1 for an example).

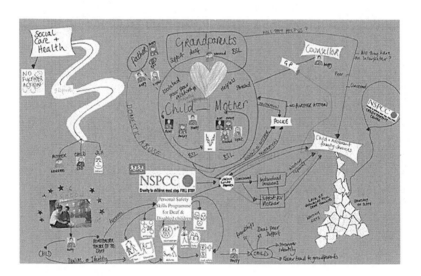

Figure 8.1 Conveying the experiences of a deaf child and his family experiences using visuals to support systemic inquiry in Children's Services (from Percy-Smith & Walsh, 2006, p. 33).

There is a key challenge, therefore, with facilitating the participation of children in ways that are meaningful and effective, in terms of having impact. The challenge, as Kemmis (2001) argues, drawing on Habermas (1987), is to bridge lifeworlds and systems through developing an 'appropriate' *communicative action space.* Visuals have been shown to be both an appropriate way for children to articulate their perspectives, but equally can be effective in communicating the message in an impactful way (Percy-Smith & Walsh, 2006). If the medium helps maximize the impact of the message, this can initiate learning for professionals and service providers and stimulate reflection on their own, taken-for-granted assumptions, about children's needs and how their services should respond (see example in Figure 8.1). But children also need to be able to participate and share their perspectives on terms that matter to them and when they feel the need to communicate needs, issues, ideas and concerns, not just when it suits service providers. The extent to which participation is meaningful and effective or not is dependent on whose agenda participation is for. So often participation is driven by an adult agenda, yet if children want to have a say about an issue that they feel is important according to their own agenda, this may be more difficult.

Reflection on whether children's perspectives have an impact or influence decision-making challenges us to think of children's perspectives not just as the contribution of new data, but as a critically reflexive process of learning for change, as the expression of lifeworld experiences engages with systems in a dynamic way. For this to happen, the position, interrelationship and response of adults is critical. In this sense we need to understand children's perspectives relationally.

Children's perspectives as a relational concept

According to Lundy's second proposition – *audience* – we need to understand the significance of children's voice in relation to others. Because of the power inequalities which tend to be inherent in relationships with adults (in particular, adults driven by target pressures), children's perspectives tend to be articulated in contexts of inequality. By implication the role of adults and quality of adult–child relations are arguably more important than structures and approaches for 'coming to know' the perspectives of children. If we are to understand children's perspectives in relation to others, we need to attend to 'the relational and mutual nature of participation and to the dialogical space within which norms of recognition and inter-subjectivity are constituted and negotiated' (Fitzgerald, Graham, Smith & Taylor, 2010, p. 301).

Fielding (2007, p. 307) similarly argues that we need to move to a more participatory form of engaging children's perspectives characterized by:

an intended mutuality, a disposition to see difference as a potentially creative resource, and more overt commitment to co-construction which requires quite different relationships and spaces and a different linguistic schema to form such aspirations.

By extending ideas of children's perspectives in terms of a relational *social learning* process (Percy-Smith, 2006), we need to think about what listening to a child's perspective really means in practice. Recognition of a child's perspective should not simply involve hearing a set of ideas. Rather it involves connecting with the whole 'experience' of that person's world and appreciating the significance of that view or experience in the context of the child's life. Warming (2006) uses Honneth's (1995) theory of recognition to understand professional relationships with children. She differentiates between *realization* – in which there is a cognitive appreciation of the knowledge children share – and *recognition* – a deeper process of 'coming to know' the child's position, which Honneth proposes is facilitated or negotiated through dialogue and mutual recognition. As Boylan and Dalrymple (2009, p. 75) state:

> By listening to children and young people we can gain the information we need for a fuller understanding of the issues that affect their lives. By dealing with voices, we are affecting power relations. To listen to people is to empower them … If we were to really listen to children and hear what they have to say, it would result in the need to radically change many of the services that are currently provided. … the starting point… is to continue to make visible the paradoxical discourses, which come from the exercise of adult power.

Participation is about power, and as Gallagher (2008), drawing on Foucault, argues: power is always negotiated in specific contexts of action. In seeking children's perspectives we need to think about the extent to which children can negotiate power in relations with adults. For Janssens, Percy-Smith, Jans and Wildemeersch (2000), this challenge for professionals involves a transition from the *expert* to a more *interpretive* professional practice. Drawing on the principles of the *interpretive professional*, Percy-Smith and Weil (2003) has developed an understanding of what it might mean to 'democratize the encounter space' between child and adult in a dynamic process of mutual learning and recognition, adapted here for the purpose of this chapter (see Figure 8.2).

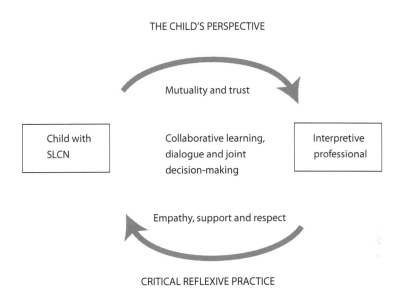

THE CHILD'S PERSECTIVE

Mutuality and trust

| Child with SLCN | Collaborative learning, dialogue and joint decision-making | Interpretive professional |

Empathy, support and respect

CRITICAL REFLEXIVE PRACTICE

Figure 8.2 Creating a communicative action space between adult professionals and children with speech, language and communication needs (SLCN).

Reconceptualizing adult–child relations in this way has implications for how spaces are created for children to share their perspective (Percy-Smith, 2010a). Structures such as school councils may be limited in appeal as contexts for children to share their perspectives in a meaningful way. Children may not wish to take issues that affect them in their day-to-day reality to a decision-making forum, and instead may seek more immediate attention. In contrast, more informal approaches – for example, through small groups and one-to-one communications – can often provide a more conducive environment for children with speech, language and communication needs to participate in relationships of trust, respect and mutual reciprocity. For example, in the UK the Parent Support Advisors service[5] involves practitioners working in a person-centred way with children and families where, through building relationships of trust, children can voice their innermost concerns and receive empathic support in response to the child's needs (Percy-Smith, 2010b).

5   Parent Support Advisors are employed by schools and work within schools, and also undertake outreach work with families in their homes.

Rethinking *spaces* for children's perspectives in the context of everyday life

By recognizing that children's perspectives need to be understood in relation to adults, the previous section highlights the importance of the *spaces* in which children share their perspectives. Spaces for children's participation tend to be dominated by more formalized structures and processes driven by service development, commissioning and research agenda (Percy-Smith, 2010a). There is an assumption that through 'having a say' in local authority decision-making, group interests are represented, individuals are 'empowered' and the excluded become included. The underlying rationale seems to be that inclusion and empowerment only happen through mainstream public sector decision-making. Yet evidence suggests that children are more likely to feel empowered when they feel they have been able to have an influence on decisions and choices being made or simply by deriving a sense of value and esteem from being involved (Percy-Smith, 2007; Thomas & Percy-Smith, 2011). Many of the choices and actions which characterize, shape and give meaning in people's lives are taken outside of public sector service and governance contexts within everyday life contexts. This suggests that if the goal of seeking children's perspectives is to bring about a greater sense of inclusion, then we also need to look at how children's perspectives and contributions are 'accommodated' in everyday relationships and activities.

Fielding (2006) echoes these sentiments by arguing against the current (managerialist) emphasis on participation for effective services and organizations and suggests instead that we focus on participation for the benefit and wellbeing of human communities. What is important is not children's perspectives per se, rather the benefits and realities for children. Moss and Petrie (2002, pp. 12–13), in turn, argue for the need to shift thinking from the instrumental provision of *children's services* to *children's spaces*, where children and adults engage together on projects of mutual significance. Space or context for children to actively contribute their perspective is important here, not just as a physical space, but a social space characterized by a quality of relationships between children and others within which children can meaningfully articulate their perspectives in multiple ways.

Conclusions

This chapter has explored some of the key issues and challenges that characterize the way in which children's perspectives are understood and approached in practice. The chapter argues for the need to look beyond the 'simple' act of children voicing a view, to understanding the significance of children's perspectives in relation to others. At an individual level, this needs to happen in relationships of trust and mutual recognition. At the level of policy, children with speech, language and communication needs should be able to articulate their perspectives, needs and desires as a collective along with, and in competition with, those of others. Increasingly we are seeing a greater acknowledgement of the need to be more aware of whether and how we are hearing and including the voices of *all* children, including those with specific speech, language and communication needs, in appropriate ways. Whilst the chapters in this book provide valuable examples of hearing the perspectives of children with speech, language and communication needs, we need to be cognizant of the extent to which these perspectives are influencing decision-making and service development and providing benefits in children's lives. The chapter argues that children with speech, language and communication needs should be more actively involved in all phases of the decision-making or commissioning cycle, including developing a better understanding of the issues, working with adults to consider different decisions and evaluating the changes that have been made.

However, this chapter has also highlighted the tendency to focus attention disproportionately on children's involvement in local authority decision-making dominated by the agenda of service providers. For children with speech, language and communication needs to feel a sense of value, inclusion and equality, attention also needs to be focused on everyday interactions, relationships and contexts. Accordingly I have argued that paying attention to the quality of everyday adult–child relationships is central to hearing the perspectives of children, and for children to feel valued and included in society rather than just being represented in decision-making. Key to involving children with speech, language and communication needs in a meaningful and effective way is the imperative of developing appropriate contexts, media and relationships together. These will be explored further in subsequent chapters.

References

Boylan, J. & Dalrymple, J. (2009) *Understanding advocacy for children and young people.* Milton Keynes: Open University Press.

Christensen, P. (2004). Children's participation in research: Issues of power and representation. *Children and Society, 18:28,* 165–176.

Clark, A. and Moss, P. (2001) *Listening to young children: The Mosaic approach.* London: National Children's Bureau

Coad, J. & Hambly, H. (2011). Listening to children with speech, language and communication needs through arts-based methods. In S. Roulstone & S. McLeod (Eds), *Listening to children and young people with speech language and communication needs*. London: J&R Press.

Cockburn, T. (1998). Children and citizenship in Britain: A case for a socially interdependent model of citizenship. *Childhood, 5:1*, 99–117.

Fielding, M. (2006) Leadership, radical student engagement and the necessity of person-centred education. *International Journal of Leadership in Education, 9:4*, 299–313.

Fielding, M. (2007) Beyond voice: New roles, relations, and contexts in researching with young people, *Discourse: Studies in the Cultural Politics of Education, 28:3*, 301–310.

Fitzgerald, R., Graham, A., Smith, A. & Taylor, N. (2010) Children's participation as a struggle over recognition: exploring the promise of dialogue. In B. Percy-Smith & N. Thomas (Eds), *A handbook of children and young people's participation: perspectives from theory and practice* (pp. 293–305). London: Routledge.

Gallagher, M. (2008) Foucault, power and participation. *International Journal of Children's Rights, 16:3*, 379–394.

Habermas, J. (1987) *The theory of communicative action,* Vol. 2, *Lifeworld and system: A critique of Functionalist Reason.* Boston, MA: Beacon Press.

Honneth, A. (1995) *The struggle for recognition.* Trans J. Anderson. Cambridge: Polity Press.

James, A. & Prout, A. (1990) *Constructing and reconstructing childhood.* Basingstoke: Falmer.

Janssens, C., Percy-Smith, B., Jans, M. & Wildemeersch, D. (2000) *Towards an interpretive education, training and guidance practice. Final report, balancing competencies.* Leuven: TSER EU Fourth Framework Programme.

Kellett, M. (2005) *How to develop children as researchers.* London: Paul Chapman.

Kemmis, S. (2001) Exploring the relevance of critical theory for action research: Emancipatory action research in the footsteps of Jurgen Habermas. In P. Reason & H. Bradbury (Eds), *Handbook of action research: Participative inquiry and practice* (pp. 91–102). London: Sage.

Lansdown, G. (2006) International developments in children's participation: Lessons and challenges. In E. Kay, M. Tisdall, J. M. Davis, M. Hill & A. Prout (Eds), *Children, young people and social inclusion: Participation for what?* (pp. 139–158). Bristol: Policy Press.

Lundy, L. (2007) 'Voice' is not enough: Conceptualising Article 12 of the United Nations Convention on the Rights of the Child. *British Education Research Journal, 33:63*, 927–942.

Mannion, G. (2007) Going spatial, going relational: Why 'listening to children' and children's participation needs reframing. *Discourse: Studies in the Cultural Politics of Education, 28:3*, 405–420.

Moss, P. & Petrie, P. (2003) *From children's services to children's spaces.* London: RoutledgeFalmer.

Percy-Smith, B. (2006) From consultation to social learning in community participation with young people. *Children Youth and Environments, 16:2,* 153–179.

Percy-Smith, B. (2007) *Evaluating the development of children's participation plans in two Children's Trusts. Year one report.* Leicester: National Youth Agency.

Percy-Smith, B. (2009) *Evaluating the development of young people's participation in two Children's Trusts. Year Two report.* Leicester: National Youth Agency.

Percy-Smith, B. (2010a) Councils, consultation and community: Rethinking the spaces for children and young people's participation. *Children's Geographies 8:2,* 107–122.

Percy-Smith, B. (2010b) *Evaluation of the Northamptonshire Parent Support Advisor service, evaluation report,* Bristol: University of the West of England/Northants County Council.

Percy-Smith, B. & Walsh, D. (2006) *Improving services for children and families: Listening and learning, Report from a systemic action inquiry evaluation process.* Northampton: Children's Fund Northamptonshire/ SOLAR.

Percy-Smith, B. & Weil, S. (2003) Practice-based research as development: innovation and empowerment in youth intervention initiatives using collaborative action inquiry. In A. Bennett, M. Cieslik, & S. Miles (Eds), *Researching youth.* (pp. 66–84). Basingstoke: Palgrave Publishing.

Thomas, N. & Percy-Smith, B. (2007) Towards a Theory of Children's Participationn. *International Journal of Children's Rights, 15,* 199–218.

Thomas, N. & Percy-Smith, B. (2011) 'It's about changing services and building relationships': Evaluation of the development of Children in Care Councils. Manuscript in submission.

Tisdall, E.K.M. & Davis, J. (2004) Making a difference? Bringing children's and young people's views into policy making. *Children and Society, 18:2,* 131–142.

United Nations Committee on the Rights of the Child (UNCRC) (2009) *General Comment No. 12 (The right of the child to be heard).* Geneva: Office of the United Nations High Commissioner for Human Rights.

Warming, H. (2006) 'How can you know? You're not a foster child': Dilemmas and possibilities of giving voice to children in foster care. *Children Youth and Environments, 16:2,* 28–50.

Wulff, H. (1995) The state of the art and new possibilities. In V. Amit-Talai, & H. Wulff (Eds.). (1995). *Youth cultures: A cross cultural perspective.* (pp. 1–18). London: Routledge.

9 The Importance of Silence When Hearing the Views of Children and Young People with Speech, Language and Communication Needs

Ann Lewis

Abstract

Hearing children's views has become ubiquitous across a range of contexts, including work with children and young people with speech, language and communication needs. This emphasis on 'voice' underplays the concurrent significance of silence. It is argued here that such silence should be recognized and explored. A series of eight pointers for doing so are provided which, through fostering reflectivity about both 'voice' and silence, can benefit practice in this field across research, evaluation and professional contexts.

Counterintuitively, silence can be the most powerful form of 'voice'. How is this potential power to be recognized in, and so exercised productively by, children and young people with speech, language and communication needs? This is the question at the heart of this chapter. It is a critical question, distinctive in its application to this group of children, because their silences may too readily be assumed to be involuntary. In seeking to understand the views of children with speech, language and communication needs we need to be finely attuned to the warp and weft of their silences. In analogous textual terms this is about recognizing, acknowledging, interpreting and reflecting the spaces between words, as well as decoding the words themselves.

First, a brief note about speech, language and communication needs terminology is needed. In the UK, one of the repercussions of the policy shift in education away from *Special Educational Needs* and towards *Special Educational Needs and Disabilities* has been a subtle redefining of individual disability categories. The trend has been to make individual *disability* terms, or categories, wider and more fluid (Lewis, 2010a). For example, conventionally speech, language and communication needs have been defined tightly as *communication disability* or specific language impairment (Martin, 2005). In contrast, *The Bercow Report* (Bercow, 2008) noted that 'The term speech, language and communication needs encompasses a wide range of difficulties related to all aspects of communication in young children. These can include difficulties with fluency, forming sounds and words, formulating sentences, understanding what others say, and using language socially' (p. 13). A similarly broad definition was taken by the extensive post-Bercow investigation into speech, language and communication needs (Lindsay, Dockrell, Law, Roulstone & Vignoles, 2009). This definitional point is relevant here because of the various ensuing interpretations of silence. The wider (Bercow) definition of speech, language and communication needs implies a very diverse range of possible reasons for, and hence responses to, silence.

Pushing the boundaries: The growing body of research on 'voice' and children with speech, language and communication needs

The large and expanding set of research, evaluation and practice literature on hearing the views of children with speech, language and communication needs shows that views are sought from an ever-widening group of children. Through this work, the assumption that at least some children with speech, language and communication needs will be unable to communicate their views in authentic and trustworthy ways has been strongly challenged.

A flavour of this work is conveyed in separate studies by (Abbott & Carpenter, 2010, 2011; Clarke & Wilkinson, 2008; Wickenden, 2011, Chapter 20 in this volume). These sets of research involved systematic attempts to hear from children and young people with speech, language and communication needs who, probably even as little as a decade previously, would not have been readily included as unmediated participants (i.e. without facilitators) in studies on disability and 'voice'.

The need for transparency and reflection concerning silence in research/evaluation interviews

A series of generic publications has explored our need for silence (e.g. George Foy's (2010) *Zero decibels: The quest for absolute silence*; Tim Parks (2009) *Teach us to sit still*; and Sara Maitland's (2008) *A book of silence*)). Yet the more that policy initiatives require evaluation from users, the stronger the pressures towards verbal, or narrowly interpreted visual, means of communication. In this context, choosing silence (i.e., in conventional terms, not to express a view) becomes an act of defiance. It seems that we both need, and fear, silence. We need silence as part of a reflective, often solitary, space but we also fear silence because of the conceptual proximity of silence with loneliness or isolation. Interestingly, silence was the focus of a recent special issue of the *Journal of Pragmatics* (Kurzon, 2010) reflecting the burgeoning interest in this topic within linguistics and philosophy, stimulated by research and scholarship such as that on typologies of silence (Ephratt, 2008).

Scrutiny of how the principle of giving disabled children (including those with speech, language and communication needs) a voice has been translated into practice suggests that considerable progress has been made in rights-based arguments and in developing approaches. However, there has also been a blurring of purpose, insufficient regard to ethical issues, an overemphasis on procedures and a lack of consideration of impact. The last – consideration of impact – includes asking, first, what, if any, is the impact of hearing children's views; and second (less obviously), whether to seek impact is in itself ethical, relevant or reasonable.

Reflecting these points, a series of commentators have taken a more critical look at child 'voice' as well as consultation with children in general (Fielding, 2004; Komulainen, 2007; Lewis, 2010b). Komulainen cautions against 'too simplistic and/or sensationalised a usage of the term "voice"' (p. 22) and the taken-for-granted view that 'children have message-like thoughts that can be exchanged, and intentions that match the situations defined by adults; and that these can be researched in an ethical fashion' (p. 25). Such work points to potential problems in operationalizing 'voice' if this does not take into account multiple and changing notions of self. Reflecting this, Cruddas (2006) avoids the term 'voice' preferring the concept of 'engaged voices' operating within a socially constructed space. One strength of such a stance is that it prompts examination of adult-focused, as well as child-focused, elements in that situation, not just an adult-dominated listening to children. Abbott (in Abbott & Carpenter, 2011) articulates this position powerfully:

I have a concern that I (and perhaps others in the field of childhood disability studies) have sometimes been so in thrall at accessing 'voice' (given many of the barriers which we know exist around involving disabled children and young people in research) that I report what children and young people say in a very 'straightforward way' – possibly lacking in reflection or critique. Much of my applied, thematic analysis cuts or slices across people's accounts/voices/lives and produces themes and findings which are the composite of that 'talk'. It's a perfectly useful and valid exercise especially when linked to political action but what gets lost?

Including an account of silence in the context of children and young people with speech, language and communication needs

A preference by children for silence, despite elaborate ethical protocols and careful procedures to facilitate their voicing of views, warrants more notice. At one level it is merely a more clear statement of reality: the best ethical protocols and sensitive methods will still only generate a partial picture of children's worlds. It is still unusual to read published accounts in which the anticipated processes concerning children's possible withdrawal, actual withdrawal from the research or partial withdrawal (such as requests for audio or video recorders to be turned off), are reported and discussed reflectively.

Whatever data are collected and whatever conclusions are drawn, much remains undisclosed. It would make the work more transparent if all research (and evaluations) involving 'child voice' included an explicit account of why and how children's silences were recognized, noted, responded to and interpreted.

Such a methodological account might include the following eight elements:

1. A statement of epistemological position in relation to the interpretation of silence. For example, is silence ignored as merely a gap between responses or is it seen, rather, as an integral part of the co-construction of the encounter?

2. Reference to the multilayered cultural context of the interaction and the implications for silence. For example, if silence is associated with politeness (as in the Japanese culture) and this is not recognized, then the interviewer might make a series of inappropriate and recurrently

counterproductive initiations in order to speed a response. While this example is fairly obvious (almost a cliché´ – with the accompanying danger of overgeneralization), similar cultural differences may be less transparent.

3. Clarity about the researcher's responses (verbal and non-verbal; beforehand, contemporaneously and subsequently) to silence in the light of (1) and (2) above and including the use, or avoidance, of 'incentives' to participate.

4. Scrutiny of silence within the encounter in the context of the evolving power relationships between researcher and researched. Each 'side' may use or manipulate silences for their own ends. For example, the researcher may use silence to (perhaps unwittingly) put pressure on a child to give some response and advice to researchers to wait (e.g. at least 10 seconds) for a response could be interpreted as a way of increasing their hold over the interaction, rather than accepting silence as reflecting a child's valid wish not to respond.

5. Examination of the silence explicitly from the child's point of view. For example, the language around the silence may point to the child using the space to ponder their views, to give space, to conjecture the speaker's intentions, to take over control of the interaction or even to get in touch with an unseen 'other'.

6. How the silence is managed by both adult and child (linking with the third example in this list). For example, Beresford (1997) suggests using a squeaky toy which could be squeezed by the child for a 'no response'. This shifts the emphasis from silence as a non-reply to silence as a positive choice and so making that silence more apparent.

7. How the silences are coded – that is, the place of silence or gaps in interpreting talk. Rogers (2005, p. 164) describes the use of 'interpretive poetics' and illustrates this approach through the identifying of story threads and 'tearing' in transcripts of talk from an individual child. This is in line with approaches to 'child voice' as co-constructed in specific contexts.

8. How the silences are reported, including any respondent validation approaches or other ways, consistent with the epistemological stance, of re-visiting 'voice'. If agreeing about the interpretations of words is

fraught (how to cohere speaker's, listener's and observer's views?) how much harder must it be to agree about what a nebulous silence may convey'?

Such an eightfold account would help to avoid treating child 'voice' (particularly the aspects of silence) in a simplistic way. Over time, it could contribute to the development of methodologies of silence alongside methodologies of 'voice'.

Concluding note

Those working in the context of 'voice' with children who have speech, language and communication needs need to sustain a recursive and reflective approach. This operates across all paradigms and contexts. It is a guard against the muddying of purpose which subverts child 'voice' into others' agendas. Reflectivity should also prompt clarity in context (a listening culture) and progress in methods so that these become more authentic (the child is communicating a genuine view) and valid (we are correctly interpreting the child's message).

An overarching issue emerging from the plethora of work on 'voice' and children with speech, language and communication needs is the fragmentation of these children's voices. They tend to be sought within the remit of a particular project or with a specific narrow focus (but see Wickenden, 2011), perhaps reflecting the funding constraints or service foci. This means that the more holistic understanding of the child's views – along with inevitable fluidities and ambiguities – may be missed. Integrating those views into policy and provision requires a listening culture that permeates all children's services and experiences.

All children should have the chance to have their voices heard. The onus is on adults to find ways to facilitate this process. Methods for hearing the views of children with speech, language and communication needs are constrained more by researchers' and evaluators' imaginations than by children's capabilities. Limits to voice have been repeatedly overridden (see above) and a 'can-do' approach will push boundaries further. However, in pushing out these boundaries, the wider context of overlapping disadvantage and disability needs to be recognized. Checks need to be made that the fostering of voice for children with speech, language and communication needs is having an impact for all those children and not just a subset whose personal circumstances privilege their voices.

Key references

Fielding, M. (2004) Transformative approaches to student voice: theoretical underpinnings, recalcitrant realities. *British Educational Research Journal, 30*, 295–311.

Komulainen, S. (2007) The ambiguity of the child's 'voice' in social research. *Childhood, 14*, 11–28.

Lewis, A. (2010b) Silence in the context of child 'voice'. *Children and Society, 24*, 14–23.

References

Abbott, D. & Carpenter, J. (2010) Becoming an adult – Transition for young men with Duchene Muscular Dystrophy. Retrieved from http://www.bristol.ac.uk/norahfry/resources/ online

Abbott, D. & Carpenter, J. (2011, January) 'Other voices, other rooms': Talking about transition to adulthood with young men with Duchene Muscular Dystrophy (DMD). Paper to ESRC-sponsored seminar, *Substantive issues in disabled children's lives: recent research.* University of Bristol.

Bercow, J. (2008) *The Bercow Report: A review of services for children and young people with speech, language and communication needs.* Annesley, Nottingham: Department for Children, Schools and Families.

Beresford, B. (1997) *Personal accounts: Involving disabled children in research.* York: University of York Social Policy Research Unit, Stationery Office.

Clarke, M.T. & Wilkinson, R. (2008) Interaction between children with cerebral palsy and their peers 2: Understanding initiated VOCA mediated turns. *Augmentative and Alternative Communication, 24,* 3–15.

Cruddas, L. (2006, May) 'Engaged voices' – Dialogic interaction and the construction of shared social meanings. Paper at ESRC Seminar Series, *Pupil voice and participation: Pleasures, promises and pitfalls,* Nottingham.

Ephratt, M. (2008) The functions of silence. *Journal of Pragmatics, 40:11,* 1909–1938.

Fielding, M. (2004) Transformative approaches to student voice: theoretical underpinnings, recalcitrant realities. *British Educational Research Journal, 30,* 295–311.

Foy, G. (2010) *Zero decibels: The quest for absolute silence.* New York: Scribner.

Komulainen, S. (2007) The ambiguity of the child's 'voice' in social research. *Childhood, 14,* 11–28.

Kurzon, D. (2010) On silence. *Journal of Pragmatics,* DOI: 10.1016/j.pragma.2010.11.011

Lewis, A. (2010a) Parental involvement, influence and impact concerning Special Educational Needs and Disabilities (SEND). *Journal of Research in Special Educational Needs, 10:3,* 237–254.

Lewis, A. (2010b) Silence in the context of child 'voice'. *Children and Society, 24,* 14–23.

Lindsay, G. Dockrell, J., Law, J., Roulstone, S. & Vignoles, A. (2009) *Better Communication research programme: First interim report research report RR070. London: Department for Education.*

Martin, D. (2005) English as an additional language and children with speech, language and communication needs. In A. Lewis & B. Norwich (Eds), *Special teaching for special children? Pedagogies for inclusion.* Buckingham: Open University Press.

Wickenden, M. (2011, January) 'Talk to me as a teenage girl': Experiences of friendship for disabled teenagers. Paper to ESRC-sponsored seminar, *Substantive issues in disabled children's lives: Recent research.* University of Bristol.

Wickenden, M. (2011) 'Give me time and I'll tell you': Using ethnography to investigate aspects of identity with teenagers who use Alternative and Augmentative methods in communication (AAC). In S. Roulstone and S. McLeod (Eds) *Listening to children and young people with speech, language and communication needs.* London: J&R Press.

10 Ethics, Consent and Assent When Listening to Children with Speech, Language and Communication Needs

Rosalind Merrick

Abstract

When children with speech, language and communication needs are listened to in research, particular challenges regarding ethical judgements are encountered. There are benefits to all parties, but there are also risks to be assessed in the light of principles such as respect and justice. First, there is the risk of omitting certain children unfairly. Second, there is the risk of engaging children in projects or activities to which they do not really consent. Third, there is the danger of listening but failing to hear their meaning. Reflecting on these risks is in the interests of the children and can enhance the quality of our own knowledge.

Actually I'm really enjoying doing this with you.
William was an 8-year-old boy with specific language impairment. He uttered this comment while participating in a research interview exploring the views of children about communication and speech and language therapy (Merrick, 2009).

Introduction

Listening to people would appear a relatively mundane and risk-free activity. After all, it is done every day by many people without ethical dilemma or concern. However, listening through research is a process permeated by ethical judgements, from establishing aims to reporting findings. Children at large are considered to be a vulnerable population because they are less able than adults to protect their own interests (Farrell, 2005). Research with children with speech, language and communication needs can pose a particular ethical challenge, given the importance of mutual understanding to ethical conduct. There are benefits to all parties in terms of knowledge, enjoyment and improvements to services and care. However, there are also dangers to be avoided, or at least balanced against each other in the light of principles such as respect and justice. This chapter covers three levels of risk. The first type of risk, failing to offer children the opportunity to be heard, is related to access and issues of diversity. The second type, engaging children as participants in projects without their consent, concerns notions of competence and respect for autonomy. The third type, the danger of listening without truly hearing, concerns issues of interpretation and respect for knowledge.

The opportunity to be listened to

Adults have an ethical obligation to respect children's right to participation, and also to protect them from harm. Sometimes these two principles may appear to be in conflict. The argument for limiting children's participation on grounds of protection can of course apply in a variety of research contexts, but it is perhaps more likely to be used where the level of vulnerability is high. Given the vulnerability of children with speech, language and communication needs, researchers and gatekeepers such as parents and teachers have a particular protective role. They will wish, for example, to shield children from research procedures that risk stirring up negative emotions. However, overprotection from gatekeepers and the blocking of access can impede children's opportunities to be heard (Balen, Blyth, Calabretto, Fraser, Horrocks & Manby, 2006) and deprive children of the chance to opt into projects that are in their interests (Robson, 2009).

It is misleading and unfair for mainstream research to claim to be representative of children at large, yet fail to include children with speech, language and communication needs. Yet researchers are often reluctant to plan a project to include children with learning or communication difficulties, because of ideas about the degrees of competence required to understand the project, consent and take part (Cuskelly, 2005). Participation may be facilitated even where children are profoundly disabled, although special arrangements may be necessary to include them (e.g. Wickenden, 2011, Chapter 20 in this volume). In order to be heard, children with speech, language and communication difficulties need a context where they can communicate effectively and confidently. The involvement of parents and carers is an obvious and sometimes vital strategy for overcoming the difficulties of an unfamiliar researcher communicating directly with the child. For this reason, parents and carers are often asked for their views alongside those of their children. This is proposed, for example, in Clark and Moss' (2001) Mosaic approach, which has been applied to children with speech difficulty (Daniel & McLeod, 2006). The involvement of a familiar and valued person can provide the emotional support that some children will need, in order to believe that their views will be understood and valued (Lewis & Porter, 2004). They may, moreover, have a practical role in facilitating effective communication. The risk to be avoided here, however, is giving undue weight to adult accounts because of their relative accessibility or intelligibility. Adults closest to a child are likely to be reliable proxies, but also to have strong views of their own (Ware, 2004; see also Goldbart & Marshall, 2011, Chapter 13 in this volume).

Another possible source of injustice is where the views of some children are subsumed among the voices of others. Children with speech, language and communication needs are not a homogeneous group, and there is a danger of overgeneralizing and assuming that some children (for example, those who are older, more confident or who meet clear criteria for a particular diagnostic category) speak for others. Children themselves are aware of this issue of unfairness, where some children never 'get picked' (Hill, 2006, p. 77).

Consent and assent

Alongside the ethical concern not to exclude children is, conversely, the danger of engaging them as participants without their true consent. Prospective participants in research have the right to be well informed, to have choice and to decline from participation should they so wish. Establishing informed consent is a cornerstone of ethical research with adults as well as children. Legally, the informed consent of participants is required for all research. Where children are under 16 and considered incapable of giving agreement which is fully informed, consent is sought from a parent or carer. In English law, minors can give valid consent themselves as long as they have the competence to understand what is proposed and the discretion to make a wise choice (Alderson & Morrow, 2004). This model of informed consent comes from medical practice with adults, who can reasonably be expected to understand appropriately presented materials and communicate their wishes (Allen, 2005). Children's capacity to consent and participate actively should not be underestimated, and has been demonstrated even in very young children (Alderson, 1993; Flewitt, 2005). It is also the case, however, that a rigid interpretation of informed consent has limited relevance to children who lack prerequisite skills, or for whom making informed rational choices and sticking to them is simply not the way they do things.

It is generally recognized that, where children are considered incapable of giving fully informed consent, the researcher should still do everything possible to ascertain their level of agreement or disagreement (Morris, 2003; Harcourt & Conroy, 2005). The term 'assent' is often used in place of 'consent' when children are willing to participate in research even though they may not fully understand its nature and purpose. Hurley and Underwood (2002) found that abstract features such as research goals and confidentiality were not always easily understood by the schoolchildren in their study, but the activities and voluntary nature of participation were communicated more effectively. Assent is required at the beginning of a project and, just as importantly, should be ongoing throughout the listening process, as children often need to try something before forming an opinion (Lewis & Porter, 2004). William, quoted at the beginning of this chapter, was not necessarily sure at the beginning what participation in a project was going to be like, but his expression of enjoyment provides an example of positive assent.

While informed consent depends upon children's competence, assent is a notion that depends upon responsiveness on the part of the researcher (Cocks, 2006). Older generations typically exercise control over children, and the adult researcher is in an inherently powerful position relative to the child (Mayall, 2008). Children have a particular deference to adult authority and an eagerness to please, which makes them more vulnerable than adults to controlling influence (Ceci & Bruck, 1998). They might find their choice to participate and right to withdraw difficult to believe or to remember. They may also perceive covert penalties for non-participation (Aubrey, David, Godfrey

& Thompson, 2000). Aware of this, researchers advocate techniques that seek to go some way towards redressing this power imbalance by encouraging children to take an active role (Morrow & Richards, 1996).

While respecting children's autonomy, one must also recognize the importance of children's social context when helping them to make decisions. Research often takes place in school, where expectations to listen and act cooperatively prevail. Children experience pressures and preferences to conform, which reduce the likelihood of questioning and dissent (Heath, Charles, Crow & Wiles, 2007). Perhaps particularly for children with disabilities, decision-making is embedded in interdependent relationships with parents, teachers or carers (Clegg, 2004). Encouragement can merge into coercion; there is a fine line between on the one hand giving needed reassurance, arousing interest and sharing enjoyment and, on the other hand, conveying expectations of participation that a child feels pressurized to fulfil. Trust and social factors, such as the activities of friends, are as influential as cognitive and linguistic skills in consent-giving (Alderson, 1992).

In children's health and education there are times when the principle of beneficence – that is, promoting the wellbeing of others – carries more weight than that of respect for autonomy. Teachers, healthcare professionals and parents take responsibility for judging what is in the best interests of the child. Allmark (2002) warned that, in the context of healthcare, some adults are accustomed to hearing and overruling children's protests against certain treatments, and there is a danger of doing this in research. Children have many ways of expressing dissent, being prepared to switch the topic of conversation, look away or move away when disinterested or uncomfortable. They can also respond with silence to a question or invitation. Lewis (2010, 2011, Chapter 9 in this volume) has emphasized the ethical importance of accepting and interpreting verbal non-responses. The challenge for researchers is to design a study in which dissent is a socially acceptable option, so that there are no negative repercussions for the child among peers or from gatekeepers. It should be added, however, that pauses, silences and topic shifts can indicate difficulty with understanding or social interaction, not necessarily dissent or discomfort with the question (Gallagher, 2009).

During the course of the research process, codes of ethical conduct sometimes come into direct conflict with children's expressed interests and priorities. For example, data should be treated as anonymous, in order to protect children's identity, and yet participants sometimes want to be identified with their work (Conroy & Harcourt, 2009). Principles of confidentiality work against children having the freedom to disseminate firsthand to policy-makers and practitioners (Cree, Kay & Tisdall, 2002). Ethics committees typically stipulate that full information be provided at the beginning of the study, before the participants agree to participate. Yet children are sometimes not interested in preamble and just want to try something to see for themselves (Gallagher, Haywood, Jones & Milne, 2010). Children's use of time is often controlled by adults, and their free time is a precious resource (Christensen, 2002). Their views on what activities they want to miss in order to participate in the research might well differ from those of their gatekeepers, such as parents, teachers or headteachers. There are no simple answers to these dilemmas. Flexibility depends in part upon the research design and methodology. However, any solutions will involve consideration of the way in which researchers communicate with participants and manage their expectations.

Children's meanings

Truly listening to children means being prepared to be surprised by them. Alderson (2004) argues that, if research aims to demonstrate children's problems and deficits, there is a danger of overstating their need for help as opposed to showing their competences. Children are likely to have views and meanings that adults cannot take for granted, and research methods need to be sensitive enough to capture these.

Researchers listening to children have an ethical duty to understand, interpret and report the children's views in a way that is fair and accurate. When gathering data through interviews, strategies can be employed to support mutual intelligibility; for example, using materials and activities that give immediacy to the conversation and provide a shared context. The sense that children make of the research enterprise will influence their contributions to it. Familiarity and time spent building a relationship are likely to help researcher and participants to understand one another and work from common assumptions about the nature and purpose of the research. Repeated contacts offer more scope than one-off consultations for verifying the validity of findings with the participants themselves.

Children can interpret the same project in different ways. For example, children in interviews about communication drew on the conventions of a lesson, a heart-to-heart or fun and games (Merrick, 2009). The impact of unspoken assumptions seems particularly poignant in the case of children who have difficulties with verbal communication, especially as misunderstandings carry the potential for disappointment and disillusionment. For example, children may hope for action in response to what they say, and have a certain time frame in mind. Or they may interpret interest from the researcher as a sign of friendship that they wish to continue. Christensen (2004) described the importance of tuning in to children's 'cultures of communication' when seeking to establish dialogue with them. By this, she meant being aware of children's own patterns of language use, and developing research methods that are in line with their experiences, interests, values and routines.

Even where effective dialogue and mutual understanding is established, there remain the challenges of fair interpretation and reporting. Reflexive thinking is perhaps the ultimate ethical safeguard in this process, and a matter of integrity for the researcher. Reflexivity refers to the technique of examining one's own preconceptions and their potential influence, in order to appreciate diversity among participants and be open to learning from them (Davis, 1998). Without it, there is a danger of using children's words to back up one's own arguments rather than being genuinely open to the children's interests (Roberts, 2008).

Conclusion

Communication with children lies at the heart of ethical practice. Truly inclusive research takes a positive view of children's capacity to actively participate, and employs practical strategies to facilitate this. Traditional definitions of informed consent depend upon communicative competence, and thus formal consent-giving is often the prerogative of parents rather than children with speech, language and communication needs. The notion of assent is useful in extending to all children the right to express agreement or disagreement to participate. Participatory methods that allow time for the development of relationships and mutual understanding offer scope for children to knowingly and willingly contribute their perspectives and influence interpretation. When listening to children with speech, language and communication needs, principles of respect and justice go hand in hand with reflexive thinking and practical responsiveness to children in context.

Key references on this topic

Alderson, P. & Morrow, V. (2004) *Ethics, social research and consulting with children and young people.* Ilford: Barnardos.

Christensen, P. & James, A. (Eds). (2008) *Research with children: Perspectives and practices* (2nd ed.). Abingdon: Routledge.

Farrell, A. (Ed.). (2005) *Ethical research with children*. Maidenhead: Open University Press.

Fraser, S., Lewis, V., Ding, S., Kellett, M. & Robinson, C. (Eds) (2004) *Doing research with children and young people*. London: Sage.

Harcourt, D., Perry, B. & Waller, T. (Eds) (2011) *Researching young children's perspectives: Debating the ethics and dilemmas of educational research with children*. Abingdon: Routledge.

Lewis, A. & Lindsay, G. (Eds) (2000) *Researching children's perspectives*. Buckingham: Open University Press.

Mauthner, M., Birch, M., Jessop, J. & Miller, T. (Eds) (2002) *Ethics in qualitative research*. London: Sage.

Tisdall, E.K.M., Davis, J.M. & Gallagher, M. (Eds) (2009) *Researching with children and young people: Research design, methods and analysis*. London: Sage

References

Alderson, P. (1992) In the genes or in the stars? Children's competence to consent. *Journal of Medical Ethics, 18*, 119–124.

Alderson, P. (1993) *Children's consent to surgery*. Buckingham: Open University Press.

Alderson, P. (2004) Ethics. In S. Fraser, V. Lewis, S. Ding, M. Kellett & C. Robinson (Eds), *Doing research with children and young people* (pp. 97–112). London: Sage.

Alderson, P. & Morrow, V. (2004) *Ethics, social research and consulting with children and young people*. Ilford: Barnardos.

Allen, G. (2005) Research ethics in a culture of risk. In A. Farrell (Ed.), *Ethical research with children* (pp. 15–26). Maidenhead: Open University Press.

Allmark, P. (2002) The ethics of research with children. *Nurse Researcher, 10:2*, 7–19.

Aubrey, C., David, T., Godfrey, R. & Thompson, L. (2000) *Early childhood educational research: Issues in methodology and ethics*. London: RoutledgeFalmer.

Balen, R., Blyth, E., Calabretto, H., Fraser, C., Horrocks, C. & Manby, M. (2006) Involving children in health and social research. *Childhood, 13:1*, 29–48.

Ceci, S. J., & Bruck, M. (1998) Children's testimony. In W. Damon (Ed.), *Handbook of child psychology* (Vol. 4, pp. 713–774). New York: Wiley.

Christensen, P. H. (2002) Why more 'quality time' is not on the top of children's lists: The 'qualities of time' for children. *Children and Society, 16*, 77–88.

Christensen, P. H. (2004). Children's participation in ethnographic research: Issues of power and representation. *Children and Society, 18:2*, 165–176.

Clark, A. & Moss, P. (2001) *Listening to young children: The mosaic approach*. London: National Children's Bureau and Joseph Rowntree Foundation.

Clegg, J. (2004) Practice in focus: A hermeneutic approach to research ethics. *British Journal of Learning Disabilities, 32*, 186–190.

Cocks, A.J. (2006) The ethical maze. *Childhood, 13:2*, 247–266.

Conroy, H. & Harcourt, D. (2009) Informed agreement to participate: Beginning the partnership with children in research. *Early Child Development and Care, 179:2*, 157–165.

Cree, V.E., Kay, H. & Tisdall, K. (2002) Research with children: Sharing the dilemmas. *Child and Family Social Work, 7:1*, 47–56.

Cuskelly, M. (2005) Ethical inclusion of children with disabilities in research. In A. Farrell (Ed.), *Ethical research with children* (pp. 97–111). Maidenhead: Open University Press.

Daniel, G. & McLeod, S. (2006) Listening to the voice of children with a communication impairment. In G. Whiteford (Ed.), *Proceedings of the qualitative research as interpretive practice conference: Voice, identity and reflexivity* (pp. 187–200). Albury: Charles Sturt University.

Davis, J. (1998) Understanding the meanings of children: A reflexive process. *Children and Society, 12:5*, 325–335.

Farrell, A. (Ed.) (2005) *Ethical research with children*. Maidenhead: Open University Press.

Flewitt, R. (2005) Conducting research with young children: Some ethical considerations. *Early Child Development and Care, 175:6*, 553–565.

Gallagher, M. (2009). Ethics. In E.K.M. Tisdall, J.M. Davis & M. Gallagher (Eds), *Researching with children and young people* (pp. 11–64). London: Sage.

Gallagher, M., Haywood, S.L., Jones, M.W. & Milne, S. (2010) Negotiating informed consent with children in school-based research: A critical review. *Children and Society 24:6*, 471–482.

Goldbart, J. & Marshall, J. (2011). Listening to proxies for children with speech, language and communication needs. In S. Roulstone & S. McLeod (Eds), *Listening to children and young people with speech, language and communication needs*. London: J&R Press.

Harcourt, D. & Conroy, H. (2005) Informed assent: Ethics and processes when researching with young children. *Early Child Development and Care, 175:6*, 567–577.

Heath, S., Charles, V., Crow, G. & Wiles, R. (2007) Informed consent, gatekeepers and go-betweens: Negotiating consent in child- and youth-orientated institutions. *British Educational Research Journal, 33:3*, 403–417.

Hill, M. (2006) Children's voices on ways of having a voice. *Childhood, 13:1*, 69–89.

Hurley, J.C. & Underwood, M.K. (2002) Children's understanding of their research rights before and after debriefing: Informed assent, confidentiality and stopping participation. *Child Development, 73*, 132–143.

Lewis, A. (2010) Silence in the context of 'child voice'. *Children & Society, 24:1*, 14–23.

Lewis, A. (2011) The importance of silence when hearing the views of children and young people with speech, language and communication needs. In S. Roulstone & S. McLeod (Eds), *Listening to children and young people with speech, language and communication needs.* London: J&R Press.

Lewis, A. & Porter, J. (2004) Interviewing children and young people with learning disabilities: Guidelines for researchers and multi-professional practice. *British Journal of Learning Disabilities, 32:4*, 191–197.

Mayall, B. (2008). Conversations with children: Working with generational issues. In P. Christensen & A. James (Eds), *Research with children: Perspectives and practices* (2nd ed., pp. 109–124). Abingdon: Routledge.

Merrick, R. (2009) Children's views of speech and language therapy. Unpublished doctoral thesis, University of the West of England, Bristol.

Morris, J. (2003) Including all children: Finding out about the experiences of children with communication and/or cognitive impairments. *Children and Society, 17*, 337–348.

Morrow, V. & Richards, M. (1996) The ethics of social research with children. *Children and Society, 10*, 90–105.

Roberts, H. (2008) Listening to children: And hearing them. In P. Christensen & A. James (Eds), *Research with children: Perspectives and practices* (2nd ed., pp. 260–273). Abingdon: Routledge.

Robson, S. (2009) Producing and using video data in the early years: Ethical questions and practical consequences in research with young children. *Children and Society, 25:3*, 179–189.

Ware, J. (2004) Ascertaining the views of people with profound and multiple learning disabilities. *British Journal of Learning Disabilities, 32:4*, 175–179.

Wickenden, M. (2011) 'Give me time and I'll tell you': Using ethnography to investigate aspects of identity with teenagers who use alternative and augmentative methods of communication (AAC). In S. Roulstone & S. McLeod (Eds), *Listening to children and young people with speech, language and communication needs.* London: J&R Press.

11 Issues and Assumptions of Participatory Research with Children and Young People with Speech, Language and Communication Needs

Clodagh Miskelly and Sue Roulstone

Abstract

Participatory research entails a commitment to working with people to investigate an issue that affects them. Participants are encouraged to take control of aspects of planning, implementing and reporting the research. Acknowledgement and disbursement of the power differential between the researcher and participants via constant negotiation is a key to the success of participatory research. In this chapter, a case example is unpacked to provide a rich understanding of general and specific issues in the participatory research process when researching with children and young people with speech, language and communication needs.

What is participatory research?

Participatory research is as much an attitude to research as it is a set of methods. It entails a commitment not only to undertaking research with people to investigate issues that affect or concern them but also to people being able to influence change in those issues. Reflecting on the knowledge that people gain through lived experience leads to insights and reveals the nuances of social issues. Participatory research highlights traditionally undervalued knowledge which is nonetheless important to the research process. It also tends to place emphasis on advocacy. That is, reflection and analysis of an issue leads into identifying ways to make changes and into communicating the need for change to health professionals, educators, or policy-makers (Cornwall & Jewkes, 1995).

One form of participatory research is called *participatory action research* and is grounded in the actuality of people's lives, working to take action as well as enhance understanding. Participatory action research is an 'approach characterized by the active participation of researchers and participants in the co-construction of knowledge; the promotion of self- and critical awareness that lead to individual, collective, and/or social change; and an emphasis on a co-learning process where researchers and participants plan, implement, and establish a process for disseminating information gathered in the research project' (McIntyre, 2008, p. 5). In practice the nature and extent of participation varies at different times and stages of a project, and participation in all aspects of a project is relatively rare.

The enhanced role of the participant

In participatory research projects everyone is a researcher. However, most often projects are initiated by professional researchers who work with a group of people connected to the research focus. For brevity in this chapter we will refer to professional researchers as 'researchers' and other participants as 'participants'. In participatory research, participants might take an active role in shaping all aspects of a research process, from identifying what is to be researched through to disseminating findings or initiating action to influence changes based on the research findings. Since participants shape the process, the outcomes are not always consistent with the original purposes or starting point of the project.

Research that is shaped by and conducted with participants is context-specific and approaches to designing, practising and implementing participatory research projects need to be responsive to participants' needs and to an evolving process. Frequently, people are involved who have little experience of collective reflection or of being listened to; therefore a wide range of methods may be necessary to enable participants to express, reflect on and document experience, knowledge and ideas which aim to take into account that there are different ways of knowing (McIntyre, 2008). These include using different media and a range of approaches for describing, categorizing and making sense of knowledge and experience. There are no fixed methods and no single theoretical framework for undertaking participatory research (McIntyre, 2008).

Negotiation and power in participatory research

Participatory research can require participants to step into processes of investigation and reflection which are unfamiliar and even uncomfortable. It can take a while for any sense of the value of the process to be clear, or for themes or ideas for action to emerge (Cornwall & Jewkes, 1995). The process has to be fitted around other demands in the lives of participants. Furthermore, groups include diverse sets of people, and different participants will engage at different times or to different degrees with different methods or themes. This requires both researchers and participants to be open to what will happen next and researchers to be responsive in the choice of methods. McIntyre suggests a 'commonsense' approach where researchers and participants take joint responsibility, working together to develop feasible ways of participating, reducing the pressure to conform to particular ways of participating. 'In that way, participation is viewed as a choice, not an imposition' (McIntyre, 2008, p. 19).

Participatory research requires attention to relationships of power between professional researchers and research participants and usually involves a shift of control from the researchers to participants. Researchers usually come to the project with control of resources, and with their expertise and status recognized both socially and through their salaried position. Participants may feel obliged to go along with them, especially if they are concerned about sanction or loss of resources, or they may lack confidence to challenge. Researchers need to acknowledge and attempt to mitigate against these power dynamics which otherwise can undermine the very aspects of participatory research that are intended to include and empower (Cooke & Kothari, 2001).

Thus the process of ongoing negotiation between participants and researchers as to what, why, when and how they are researching is rarely neat and can be challenging. It requires researchers to consciously step away from being in control and to be reflexive about their own motives, goals and attitudes. Throughout the process researchers need to be aware of how their 'biography informs [their] ability to listen, question, synthesize, analyse, and interpret knowledge' (McIntyre, 2008, p. 8). For example, a speech and language therapist might reflect on how their professional knowledge and experience shapes their judgements of participants' actions or comments. Participatory researchers accept that human beings are subjective in their interactions with others rather than trying to impose objectivity on these situations; they advocate acknowledging our biases. For example, feminist qualitative researchers argue for considering biases as resources that researchers bring to a context and that can be useful in shaping or making sense of the process provided that they are explicitly acknowledged (Olesen, 1994, p. 165).

Reflexivity extends to how researchers use and present findings. Ideally participants should co-author publications with researchers, but this is not always possible. Where there is no co-authoring, to keep to the principle of researching with, rather than about, participants, it is important to retain and make visible participant voices (or silences) within the presentation of the research; the researcher's own role and position in relation to the participants should be clear.

Frameworks and models to guide participatory research

There are a range of different frameworks and models to help assess or guide participatory processes. Some focus on the process, such as the cycles of exploration, knowledge construction and action in participatory action research, (McIntyre, 2008; Reason, 1994) and others focus on the extent or nature of participation (Arnstein, 1969; Hart, 1992). Perhaps the most commonly adopted model, Arnstein's ladder focuses on the extent or nature of participation. In this model each rung of the ladder presents different degrees of participation – from manipulation and therapy, which are classed as non participation; through informing, consultation and placation, which Arnstein classes as tokenism; through to citizen power, available through partnership, delegated powers and citizen control (Arnstein, 1969).

Applying frameworks and models to participatory research with children

The majority of frameworks and models for participatory research have been designed for adult participation and are usually designed by adults. Even when they are adapted for young people (e.g. Hart, 1992), they tend to be weak on the realities of adult–child power relations and in acknowledging and respecting children's agency as well as different ways of being, acting or expressing in participatory projects. They leave us with 'a limited and fragmentary conceptualisation of children's participation' (Malone & Hartung, 2010. p. 28). Participation is not as neat or sequential as a ladder (cf. Arnstein, 1969; Hart, 1992) might suggest (even Hart has critiqued the use of his model as a comprehensive tool for assessing projects; see Malone & Hartung, 2010). Other participatory models explain different aspects of children's participation but largely continue to impose adult frameworks on to children rather than 'acknowledging that children are participating everyday through their own cultural practices and their remaking of themselves and their environments' (Malone & Hartung, 2010, p. 35). Malone and Hartung advocate for more creative approaches to interacting with children which open up dialogue, and being open to 'all the possibilities of children's participation, even those [adults] haven't thought of' (Malone & Hartung, 2010, p. 36).

Participatory research with children and young people, particularly those with speech, language and communication needs

Research with children and young people, particularly those with speech, language and communication needs, has its own set of concerns regarding methods, process and power relationships. If children are to be able to participate meaningfully in research, then care should be taken not to measure or value the formation and communication of views by children according to how they conform to adult norms: 'Too often, adults underestimate children's capacities or fail to appreciate the value of their perspectives, because they are not expressed in ways which would be used by adults' (Lansdown, 2010, p. 15). Openness to a range of ways of communicating views is of particular importance when working with children and young people with speech, language and communication needs, and recognition and respect for non-verbal forms of communication as well as a range of verbal forms is required (Lansdown, 2010). A failure to recognize children's contribution because they do not fit with adult norms can lead to a failure to allow children to take any control of the research process and can undermine its value.

Researchers need to consider children and young people with speech, language and communication needs in terms of what they can do rather than what they cannot, to treat them as competent social actors in their own right rather than as less than adult, and to use and develop methods that build on how, rather than whether, a child can participate. Rather than expecting children to fit in with adult structures or notions of 'ideal participation', participation should be viewed flexibly using methods that are accessible and suitable for each child (Martin & Franklin, 2010).

Participatory research can provide opportunities for children to reflect and communicate on their experience, knowledge and opinions and to be involved in decisions that affect them. However, recognizing the right to participate and creating an opportunity for that to happen neither automatically advances knowledge nor empowers young people.

A case example of participatory research: 'What's it like to be a teenager with communication difficulties?'

To consider the value and challenges of participatory research with young people with SLCN, we describe *The Bristol Project* (Speech & Language Therapy Research Unit, 2010), which aimed to explore the views of some young people with speech, language and communication needs. To read more about the whole project, including an account by one of the young participants, see Roulstone, Miskelly and Simons (2011, Chapter 32 in this volume). The project aimed to communicate a greater understanding of what it is like to be a young person with speech, language and communication needs, and the aim was that the young participants would have some control over the process and its outcomes in order to address the issue from their own perspective and in their own way. It was intended that the research themes could be shaped by their contributions, views, reflection and analysis of their own situation. Five teenage boys participated. During five half-day and three full-day workshops, we tried out a range of activities, which were intended as a framework to enable the participants to reflect on their experience and express views. Activities were developed, adapted and chosen in response to what happened in previous workshops, drawing on participants' suggestions and enthusiasm but balancing that with an attempt to focus on the research question. Activities included video diaries, collage, photography, maps, journals, storyboards, improvisation and interviewing.

Developing a shared understanding of the research question

In participatory research projects, it is not uncommon to find that the project is researcher-initiated, where a theme has been identified through literature reviews, research or policy and/or certain young people have been identified as seldom heard. Projects may emerge out of concerns identified close at hand to the children and young people concerned, but this should not be confused with child-initiated participation where children themselves have identified an issue of concern or initiate activities. Participants are often happy to use methods and resources to address the issue that has brought them together even when they have not initiated the project.

The Bristol Project was a researcher-initiated project. The question 'What's it like to be a teenager with speech and language difficulties?' was the basis on which participants were recruited and introduced to the project. However, the boys were not asked to explain why they came to the workshops, although they were certainly encouraged to participate by parents. The opportunity to make a film, take part in creative activities and spend time with other young people may have been enough motivation to get, and to stay, involved and the boys generally expressed enjoyment in the sessions. The researchers made decisions about the different activities that were undertaken broadly in relation to how they might help answer that research question. We assumed that communication difficulties were likely to be part of their daily lives and hoped that initial workshop activities aimed at exploring their daily life would lead them into talking about or showing what it is like to be a teenager with communication difficulties.

The participants were able to say what research is and were aware of the question we were asking. However, they did not talk about communication difficulties and did not appear to see the research topic as something of particular interest. They only mentioned it if prompted and then there was evasion, puzzlement and evident discomfort. As one participant put it, 'Talking about talking – that's weird.' Furthermore, they were puzzled by the idea that people might be interested to watch a film about them and felt that a film about something interesting (notably, the things that interested them, such as sport, trains, popular culture) would have wider appeal. As one participant commented, 'Why would anyone watch a film about me? I'm not famous.' We tried different approaches, thinking that if we just asked the right kinds of questions or chose the right activity, then they would or could answer the question 'What's it like to be a teenager with speech and language difficulties?' Eventually we understood that we were asking the wrong question.

We were expecting or wanting a self-analysis that was premised on the young people having some understanding of how communication is not working for them. However, the boys did not appear to see themselves as having a difficulty in the way that we thought of them as having one. This was not to say that the boys did not perceive themselves as different or as encountering difficulty. One boy described himself as having 'behaviour problems'; another talked about his 'bad luck'; and there were regular references to bullying and bullies, which revealed difficult experiences at school.

While we cannot be sure why participants did not take an interest in the research question, it may be for some or all of the following reasons depending on the participant:

- They lacked sufficient ability for introspection or were not sufficiently self-aware to reflect on or critique their own communication or difficulties in interacting with others.

- They were not interested in talking about communication or their own difficulties and saw no appeal in the proposed topic of the film.

- They found it too difficult to talk about sensitive and personal issues.

- They did not see themselves as having difficulties – or considered that the difficulty lay in how others interacted with them.

- The research methods and questions were not sufficient.

The participants were there because they had been identified as having speech, language and communication needs by other people, but this was not necessarily how they saw themselves. Robbie's report (Roulstone et al., 2011, Chapter 32 in this volume) provides his perspective on why he attended the workshops.

Nevertheless, *The Bristol Project* did explore what it is like to be these young people. The boys communicated certain things about their ways of being in the world, their interests and ways of interacting with others. They did so largely on their terms, and in doing so we learned something about what life is like for some young people who have been identified as having speech, language and communication needs, as well as how we might research with, and listen better to, these young people.

How young people and researchers can shape the research process

It is important to be alert throughout the research process to when and how children and young people can exercise choice, especially since they may have limited experience of doing so. In school, which constitutes a significant part of their lives, children and young people are encouraged to conform to adult norms, and rewarded for it, and their lives outside are largely organized around the decisions of parents or other adults (Gallacher & Gallagher, 2008). Given this context, it can be unreasonable to expect young people to quickly and directly take a lead in a research process. It is not always enough to create opportunities or provide activities to frame young people's participation. Time is needed to get used to the situation, along with trial and error to see what works for a particular group. Activities should be chosen, developed and adapted, taking into consideration suggestions from the participants as well as observations as to what appear to be the participants' preferred way of working.

In *The Bristol Project*, the participants shaped the research process and outcomes by following their own interests and not conforming to adult expectations and structures. Initially the boys tended to accept the structures, practices and activities that adults had introduced – sometimes willingly, sometimes with less enthusiasm and, in the case of one participant, with frequent objections. We had established ground rules as a group, including the rule that anyone (adults or young people) could opt out of any activity, at any time, and to facilitate them in keeping control of their participation. Most of the boys chose to opt out at times.

Researchers, as reflective practitioners, should also be attentive to the ways in which power and control are implied or subtly manifested. The shift in this project towards young people's interests did not happen in an articulated or explicit way. The adults' behaviour and communications enabled the boys to take more control of some aspects of the project. The adults would participate in activities alongside the young people; in this way, we also tried to equalize how information flowed between researchers and participants and to show that we wanted to hear their views and about their lives. The participants became more confident, to the point where they would criticize our methods and remind us, or each other, of the project ground rules. We, in turn, became more relaxed, more open to the boys taking over the timing, content, form and terms of engagement. This can be illustrated through the role of video and the video camera in *The Bristol Project*.

Initially we set up a video camera in the workshop in order to record what happened, so we could review it as part of the research. However, the boys were immediately interested by the camera and wanted to try it out or perform in front of it. We were concerned about our research record and at first discouraged the boys from engaging directly with the video. In the second workshop, at the boys' request, we made video diaries and the boys were involved in filming each other. Subsequently, it was untenable to maintain control of the camera, so we started to bring two cameras, and maintained one to record what happened and a second that the boys would pick up and use when they wanted to video. The subsequent film (DVD) we made contains some of the footage recorded by the boys in the workshops.

These shifts and ways of influencing *The Bristol Project* were as much to do with relationships of power between children and adults as with particular activities. The researchers both consciously and indirectly gradually ceded control to the young people by adapting activities or changing how the workshops were organized. We moved to accommodate the participants in terms of topics of investigation, process and activities. For example, the boys enjoyed role play and improvised drama activities, so on a number of occasions we followed their lead on this, in order to further understand their perspectives on their lives and how they would play out both real and imagined scenarios. For some of the boys, role play was a preferred option to storyboard techniques, which we introduced for planning potential scenes in the film. While it might be a strength of our approach that the young people's actions shaped how the project developed, there was throughout a tension between how the boys could, and the researchers intended them to, shape the process, research direction and themes.

It isn't just participation when the adults say so

All aspects of people's engagement with a participatory research workshop can influence the process, research findings and outcomes. It is important to look beyond what we think of as the 'research process' and participation. We need to think about how these activities sit within a young person's world and how relevant or interesting they might be. Practitioners of participatory research need to be reflexive (Reason, 1994). They need to be aware of their own role and how they may be seen from the participants' perspective – for example, as a teacher-like, authority figure. Even when adults work hard to relinquish control, acknowledge the power relationships and take a broader understanding of how children choose to participate or not, this participation tends to take place within wider adult-led and devised structures of action and decision-making (Malone & Hartung, 2010). Adults set many of the conventions of the workshop, such as scheduling, boundaries of activities, involvement and conduct. These can be valuable and useful aspects of the adult role, without which there might not be any workshops. This is particularly the case early in the process, when young people would not have had time to get used to the project and assert themselves.

Although researchers tend to hold the resources and initiate research, they need to make choices which are intended to cede control of the project while also attempting to keep to the interests of the research and the participants. In our project, we tried out some activities that the boys had suggested, but attempted to keep the content to areas that would shed light on the research topic. So we did make a video diary, but did not go bowling or play chess.

Participatory research with children can be critiqued for having too narrow a conception of what constitutes participation. This is the case where only activities that have been devised by researchers are considered to be part of the research. This can be counterproductive when attempting to access young people's perspectives and does not recognize their right to freely participate (Gallacher & Gallagher, 2008; Malone & Hartung, 2010). It is important to avoid equating a successful participatory process with obedience to adult researchers. Only to consider the pre-planned and/or adult-initiated activities as 'the participation' limits the learning from a project, as well as young people's opportunities to shape that learning. For example, even when young people opted out of activities, they did not become invisible; they were still present and sometimes got involved in other ways. One boy would video what we were doing; another would read a book but occasionally join in the conversation if it took his interest.

The ways in which participants appropriate the workshop's conventions or resources for their own purposes should be considered an important part of the learning process. The boy who would pick up the video when he opted out of an activity was often reluctant to be the focus of attention. He could avoid this by staying behind the camera, but he could also film what interested him rather than necessarily recording the workshop activities. He was very interested by CCTV and surveillance and sometimes he hid the camera or filmed passers-by out the window. The video and other media technology was also a mechanism for him to interact with the adults. He would take on the role of assistant, checking batteries or moving the camera around.

Researchers can learn more with, and from, and about, the young people by looking at all aspects of a project, including the conventions that evolve as part of workshop practice, the use of the ground rules, and activities or actions initiated by young people. We hope and think that the young people in *The Bristol Project* also gained something from both the activities they introduced and the ones we introduced.

By only focusing on adult-initiated events, there is a danger of falling into assumptions that 'children require to be "empowered" by adults if they are to act in the world' (Gallacher & Gallagher, 2008, p. 503). As this project illustrates, children and young people act and participate in ways which go beyond the limits of the techniques and frameworks introduced by adults (Gallacher & Gallagher, 2008).

Conclusion

Participatory research involves working with people to investigate an issue that affects them. This requires an active commitment to participants taking control of aspects of the research, and means having an awareness of who holds power and authority and how it is manifested. How the research unfolds depends on the context, a rich understanding of the context and how it changes during the research. Researchers need to reflect on their own practice and views, as well as the participants', and should be open to their assumptions being challenged as they listen and learn in the process. They should work to move beyond preconceived ideas and expectations.

In the case example of *The Bristol Project*, it was clear that by resisting our research question the participants took us past our framing of their experience in terms of 'difficulties' to work with them in representing themselves on their own terms and learning about their tactics for coping with the world. They challenged our assumptions about their communication. The young people were not involved in analysis of what we produced or discussed in workshops. Instead there was a second part to the project involving a researcher-only analysis phase, albeit one which reflected on all aspects of the process. In doing so, we tried to focus on what the boys were explicitly telling us and to avoid placing our interpretations on their communication and what might be perceived as difficulties.

The Bristol Project originally asked young people to reflect on their own communication, which required self-awareness and introspection and being able to discuss feelings and (to some degree) perceptions of others. For most people, this is difficult; for young people with social and cognitive communication difficulties, it is even more difficult. While projects with themes requiring less introspection may be able to achieve more involvement from young people in making sense of what emerges through the process, this is also reliant on the choice of appropriate and innovative methods.

References

Arnstein, S.R. (1969) A ladder of citizen participation. *Journal of the American Planning Association, 35*:4, 216–224.

Cooke, B. & Kothari, U. (Eds) (2001) *Participation: The new tyranny?* London: Zed Books.

Cornwall, A. & Jewkes, R. (1995) What is participatory research? *Social Science and Medicine, 41:12,* 1667–1676.

Gallacher, L. & Gallagher, M. (2008) Methodological immaturity in childhood research?: Thinking through 'participatory methods'. *Childhood,* 15, 499.

Hart, R.A. (1992) *Children's participation, from tokenism to citizenship.* Florence: UNICEF.

Lansdown, G. (2010) The realisation of children's participation rights: Critical reflections. In B. Percy-Smith & N. Thomas (Eds), *A handbook of children and young people's participation* (pp. 11–23). London: Routledge.

McIntyre, A. (2008) *Participatory action research.* Thousand Oaks, CA: Sage.

Malone, K. & Hartung, C. (2010) Challenges of participatory practice with children. In B. Percy-Smith & N. Thomas (Eds), *A handbook of children and young people's participation* (pp. 24–38). London: Routledge.

Martin, K. & Franklin, A. (2010) Disabled children and participation in the UK: Reality or rhetoric? In B. Percy-Smith & N. Thomas (Eds), *A handbook of children and young people's participation* (pp. 97–104). London: Routledge.

Olesen, V. (1994) Feminisms and models of Qualitative Research. In N.K. Denzin & Y.S. Lincoln, (Eds), *Handbook of qualitative research* (pp. 158–174) Thousand Oaks, CA: Sage Publications.

Reason, P. (1994) Three approaches to participative inquiry. In N.K. Denzin & Y.S. Lincoln (Eds), *Handbook of qualitative research* (pp. 324–339). Thousand Oaks, CA: Sage.

Roulstone, S., Miskelly, C. & Simons, R. (2011) Making a film as a means of listening to young people. In S. Roulstone & S. McLeod (Eds), *Listening to children and young people with speech, language and communication needs.* London: J&R Press.

Speech & Language Therapy Research Unit (2010) *The Bristol project* [DVD]. Bristol: Author. Available from http://www.speech-therapy.btck.co.uk/News/Film

12 Independent Advocacy and Listening to Children with Speech, Language and Communication Needs

Jane Dalrymple

Abstract

Children with speech, language and communication needs can sometimes find communicating with adults stressful: 'If I'm trying to explain something, when I get frustrated I start to babble,' says Bryn; while Shona states, 'I tried to get a pen and paper to write down but then I'd scribble because I couldn't think what to say' (Dalrymple, 2008, p. 16). Carl explains, 'Most adults don't seem to understand children a lot. They don't seem to want to listen. It's different with [the advocate] because she really does help me get my point across – she is the exception' (Dalrymple, 2008, p. 18). When children feel powerless or without a voice, feelings of frustration may be exacerbated, and access to an independent advocate is one way of enabling children to feel able to have a voice.

Understanding the need for independent advocacy

Independent advocacy services for children and young people have developed over the last two decades as the benefits of listening to children have become recognized and advocacy has been a focus of government initiatives (Department of Health, 1998). Advocacy can broadly be defined as supporting or speaking up for someone and has its origins in the Latin word *advocatus*, which means 'legal advocate' (NSPCC, no date). Inevitably advocacy is therefore best known and understood in a *formal* way in relation to legal services where the role of advocates in court (lawyers) is to represent the interests of their clients, speak up on their behalf and protect their rights (Wertheimer, 1996). However, advocacy is also a natural part of being a parent or carer, and can be undertaken by any person who wants to support a friend, relative or colleague, for example. Health and social care practitioners often act as advocates for service users, and paid carers (foster carers or key workers in residential homes) will advocate for the children they are looking after. However, parents, carers and professionals may find it difficult to advocate the wishes and feelings of a child while also feeling that they need to make decisions based on their best interests. Furthermore, it can be disempowering for both the child and the professional, who acts as an advocate but feels constrained by their employer: 'those who exhibit a willingness to stand up on behalf of the people they serve, frequently find themselves in trouble with the employing body' (Kennedy, 1990, p. 17). Similarly parents, foster carers or key workers can find it difficult to advocate if their own needs conflict with the needs of the child they are caring for. It is likely that a child or young person will find it more disempowering when someone appears to be acting as an advocate and yet continues to act in their own role. In such circumstances specialist advocacy services provided by independent advocates have a valuable role to play in supporting children when decisions are being made that concern their lives.

What is independent advocacy?

A key element of listening to children and young people is finding out what their views are (McLeod, 2008), which in turn enables their participation. The role of advocates in this process can be described as providing 'an enabling environment where young people can evolve their own means of expression and participation' (Percy-Smith & Thomas, 2010, p. 362). The starting point is to recognize that children and young people have a perspective that can be shared, based on the sociological perspective that children are social actors who should therefore be 'active in the construction and determination of their own lives... not just the passive subjects of social structures and processes' (James & Prout, 1990, p. 8). Rather than assume a child cannot communicate their views, adults need to find out what the child's views are. This not only means using a range of communication techniques, but also requires adults to rethink their attitudes towards children. Such thinking involves moving away from practice where adults make decisions based solely on what they consider to be in the best interests of a child to one where the starting point is to find out the views, wishes or feelings of the child (Boylan & Dalrymple, 2009; McLeod, 2008).

Independent advocacy is usefully defined by the Scottish Independent Advocacy Alliance as:

> a crucial element in achieving social justice. It is a way to ensure that everyone matters and everyone is heard – including people who are at risk of exclusion and people who have particular difficulties in making their views known (Scottish Independent Advocacy Alliance, 2010, p. 4).

The Alliance guide to commissioners of independent advocacy services explores the power relations that exist in the provision of services, recognizing that professionals are in a powerful position because they are often expected to make judgements that impact on the lives of service users and control resources. Independent advocates are in a position to challenge the power relations through promoting the right of children to be involved in decision-making and to have their views valued and listened to with equal importance, however they are expressed (Martin & Franklin, 2010). This does not make advocates better people; it means that 'they just stand in a different place and see things from a different perspective' (Scottish Independent Advocacy Alliance, 2010, p. 21). Different power relations can make it difficult for all children to participate in decision-making – both within adult–child relations and because of the structural power of organizations providing services. Children and young people with speech, language and communication needs may also have to rely more on adults to facilitate their communication and participation. It is particularly important in this respect that the role of the advocate, to be their champion and explore their views, is managed without disrupting their existing networks of support (Knight & Oliver, 2008). Knight and Oliver point out that the advocacy relationship can produce dilemmas and tensions for children with specific communication needs, and independent advocates find that it may be necessary to work alongside other key people in the life of a child in order to build up a picture of their life. The following commentary from an independent advocate illustrates the point:

> Most young people we work with have their own idiosyncratic communication systems, so we may also need to work with other people in their lives to understand how they communicate – for example with their carer, speech therapist or college. The way

in which these people, who have daily contact with the young person, communicate with him or her can hold the key to effective advocacy. Young people who do not communicate verbally still use language, but each situation is different and it is important to make time for an advocate to get to know and understand a young person and also for that young person to get to know and trust the advocate. We are committed to continuing to gain the skills we need to communicate with young people who use different ways of expressing themselves and we believe that the central tenets of advocacy should not be compromised to accommodate our own lack of skills as workers (Boylan & Dalrymple, 2006, p. 29).

The key role of an advocate is to make sure that all those involved in the life of a child with speech, language or communication needs hear and consider the view of the child. The advocate may disagree with the child and understand the reasons for the views of the adults in that child's life, but their role is to stand alongside the child and ensure that their views and feelings are heard and listened to, not to express a personal opinion.

There is, however, a wider element of independent advocacy which, as the definition above indicates, goes beyond the individual to a wider systemic role. This means that advocacy has a political role to promote equality, social justice and social inclusion (Boylan & Dalrymple, 2009; Henderson & Pochin, 2001). For children with speech, language and communication needs, this means challenging the discrimination and oppression they may face, not only because they are children but because, compared to children who do not have such needs, they may experience multiple discrimination, low expectations and social exclusion – defined by what they cannot do rather than what they can do (Martin & Franklin, 2010).

While many independent advocacy services concentrate on case advocacy, the empowering potential of advocacy can best be understood in terms of the relationship between individual or case advocacy and the wider systemic or cause advocacy which identifies how advocacy can contribute to changing policy, legislation and practice. A framework for understanding advocacy links case and systemic advocacy together (Office of the Child Youth and Family Advocate, 1997) and demonstrates that if children with speech, language and communication needs are to have access to services which meet their needs, to be protected and to have a voice in the decisions which affect their lives, both elements of advocacy practice are needed (see Figure 12.1).

Root causes of many problems experienced by children and young people are systemic.
Systemic change should support better case solutions

Systemic Advocacy

Case Advocacy

*Public, Political and
Bureaucratic*

Formal and Informal

Many cases cannot be resolved within the current system.
Case advocacy 'informs' our systemic advocacy and tells us what changes are needed.

Figure 12.1 Framework for understanding advocacy.

Policy and legislation

Despite increasing emphasis on ensuring the participation of children and young people in decision-making, it can be difficult for many children to find their voice in adult-led decision-making processes and in practice it has been found that children may need advocacy support if they are to participate in a meaningful way. Research indicates that children can feel marginalized and disempowered in processes such as reviews (Boylan, 2009), child protection conferences (Dalrymple, 2005; Wyllie, 1999), and family group conferences (Laws & Kirby, 2007). As well as not feeling listened to, the experience of adult-led meetings for children can be difficult:

> I feel bombarded at meetings – it is better with [the advocate]… she can put my views across to everyone and they listen to what I want ('Bryn' in Dalrymple, 2008, p. 16).

Independent advocacy services for children and young people have therefore developed as a response to such experiences and the need for access to independent advocacy to support young people is now written into government policy.

The United Nations Convention on the Rights of the Child (1989) has been a key tool to promote children's participatory rights. The participation elements of the Convention include Article 12, which upholds the right for children and young people to be heard in decisions that concern their lives. This Article has provided the impetus and justification for the development of independent advocacy services for children in the UK. The Convention influenced key legislation for children across the UK (the Children Act 1989 in England and Wales, the Children (Scotland) Act 1995 and the Children (Northern Ireland) Act) and brought a participatory decision-making framework into the work of professionals working in children's services. The legislation is not without its shortcomings and each of the four nations of the UK has its own history in developing services for children and young people. Nevertheless it is fair to say that the emergence of a range of policy and legislative frameworks has recognized children and young people as social actors and experts in their own lives, whose views should be respected and taken into account (Percy-Smith & Thomas, 2010).

For children and young people with speech, language and communication needs it is likely that their views may be sought when they are identified as having special educational needs as part of the statutory annual review process, within Individual Education Plans as well as other assessment and review. The Special Educational Needs Code of Practice, which applies to children with speech, language and communication needs, recognizes the difficulties in such decision-making processes and acknowledges that:

> Some young people may wish for personal support and may prefer to express their views through a parent or other family member or an independent supporter such as an advocate, Connexions Personal Adviser, counsellor, social worker or health professional or through peer support (3.15 Code of Practice, p. 29).

Acknowledgement that children with speech, language and communication needs should have specific access to advocacy is recognized in Issue 6 of the *I CAN* talk series. Identifying that collaboration between health and social care practitioners and parents is an important part of supporting children with speech, language and communication needs, it suggests that if this is to work, then:

> Children and young people need to have their needs understood, to
> be consulted and involved in decision concerning then and to have an
> advocate within their learning environment (Lee, 2008, p. 13).

Clearly the need to have a 'team around the child' (Children's Workforce
Development Council, 2009) is important if the needs of children with speech,
language and communication needs are to be recognized and met. This is
reflected in government initiatives to promote integrated services. However,
an advocate is able to ensure that the needs of the child are not subsumed
into either into the needs of parents or carers or the constraints of service
providers. Advocacy ensures the centrality of the child within the processes of
multi-agency working. It is suggested therefore that collaboration works best
if children feel listened to and heard; teachers feel supported in developing the
knowledge and skills that they need to work with children who have speech,
language and communication needs; parents feel that the needs of their child
are being understood and provided for and speech and language therapists
understand the school community, curricular demands and family context –
which includes accepting the need for advocacy support (Lee, 2008).

The *National Standards for the Provision of Children's Advocacy Services*
(Department of Health, 2002; Welsh Assembly Government, 2003) point
out that all children should have access to advocacy services, and notes that
communication needs should not prevent them from accessing advocacy.

Forms of advocacy

Various forms of independent advocacy are now accepted ways of working
with children and young people in order to promote their voice and agency and
also to challenge social injustice (Boylan & Dalrymple, 2009). Self-advocacy,
citizen advocacy and non-directed advocacy are particularly relevant for
children with speech, language and communication needs. Often independent
advocates are professional, paid advocates. Other forms of advocacy which
cannot be examined in detail in this chapter include collective advocacy, peer
advocacy, legal advocacy and e-advocacy (Table 12.1).

Table 12.1 Forms of advocacy.

	Form of advocacy	Key characteristics	Model
Self-advocacy	Self-advocacy	Person expresses own feelings. Individual or group	Individual issue-based advocacy
	Collective advocacy	Group of people in a similar situation	Usually cause/systemic advocacy
Support by independent advocate	Citizen advocacy	A long term relationship between a person and their advocate	Individual covering any situation where a young person may need support
	Peer advocacy	Advocate has had similar experiences as the person being supported. Individual or group	Individual and often issue- based. Can also be collective systemic advocacy
	Professional advocacy	Advocate is trained and paid	Usually short term and issue-based advocacy
	Non-directed advocacy	Advocate supports people whose form of communication is difficult to interpret or who lack capacity (person-centred, human rights, best interests, watching brief)	Individual issue-based advocacy
	Legal advocacy	A contractual (and financial) relationship between advocate and person being represented	Individual issue-based advocacy
	E-advocacy		Individual issue-based or systemic advocacy

Self-advocacy

Self-advocacy simply means speaking up for oneself. Some young people with speech, language and communication needs can be supported to advocate for themselves at an individual level to gain the confidence to speak up in decision-making meetings. This may also require advocates to work with other adults in the meetings to ensure respect for the contribution of the young person involved as part of their supportive role. The difficulties for self-advocacy have been highlighted in research by Afasic Scotland (2002), who held a workshop as part of the research process. The workshop was attended by 19 young people who had a degree of speech, language or communication needs. During the course of the day they spoke about how they are treated in relation to meetings, and the responses clearly indicate the difficulties that children may face in trying to advocate for themselves:

> You're chucked out of the room and the door is slammed in your face.
>
> You're treated like idiots.
>
> You feel as if people are saying 'You shouldn't be here in your meeting. We are the experts.'
>
> (Afasic Scotland, 2002, p. 31).

As well as individual self-advocacy, some children may be part of a self-advocacy group. These often have more of a campaigning role and invariably occur within residential settings or where children are in a situation where there is a level of continuity (such as children who spend long periods in hospital). Some groups of young people are also supported to meet regularly. People First is an organization run by and for people with learning difficulties which aims to raise awareness and campaign for the rights of people with learning difficulties and to support self advocacy groups across the UK. Young People First groups have developed as part of this organization.

In some instances, self-advocacy is linked into consultations to address adult concerns about children's services. For example the Royal College of Paediatrics and Child Health promote work that they undertook to increase the participation of children in the work of the college as self-advocacy. The consultation involved listening to healthy children, children with multiple and complex health needs and those with experience of acute and chronic illness. As a result, recommendations to improve how the college used the views of children to improve the work of the health system were made and actively taken forward by a participation manager (RCPCH, 2008).

Citizen advocacy

Citizen advocacy is a type of advocacy that involves a long-term relationship to support people who are unable to advocate for themselves or who need specific help to do so. Most recent definitions state that 'citizen advocacy is about individual active citizenship, where an ordinary member of the community makes a commitment to the rights of another who is disadvantaged and/or socially excluded' (CAIT, 2002, p. 1). For some young people with specific needs, an advocate with whom they have a long-term and more informal relationship can help them to communicate their views. It is less crisis-orientated than some forms of advocacy and, for young people whose lives often in rely on service providers, it ensures that their needs, preferences and wishes are taken into account (Ramcharan, 1995). This in turn means that they feel listened to and in more control of their lives. There are a few citizen advocacy projects that recruit young volunteers and, while this may be challenging for professionals, it is likely to be empowering for young people who have speech, language or communication needs (Sounds Good Project and Advocacy Resource Exchange, 2005).

Non-instructed advocacy

For children whose method of communication is difficult to interpret, or for those who lack capacity, non-instructed advocacy has developed as a way of ensuring that their likely views and preferences are listened to and taken into account. It is a challenging form of advocacy that has emerged with the provisions set out in the Mental Capacity Act 2005 to safeguard people who lack capacity in particular situations. Since advocacy is very much about empowering children to be involved in decision-making and working *with* then to ensure that they are listened to, a model of advocacy that supports children who are unable to instruct an advocate is difficult and contested within advocacy literature (Boylan & Dalrymple, 2006; Mercer, 2009). Within this form of advocacy there are a number of approaches and it is important for advocates with the skills to communicate with children with speech, language and communication needs (see also Goldbart and Marshall, 2011, Chapter

13). As Mercer (2009) points out, the challenge for advocates is to consistently consider the notion of 'taking instruction' and say to themselves:

> I'm not clear what this eye movement means so I'll take a human rights approach now. But I'll also commit to learning what the eye movement means, so that I can learn more about the communication style and therefore it will not be necessary to continue to rely on non-directed approaches (Mercer, 2009).

Competence to participate and the role of adults

A project for children in Nicaragua starts from 'an unshakeable belief that children and young people are capable and competent' (Shier, 2010. p. 223). Shier points out that while children may have limited tools to analyze the knowledge that they have about their lives, their families, their communities, their hopes and fears, they are the experts about their own lives. Put this alongside failures in services for children with speech, language and communication needs, the difficulties in having a voice within adult decision-making processes and the fact that the needs of children may be subsumed into, or even eclipsed by those of adults, and it is clear that they need support if they are to be heard. This is well described by Shona (Dalrymple, 2008, p. 21), who explained that the advocate 'helps me get the words and then they understand what I am trying to get through'. The case for listening to children rests both on the fact that they suffer if their needs are not met and that they have a right to participate in decision-making. It can be difficult for professionals and parents or carers to act directly as advocates for individual children, and independent advocates can therefore ensure that they are listened to and heard. In order to do this successfully, advocates tend to be 'adults with a "burning heart" and passionate commitment to young people, who understand children and young people's rights and who can assist, advise and support children and young people who are competent actors in their own lives' (Batsleer, 2010, p. 194).

Key references on this topic

Afasic Scotland (2002) *Exploring advocacy: Outcomes of Afasic's enquiry into participation by children with speech and language impairments in the process of participation in decision-making concerning their education.* Dundee: Afasic Scotland.

Boylan, J. & Dalrymple, J. (2009) *Understanding advocacy for children and young people*. Maidenhead: Open University Press.

References

Afasic Scotland (2002) *Exploring advocacy: Outcomes of Afasic's enquiry into participation by children with speech and language impairments in the process of participation in decision-making concerning their education*. Dundee: Afasic Scotland.

Batsleer, J. (2010) Commentary 4. In B. Percy-Smith & N. Thomas (Eds), *A handbook of children and young people's participation: Perspectives from theory and practice* (pp. 193–195). Abingdon: Routledge.

Boylan, J. (2008). An analysis of the role of advocacy in promoting children's participation in statutory reviews. In C.M. Oliver & J. Dalrymple (Eds), *Developing advocacy for children and young people: Current issues in research and practice* (pp. 45–63). London: Jessica Kingsley.

Boylan, J. & Dalrymple, J. (2006) Contemporary advocacy: Providing advocacy for young people with verbal communication difficulties. *ChildRight, cR225*, 2851.

Boylan, J. & Dalrymple, J. (2009) *Understanding advocacy for children and young people*. Maidenhead: Open University Press.

CAIT (2002) *Comments on the national standards for agencies providing advocacy for children and young people*.

Children's Workforce Development Council (CWDC) (2009) *The team around the child and the lead professional: A guide for practitioners*. Leeds: CWDC.

Dalrymple, J. (2005) *Child protection conferences in Wiltshire*. Bristol: UWE/Barnardos.

Dalrymple, J. (2008) *Mapping the maze: An evaluation of the maze advocacy project*. Bristol: University of the West of England (UWE).

Department of Health (1998a) *Modernising social services*. London: The Stationery Office.

Department of Health (1998b) *The quality protects programme: Transforming children's services*. London: HMSO.

Department of Health (2002) *National standards for the provision of children's advocacy services*. London: Department of Health Publications.

Goldbart, J. & Marshall, J. (2011) Listening to proxies for children with speech, language and communication needs. In S. Roulstone and S. McLeod (Eds) *Listening to children and young people with speech, language and communication needs*. London: J&R Press.

Henderson, R. & Pochin, M. (2001) *A right result? Advocacy, justice and empowerment*. Bristol: The Policy Press.

James, A. & Prout, A. (1990) A new paradigm for the sociology of childhood? Provenance, promise and problems. In A. Prout & A. James (Eds), *Constructing and reconstructing childhood. Contemporary issues in the sociological study of childhood* (pp. 7–34). Basingstoke: Falmer Press.

Kennedy, S. (1990) Politics, poverty and power. *Social Work Today,* 14 June, 16–17.

Knight, A. & Oliver, C. (2008) Providing advocacy for disabled children, including children without speech. In C. Oliver & J. Dalrymple (Eds), *Developing advocacy for children and young people: Current issues in research and practice* (pp. 116–131). London: Jessica Kingsley Publishers.

Laws, S. & Kirby, P. (2007) *Under the table or at the table? Supporting children and families in family group conferences: A summary of the Daybreak research.* Brighton and Hove: Brighton and Hove Children's Fund Partnership and Brighton and Hove Daybreak Project.

Lee, W. (2008) *Speech, language and communication needs and primary school age children.* London: I CAN.

Martin, K. & Franklin, A. (2010) Disabled children and participation in the UK: Reality or rhetoric? In B. Percy-Smith, & N. Thomas (Eds), *A handbook of children and young people's participation: Perspectives from theory and practice* (pp. 97–104). Abingdon: Routledge.

McLeod, A. (2008) *Listening to children: A practitioners guide.* London: Jessica Kingsley Publishers.

Mercer, K. (2009) Non-directed advocacy. In *Further down the rights track.* Belper: CROA.

NSPCC (no date) *Speaking out: A guide for advocates for children and young people with learning disabilities.* London: NSPCC in association with VOICE.

Office of the Child Youth and Family Advocate (1997) A framework for understanding advocacy. In *Community advocacy workshop.* Vancouver: Office of the Child Youth and Family Advocate.

Percy-Smith, B. & Thomas, N. (2010) *A handbook of children and young people's participation: Perspectives from theory and practice.* Abingdon: Routledge.

Ramcharan, P. (1995) Citizen advocacy and people with learning disabilities in Wales. In R. Jack (Ed.), *Empowerment in community care* (pp. 222–239). London: Chapman and Hall.

Royal College of Paediatrics and Child Health Advocacy Committee (2008) *Advocating for children.* London: RCPCH.

Scottish Independent Advocacy Alliance (2010) *Independent advocacy: A guide for commissioners.* Edinburgh: Scottish Independent Advocacy Alliance.

Shier, H. (2010) 'Pathways to participation' revisited: Learning from Nicaragua's child coffee-workers. In B. Percy-Smith, & N. Thomas (Eds), *A handbook of children and young people's participation: Perspectives from theory and practice* (pp. 215–229). Abingdon: Routledge.

Sounds Good Project and Advocacy Resource Exchange (2005) *Growing up speaking out: A guide to advocacy for young learning disabled people in transition.* Retrieved from www.advocacyresource.net

United Nations Convention on the Rights of the Child (2008) Retrieved 25 August 2011 from: http://www.unicef.org/crc/

Welsh Assembly Government (2003) *National standards for the provision of children's advocacy services.* Cardiff: Welsh Assembly Government.

Wertheimer, A. (1996) *Advocacy. The Rantzen Report.* London: BBS Educational Developments.

Wyllie, J. (1999) *The last rung of the ladder: An examination of the use of advocacy by children and young people in advancing participation practice within the child protection system.* London: The Children's Society.

13 Listening to Proxies for Children with Speech, Language and Communication Needs

Juliet Goldbart and Julie Marshall

Abstract

Whilst all children and young people should have the right to give their views on the services they receive, this is challenging for children and young people whose speech, language and communication needs are compounded by profound intellectual impairment and/or severe motor impairment. For these young people, proxy or surrogate views may be needed, but these views should be subject to some form of verification. The advantages and limitations of different people as proxies will be considered. Approaches to informing and validating these proxy perspectives will be presented. Implications for good practice will be briefly discussed.

Who needs proxies to represent their views?

Proxies (or surrogates; Shah, Farrow & Robinson, 2009) are people who, based on their close and detailed knowledge of the child or young person and their situation, are viewed as being able to speak on behalf of the child (Ware, 2004). The opportunity, indeed the right, to influence the services one receives is seen as an important aspect of the empowerment of people with disabilities. In the United Kingdom, this is enshrined in Government policy documents such as *Valuing People* (Department of Health, 2001) and the *Children Act* (House of Commons, 2004). As Finlay, Antaki, Walton and Stribling (2008) point out, this right should encompass a wide range of areas of influence in the lives of people with severe disabilities, from where they live to the interactions they have with caregivers. This should include the right of children and young people to give their perspectives on the speech and language therapy services they receive. There are, however, some children and young people whose capacity to give their views is severely circumscribed.

Two groups for whom this is particularly relevant, either in the long or short to medium term, are children and young people with profound intellectual impairments, and children whose ability to use speech is affected by motor difficulties such as cerebral palsy, and who are at the early stages of learning to use augmentative and alternative communication (AAC).

The tenth revision of the *International Classification of Diseases and Related Health Problems* (ICD-10; World Health Organization, 1992, p. 230) describes people with profound intellectual disability as 'severely limited in their ability to understand or comply with requests or instructions… and capable of the most rudimentary forms of non-verbal communication'. As a result, they are likely to need support in expressing their views on a long-term basis.

Children and young people learning language through AAC may have comprehension and cognitive skills within the typical range, but at early stages their output systems are likely to be limited, possibly idiosyncratic (Sigafoos et al., 2000), and only understood by very familiar people. They may, however, have, symbolic understanding, which means they can make use of photographs or pictures. As they progress, they are likely to become increasingly able to express their own views through the use of AAC.

These descriptions are perhaps rather negative, and might suggest that children and young people with these conditions have no capacity for contributing their views. This chapter, however, will describe how the views of children and young people without formal means of communication can be elicited in some circumstances, using appropriate support and the careful and planned use of proxies. The area is not particularly well researched, and this chapter will make use of studies involving adults with profound disabilities and research in related areas, such as proxy decision-making in healthcare and in quality-of-life studies, in order to explore the issue more fully. It is first necessary to consider which individuals might contribute to proxy opinion-giving and decision-making. The potential contribution of parents, siblings and other family members, peers and professionals will be considered, along with limitations of these positions. Strategies for informing and validating proxy accounts will then be presented.

Parents and other family members as proxies

Research by Goldbart and Marshall (2004) demonstrated that parents of children learning language through AAC have rich and detailed knowledge of their children's communication that allow them to make subtle and fine-grained observations of their child from which they draw inferences that are tested within family interactions. Parents' observations included comments on the level of their child's expressive and receptive skills, the topics they communicated about and the ways in which they communicated their choices. Similarly, parents of children and young people interviewed in a study by Goldbart and Caton (2010) readily identified the informal strategies their sons and daughters used to communicate. Of importance were: allowing time, becoming familiar with the person and consistency.

Parents may arguably be the best advocates or proxies for their sons and daughters. They share a culture and family life with the child or young person, are familiar with and are able to articulate their means of communication, and would be expected to have their best interests at heart. Ware (2004, p. 176), however cautions, 'Those who are most familiar with an individual and most likely to interpret their reactions appropriately are also likely to be those with the highest degree of emotional involvement.'

Parents' actions may be influenced by strongly held and subjective values which could affect the opportunities and experiences they make available to their sons and daughters. For example, Fisher, Orkin, Green and Chinchilli (2009, p. 402) found that certain types of medical examination were less likely when a person with learning disability lived with a family member rather than in another community setting. It is unclear as yet what underlies this difference. Parents also seem to be risk averse in their proxy decision-making (Brunner et al., 2003). They have also been found to judge their disabled children's quality of life lower than do their children themselves (Baca, Vickrey, Hays, Vassar & Berg, 2010; Odom, Cohen, Humble & Schwartz, 2005). Other studies have found no correlation between children and young people with disabilities' self-ratings and parental ratings (Jelsma & Ramma, 2010) or young people with disabilities' vocational choices and those of their caregivers (Martin, Woods, Sylvester & Gardner, 2005).

Families, of course, are made up of more than parents and child, with the role of different family members carrying greater or lesser weight depending on the family's culture and history. In terms of identifying appropriate advocates or proxies, it would be useful to consider the role of other adults, including grandparents, uncles and aunts.

Siblings and peers as proxies

It is also important to consider siblings or even cousins of similar ages as proxies. Both share the family's culture and traditions (White, 2001) but, being closer in age to the child or young person with communication impairment, may be more appropriate proxies for giving perspectives on some aspects of the young person's life. In particular, they are more likely to have access to the language and culture of school and leisure activities in which the young person participates and the ways in which their choices and preferences might be demonstrated.

Barr, McLeod and Daniel (2008) have explored the experiences of being a sibling of a child with speech impairment. Unlike the children who are the focus of this chapter, their participants were all siblings of children who do have formal ways of expressing their views, even if they may not always be intelligible. Whilst the role of proxy was not specifically mentioned, Barr et al.'s (2008) sibling participants described taking the role of interpreter – that is, interpreting their sibling's needs or wishes for other people who did not understand them, or even in anticipation of their not being understood. Professionals, however, need to be wary of adding to existing pressure on siblings to adopt a parent-like role (Barr et al., 2008) where the children and young people may already experience stress and 'collision of feelings' associated with their status as sibling to a child with a disability (Barr & McLeod, 2010; Barr, 2011, Chapter 33 in this volume). This may be moderated, however, by the possible benefit of increasing siblings' feeling of engagement and valuing of their contribution, although this view is speculative. Unfortunately, there is a dearth of research on the involvement of siblings as proxies for their brothers or sisters with profound intellectual impairment or complex communication needs.

Peers and friends, who share educational and/or leisure activities with the child or young person, will also have insight into activities they enjoy and how this can be inferred. Again, there seems to be an absence of research on this issue.

Involve Me, a project currently being run by the UK charity Mencap and the British Institute for Learning Disabilities, aims to develop and evaluate creative ways of involving people with profound disabilities in decision-making. One strand of this project is called *Getting to Know You*. This involves training people with learning disabilities to be peer-advocates on behalf of a person with more profound disabilities. The project, although not yet complete, suggests the potential for peers to act as proxies. Further information is available at http://www.mencap.org.uk/page.asp?id=2360.

Professionals as proxies

The final group of people who fulfil the role of proxies, surrogates or advocates are professionals, including teachers, teaching assistants, health professionals, paid carers and social workers. Feiler and Watson (2011) examined the views of teachers, teaching assistants and speech and language therapists regarding involving children and young people with severe learning and communication difficulties in decision-making in the school setting. The majority of their participants prioritized children's participation in decision-making despite acknowledging the difficulties. They suggest that the detailed knowledge that teaching assistants develop in relation to individual children puts them in a particularly strong position to support decision-making.

In examining the factors that professionals consider when making proxy decisions regarding healthcare, Fisher et al. (2009) found that staff did not take a great deal of account of the religious or spiritual affiliations of clients or their families, which seems to be in contrast to decisions made by families.

The complexities involved in the area of supporting children and young people in giving their views and making choices are acknowledged (e.g. Harris, 2003). Neither children and young people with profound intellectual impairment, nor those learning language through AAC, have easily accessed means of conveying their needs and wishes, let alone their views of therapy; a point made by the professionals interviewed by Feiler and Watson (2011). Hence, they are vulnerable to others making assumptions about their opinions. If proxies' perspectives are to be sought for children and young people with profound intellectual impairment, it is essential that proxies' interpretations of the young person's feelings or views should be subject to some form of validation. There are several strategies that can be used by proxies to validate or at least provide some support for their surrogate judgements. These are discussed below.

Validating the perspectives of proxies

Validation approaches for children and young people with profound intellectual impairment: Eliciting likes, dislikes and preferences

Two highly structured, observation-based approaches are available, both providing a framework for eliciting likes, dislikes and preferences: the *Affective Communication Assessment* (ACA) (Coupe, Barton, Collins, Levy & Murphy, 1985; Coupe-O'Kane & Goldbart, 1998) and *See What I Mean* (SWIM) (Grove, 2000; Grove, Bunning, Porter & Olsson, 1999). These are communication assessments which can be adapted to explore children's and young people's likes and dislikes, and how they demonstrate them, generating a tentative taxonomy or dictionary that others can use.

The ACA is an observation or video-based assessment. Detailed observations of the way an individual responds to a range of stimuli (e.g., smell, taste, sound, tactile), events and experiences allows evidence to be built up for identifying typical ways of responding which can be interpreted as, in the earliest stages, likes, dislikes, wants and rejection. These are regarded as hypotheses which are then tested out against the person's responses to other stimuli, events, etc. Research by Hogg, Reeves, Roberts and Mudford (2001) shows that, despite some inconsistencies, ratings of affective communication by familiar observers show some level of agreement. It could be argued, however, that this approach does not take a sufficiently robust approach to the issues of ownership of messages and ascription of meaning.

SWIM is a more recent, highly systematic, three-stage means of scrutinizing the validity of interpretations. The first stage involves collecting, sharing and discussing information about the person with a range of significant others, obviously including the person themselves, if feasible. The next stage involves checking this information across different situations and with different people, and actively seeking alternative explanations, so that they can be ruled in or out. This information can then be entered on to a summary sheet for dissemination. Useful case examples are given in Porter, Ouvry, Morgan & Downs (2001).

The information gained from either of these approaches can be collated and made accessible to other people to inform and validate proxy views through, for example, *Communication Passports* (Millar & Aitken, 2003) or *Multimedia Profiling* (Downton & Ladle, 2002).

As Ware (2004) warns, there is a considerable difference between demonstrating a preference, or even making a choice, about items that are present and giving views on more abstract, longer-term life events. Green and Reid (1996), however, have demonstrated how taking note of observationally derived 'happiness indicators' can help classroom staff to make changes in the activities they provide so as to increase the quality of life experienced by their students. Whilst the level of interpretation required by ACA and SWIM means that it is hard to regard the outcomes as active choice-making, they do provide some insight into individuals' thoughts and feelings about very concrete and specific experiences.

Vos, De Cock, Petry, van den Noortgate and Maes (2010) are developing a highly innovative approach to accessing the feelings of people with profound impairment by looking for correlates between emotional states and changes in physiological measures such as respiration. Whilst classroom application of this approach is a long way off, it is useful to consider its potential.

Validation approaches for children learning language through AAC

The greater comprehension skills and symbolic functioning of children at the early stages of learning language through AAC means that more direct approaches can be used to elicit their views and opinions, although their responses may be in a prelinguistic form. Parents of young children learning language through AAC have often devised sophisticated ways to enable their children to give their opinions. Marshall and Goldbart (2008) describe parents inviting their children to use pointing and eye pointing to choose from a restricted set of options. These parents, like the Spanish-speaking parents in McCord and Soto (2004), use their detailed knowledge of their child's non-verbal communication to elicit their views.

Talking Mats (http:/www.talkingmats.com/) is a structured approach to using symbols to elicit the views of people with communication impairments. Wright (2008) has used Talking Mats to explore young people's satisfaction with their learning experiences at school and Murphy and Cameron (2002) to elicit preferences regarding transition. A visual framework allows children and young people to rate events, situations and experiences as positive, negative or neutral, using symbols or photographs. Evaluations of the approach by Rabiee, Sloper and Beresford (2005), regarding young people's views of support services, and Murphy and Cameron (2008), confirm that Talking Mats is an effective communication resource.

Discussion

The diverse orientations of possible proxies suggest that triangulating and combining multiple perspectives across a range of proxies would be desirable. Feiler and Watson (2011) and Shah et al. (2009) argue for thorough and careful individualized approaches. Such approaches, whilst valuable, are likely to be time-consuming. Structured frameworks such as ACA, SWIM and Talking Mats can be used to inform and validate the judgements of proxies. Combining these frameworks with the views of proxies offers the best practice in enabling children and young people with complex communication needs to give their perspectives on the services they receive.

Key references on this topic

Coupe, J., Barton, L., Collins, L., Levy, D. & Murphy, D. (1985) *The Affective Communication Assessment*. Manchester: MEC. Available from Melland High School, Holmcroft Road, Manchester M18 7NG, UK.

Grove, N. (2000) *See what I mean*. Kidderminster: BILD/Mencap.

Murphy, J. & Cameron, L. (2002) Enabling young people with a learning disability to make choices at a time of transition. *British Journal of Learning Disabilities, 30:3*, 105–112.

Ware, J. (2004) Ascertaining the views of people with profound and multiple learning disabilities. *British Journal of Learning Disabilities, 32*, 175–179.

References

Baca, C., Vickrey, B., Hays, R., Vassar, S. & Berg, A. (2010) Differences in child versus parent reports of the child's Health Related Quality of Life in children with epilepsy and healthy siblings. *Value in Health, 13:6*, 778–786.

Barr, J. (2011) Listening to siblings of children with speech, language and communication needs. In S. Roulstone & S. McLeod (Eds), *Listening to children and young people with speech, language and communication needs*. London: J&R Press.

Barr, J. & McLeod, S. (2010) They never see how hard it is to be me: Siblings' observations of strangers, peers and family. *International Journal of Speech-Language Pathology, 12:2*, 162–171.

Barr, J., McLeod, S. & Daniel, G. (2008) Siblings of children with speech impairment: Cavalry on the hill. *Language, Speech, and Hearing Services in Schools, 39*, 21–32.

Brunner, H., Maker, D., Grundland, B., Young, N., Blanchette, V., Stain, A. et al. (2003) Preference-based measurement of health-related quality of life (HRQL) in children with chronic musculoskeletal disorders (MSKDs), *Medical Decision Making, 23:4*, 314–322.

Coupe-O'Kane, J. & Goldbart, J. (1998) *Communication before speech: Development and assessment.* London: David Fulton.

Department of Health (2001) *Valuing people.* London: HMSO.

Downton, K. & Ladle, J. (2002) Representation, quality and 'small things'. *PMLD Link 14*, 14–16.

Feiler, A. & Watson, D. (2011) Involving children with learning and communication difficulties: The perspectives of teachers, speech and language therapists and teaching assistants. *British Journal of Learning Disabilities, 39:2*, 113–120.

Finlay, L., Antaki, C., Walton, C. & Stribling, P. (2008) The dilemma for staff in 'playing a game' with people with a profound intellectual disability. *Sociology of Health and Illness, 30:4*, 531–549.

Fisher, K., Orkin, F., Green, M. & Chinchilli, V. (2009) Proxy healthcare decision-making for persons with intellectual disability: Perspectives of residential-agency directors. *American Journal on Intellectual and Developmental Disability, 114:6*, 401–410.

Goldbart, J. & Caton, S. (2010) *Communication and people with the most complex needs: What works and why this is essential.* London: Mencap/Department of Health.

Goldbart, J. & Marshall, J. (2004) Pushes and pulls on the parents of children using AAC. *Augmentative and Alternative Communication, 20:4*, 194–208.

Green, C. & Reid, D. (1996) Defining, validating, and increasing indices of happiness among people with profound multiple disabilities. *Journal of Applied Behavioral Analysis, 293:1*, 67–78.

Grove, N., Bunning, K., Porter, J. & Olsson, C. (1999) See what I mean: Interpreting the meaning of communication by people with severe and profound intellectual disabilities. *Journal of Applied Research in Intellectual Disability, 12*, 190–203.

Harris, J. (2003) Time to make up your mind: Why choosing is difficult. *British Journal of Learning Disabilities, 31*, 3–8.

Hogg, J., Reeves, D., Roberts, J. & Mudford, O. (2001) Consistency, context and confidence in judgements of affective communication in adults with profound intellectual and multiple disabilities. *Journal of Intellectual Disability Research, 45*, 18–29.

House of Commons (2004) *Children Act 2004.* London: HMSO.

Jelsma, J. & Ramma, L. (2010) How do children at special schools perceive their HRQoL compared to children at open schools? *Health and Quality of Life Outcomes, 8*(76).

McCord, M. & Soto, G. (2004) Perceptions of AAC: An ethnographic investigation of Mexican-American families. *Augmentative and Alternative Communication, 20,* 209–227.

Marshall, J. & Goldbart, J. (2008) 'Communication is everything I think.' Parenting a child who needs Augmentative and Alternative Communication (AAC). *International Journal of Language and Communication Disorders, 43:1,* 77–98.

Martin, J., Woods, L., Sylvester, L. & Gardner, J. (2005) A challenge to self-determination: Disagreement between the vocational choices made by individuals with severe disabilities and their caregivers. *Research and Practice for Persons with Severe Disabilities, 30:3,* 147–153.

Millar, S. & Aitken, S. (2003) *Personal communication passports: Guidelines for good practice.* Edinburgh: Call Centre.

Murphy, J. & Cameron, L. (2008) The effectiveness of Talking Mats with people with intellectual disability. *British Journal of Learning Disabilities 36,* 232–241.

Odom, J., Cohen, S., Humble, H. & Schwartz, T. (2005) Assessing vision related quality of life in school-aged patients: A comparison of child and proxy assessments. *IOVS, 46,* Suppl. S, 1908.

Porter, J., Ouvry, C., Morgan, M. & Downs, C. (2001) Interpreting the communication of people with profound and multiple learning difficulties. *British Journal of Learning Disabilities, 29,* 12–16.

Rabiee, P., Sloper, P. & Beresford, B. (2005) Doing research with children and young people who do not use speech for communication. *Children and Society, 19,* 385–396.

Shah, S., Farrow, A. & Robinson, I. (2009) The representation of healthcare end users' perspectives by surrogates in healthcare decisions: A literature review. *Scandinavian Journal of Caring Sciences, 23:4,* 809–819.

Sigafoos, J., Woodyatt, G., Keen, D., Tait, K., Tucker, M., Roberts-Pennell, D. et al. (2000) Identifying potential communicative acts in children with developmental and physical disabilities. *Communication Disorders Quarterly, 21,* 77–86.

Vos, P., De Cock, P., Petry, K., van den Noortgate, W. & Maes, B. (2010) Do you know what I feel? A first step towards a physiological measure of the subjective well-being of persons with profound intellectual and multiple disabilities. *Journal of Applied Research in Intellectual Disabilities, 23,* 366–378.

White, L. (2001) Sibling relationships over the life course: A panel analysis. *Journal of Marriage and Family, 63,* 555–568.

World Health Organization (1992) *ICD-10 classification of mental and behavioural disorders: Clinical description and diagnostic guidelines.* Geneva: Author.

Wright, K. (2008) Researching the views of pupils with multiple and complex needs. Is it worth doing and whose interests are served by it? *Support for Learning, 23:1,* 32–40.

14 Listening to Adolescents with Speech, Language and Communication Needs Who Are in Contact with the Youth Justice System

Pamela C. Snow, Dixie D. Sanger and Karen Bryan

Abstract

This chapter explores the speech, language and communication needs of young people in contact with the youth justice system. It provides evidence from across three continents that such young people represent a hidden group at high risk for speech, language and communication difficulties. Too often, these young people are identified along the single dimension of behaviour disturbance, with little or no examination of their communication needs. When considered alongside other psychosocial risks likely to exist (in particular, low academic attainment), lifelong social marginalization often awaits these young people. However, such outcomes may be avoidable, if appropriate early intervention efforts are employed and the perspectives of the young people themselves are sought.

'I need to know what words mean.'
'I started not liking school in the seventh grade. It got harder to understand. School was frustrating and I just gave up'
(Sanger, Creswell, Dworak & Schultz, 2000, p. 46).

'I remember telling mom that I was dumb. I didn't do well in subjects like social studies, math, English, or history. I tried to ask the teacher what she meant by things and sometimes I got in trouble'
(Young person, 16, with special needs)

Adolescents who come into contact with the youth justice system are among the most vulnerable in the community and represent a substantial burden on society, in financial, educational, welfare and judicial terms. This burden is realized through direct costs, but more importantly through lost opportunity and the high probability of intergenerational perpetuation of risk and vulnerability. A growing body of international literature is characterizing young offenders as a group likely to have undetected language impairments. This literature will be reviewed here, and directions for research, policy and practice will be identified.

Language competence emerges in the context of early attachment relationships and is vulnerable to a range of developmental and experiential threats during childhood and adolescence. The wider public health importance of language competence includes its pivotal role in the transition to literacy in the early school years, and the acquisition of a flexible and culturally sensitive set of social skills. Adolescence is a period of continued development of important language skills which underpin continued educational achievement and social development (Nippold, 2007).

Oral language deficits in boys may be linked with the development of externalizing behaviours, ranging from conduct difficulties through to serious and lifelong patterns of antisocial behaviour. While various cross-sectional studies have shown associations between language and behaviour problems in childhood (e.g. Cohen, Menna, Vallance, Im & Horodezky, 1998), longitudinal studies have pointed more clearly to the role of reduced oral language competence as a specific risk factor for adverse outcomes. Beitchman and co-workers (1999, 2001; Brownlie et al., 2004) have shown that unresolved developmental language problems in boys predict engagement in antisocial activity by age 19. In considering possible explanatory pathways, these workers argued that the role of language in social regulation, perspective taking and mediating interpersonal exchanges may account for the adverse psychosocial outcomes in boys with developmental language problems. Two Australian longitudinal studies of large birth cohorts (Bor, McGee & Fagan, 2004; Smart et al., 2003) have reported that poor language ability in the early years increases the risk of antisocial behaviour at age 14. This suggests that overcoming oral language deficits in the early years should be a focus of prevention and early intervention strategies aimed at reducing the prevalence of antisocial behaviour across the lifespan. Similarly, social marginalization and language impairment have been shown to be linked (e.g. Bryan, Freer & Furlong, 2007; Cohen et al., 1998; Ripley & Yuill, 2005; Snow & Sanger, 2011), though cross-sectional studies cannot resolve the 'chicken and egg' dilemma with respect to causal pathways. That is, does being born into fragile psychosocial circumstances predispose to suboptimal language development? Does suboptimal language development predispose to poor psychosocial outcomes? Or do these phenomena interact in other ways that are potentially identifiable? The circumstances under which suboptimal language development combines with a background of psychosocial disadvantage to elevate risk of offending needs to be a focus of future research.

In the United Kingdom, it was estimated in 2006 that a 16-year-old male with speech, language and social deficits would cost the community an average of £200,000, assuming a custodial sentence can be averted; if not, in excess of a further £100,000 could be added to the bill (Hartshorne, 2006). Another UK-based analysis (Barrett, Byford, Chitsabesan & Kenning, 2006) reported that an estimated £1 billion per year is spent on 'processing and dealing with young offenders' (p. 541). Thus, in addition to its wider public health significance, oral language competence has special importance for the young person's passage through the justice system, whether as a victim, a suspect or a witness. Police and other human services interviews require sophisticated auditory comprehension and narrative language abilities (Snow, Powell & Murphett, 2009), as well as the observance of subtle contextual cues around speaker authority and asymmetrical 'speaker rights' typical of exchanges that occur in the legal system. Further, interventions delivered within the justice system to address mental health and behaviour disturbances likely to interfere with community re-entry are highly verbally mediated (e.g. cognitive behaviour therapy, anger management programmes and treatment for sex offending).

Young people with communication difficulties are not commonly positioned as 'experts' with respect to their communication needs. In recently published studies, however, vulnerable young people describe ways in which they have been challenged in understanding language, literacy, curriculum and learning in school (Sanger, Deschene, Stokely & Belau, 2007; Sanger et al., 2010). Over the past two decades, researchers have collaborated to understand communication and language behaviours among marginalized young people, and have begun to document the particular difficulties they experience. These young people are overrepresented in the youth justice system across a range of Western countries. From 1993 to 2000, researchers found that in a sample of 173 incarcerated female adolescents, more than 20% (n=34) had language problems in domains such as semantics, syntax and pragmatics (Sanger, Moore-Brown & Alt, 2000). This is particularly concerning because it represents a prevalence rate that is three times that found in the general population (Larson & McKinley, 2003), yet is likely to go undetected in high-risk young people, for whom speech and language assessments are not routinely provided. Some studies have reported even higher prevalence rates of language impairment in young offenders; for example, Snow and Powell (2008) found that 52% of young male offenders on community-based orders could be classified as language impaired.

Such figures should be of concern to educators in schools as well as to correctional educators who interact with these young people on a daily basis. Qualitative research on the lived experiences of adolescent girls residing in a correctional facility reveals perspectives such as 'I need to know what words mean'; 'I started not liking school in the seventh grade. It got harder to understand. School was frustrating and I just gave up' (Sanger, Creswell et al., 2000, p. 46); and 'I remember telling mom that I was dumb. I didn't do well in subjects like social studies, math, English, or history. I tried to ask the teacher what she meant by things and sometimes I got in trouble,' (Sanger, Creswell et al., 2000, p. 46). Since as early as 1977, researchers have discussed how educators can work to reduce school violence (McPartland & McDill, 1977), but they have overlooked the central role in this endeavour of addressing the language and communication needs of adolescents. This oversight continues to plague professionals who plan academic and social aspects of school programmes.

As educators and other professionals listen to adolescents who are on the margins of society, we must consider their experiences and their views of teachers' language, classroom instruction and expected listening behaviours (Sanger et al., 2007). If carefully listened to, the voices of such young people reveal that adjustments in how we address their academic and social interactions must be made in order for them to be more successful. For example, in the study mentioned above of 31 adolescent girls residing in a correctional facility, approximately 40% indicated concern about the delivery and usefulness of information presented in core curricular classes. Specifically, their concerns related to ideas presented in class as not necessarily being important, interesting, useful, easily understood or taught in an order in which they could learn (Sanger et al., 2007). These concerns were echoed by 27 young female offenders who participated in a separate qualitative study. Via in-depth interviews, these girls reflected on how learning could be improved in school if teachers modified instruction to meet their communication needs. For example, one student reflected positively on her teacher's performance: 'She made social studies interesting and I liked this class. I was not bored and she really got us into the chapter. We would read it out loud and sometimes act it out. It is important to get the students involved' (Sanger et al., 2010).

When educators listen to the voices of adolescents on the margins of society, it becomes apparent that such students could benefit from alternative service delivery models such as Response to Intervention (RTI)[1] or, at the very least, modifications in how teachers approach curriculum to include a greater emphasis on language and communication. Even though adjudicated youths claim to not like being told what to do and seem to have trouble understanding what it is like from the teacher's perspective, there are important metalinguistic and metacognitive skills that these youths lack, and these require educators' attention. For example, a comparison of 31 young offenders' to teachers' opinions on metalinguistic skills indicated that up to half of the young people perceived their performance differently on reading and writing. Adolescents perceived they knew the different sounds that letters could make, knew that some words and phrases could have more than one meaning, understood sentences of varying length, could find the main idea in their textbooks, could predict what would happen in stories, and summarize and make judgements about what they read, read what they wrote and make changes to improve their writing. But, given that students rated their performance higher compared to teacher ratings, with statistically significant differences, this suggests serious mismatches of perceptions between the two groups, and students may not truly understand what must be accomplished to successfully complete tasks in school (Sanger, Spilker, Scheffler, Zobell & Belau, 2008). Though programme-planning challenges for this population of young people on the margins of society will not be solved quickly or simply, and directions for improvement are not always obvious, it is critical that we listen to these young people, and so position them as the experts with respect to how policy-makers and practitioners can better serve them.

An evidence-base for speech and language therapy interventions with marginalized young people is emerging, spanning universal, targeted or specialist inputs. Examples include speech and language therapy consultation to units for young people who are excluded from school (Clegg, Stackhouse, Finch, Murphy & Nicholls, 2009), and one-to-one targeted interventions for identified individuals (Joffe, 2006). That such support is needed for young people is empirically clear (Mackie & Law, 2010). However, further progress is needed to translate this evidence into policy and everyday practice. From

---

1   RTI is a method of early identification and response for children with suspected learning disabilities in the USA. RTI seeks to promote academic success and minimize behaviour difficulties through the provision of intensive, evidence-based educational approaches, with close monitoring of outcomes.

an economic perspective the cost of speech and language therapy services is modest compared to the cost of supporting a young person who might require state benefits, prison placement, public housing and mental health services over many decades (Hartshorne, 2006; Snow & Powell, 2008). The best universal intervention is early identification in educational settings of children who are not meeting developmental targets and the use of evidence-based instruction methods in early literacy, to ensure that at-risk children are not 'left behind' at a time when they could truly benefit from services (Heckman & Carneiro, 2003).

However, most high-risk or otherwise marginalized young people do not receive the support they need to develop oral language skills (Bercow, 2008). Young people with school-related problems are often identified as having behavioural problems (Cohen et al., 1998) and are unlikely, as a consequence of such characterization, to undergo speech and language assessment. Systematic screening of young people for speech, language and communication difficulties on entry to secondary school (age 11), and screening of any young people who develop problems with behaviour, would increase the likelihood of diagnosis and signposting for intervention. This should include gaining the young person's own views with respect to their language skills, their negative experiences of communication and how these impact on experiences of services such as education. Incorporating such perspectives would enable services to better engage young people who are traditionally viewed as hard to reach.

Speech and language therapy intervention for young people within the criminal justice system has also been shown to be effective. Bryan et al. (2007) showed that initiating and running a speech and language therapy service within a young offender institution was feasible. The service integrated well within the institution and was judged to enhance the regime. Referrals were made for a range of communication difficulties, including:

- language (expressive, receptive, pragmatic)

- fluency disorders

- speech (delay, disorder, dyspraxia)

- hearing impairment

- autism spectrum disorders and attention deficit hyperactivity disorder.

The intervention model employed was an individualized goal-setting approach and focused on enabling young people with language and communication problems to cope with the verbal demands of the youth justice setting. The SLT discussed communication issues with the young offenders, many of whom had some awareness of their difficulties and were willing (with support) to identify goals for improving their language skills in order to gain skills through education and work-related training schemes.

The study demonstrated the need for systematic assessment of otherwise hidden language difficulties. Half the population of one institution was screened using the verbal subtests of the *Test of Adolescent Language-3* (Hammill, Brown, Larsen & Wiederwolt, 1994). At least 60% scored below average for their age, with 80% of these scoring within the poor or very poor range (equivalent to the bottom 9% of the overall population for this age group).

Most of the young people were initially unwilling to self-refer to speech and language therapy, denying the existence of speech-language problems. This may reflect a 'lie-low' strategy that young people often adopt when coming into an institution. Trying to be invisible and not seeking help are typical aspects of the culture of young offender institutions, although many institutions try to foster more positive help-seeking. Thus while self-report was not a reliable substitute for formal assessment, it was helpful in gaining the young person's perspective on speech, language and communication issues and in establishing an initial rapport as a basis for intervention. Speech and language therapists must be skilled in eliciting particular concerns about communication, such as avoidance of certain situations, and strategies used when communication breaks down (whether appropriate or not), and other communication goals that the young person wants to achieve. Such information enabled therapy programmes to meet the young person's self-identified needs, promoting engagement and leading to demonstrable and meaningful improvements, such as managing to stay in a group until the end without disrupting proceedings.

Ninety percent of the young people in this study had left school before age 16, with 18% of these not attending by age 12 or younger. This supports the findings of Sanger et al. (2003) and Snow and Powell (2008), lending further weight to the argument that adolescents with schooling or social difficulties should have their language and communication skills properly investigated while they are still in school. Beitchman et al. (1999) found that communication difficulties tend to be misdiagnosed as behavioural problems in adolescents, at least partly explaining perhaps why speech and language therapy referrals are often not made for this group.

Young people who are held within young offender institutions represent only a very small proportion of those involved with the wider welfare system.

In the UK, young offender teams in the community manage much larger numbers of young people at-risk of involvement in criminal activity and those initially getting into trouble. Their remit is preventative with re-engagement in education or training for work as a priority. Gregory and Bryan (2011) showed that speech and language therapy could also be delivered effectively in such contexts.

This chapter deals with a very small part of the vast literature that shows that children's early relational and interpersonal experiences are foundational with respect to language development, educational attainment and the emergence of prosocial behaviours. Unless far more is done early on in the lives of vulnerable children, there is a high risk of progression to the youth justice system. This is not only costly in itself, but represents missed educational and vocational opportunities that are sometimes never made up. Language competence is a far-reaching and modifiable life asset, but appropriate assessment and intervention services must be provided in a timely, accessible and sustained manner to vulnerable young people. It is vital that speech and language therapists and policy-makers provide platforms on which the communication experiences and perspectives of young offenders can be shared, so that the life trajectories of their younger peers can be improved.

References

Barrett, B., Byford, S., Chitsabesan, P. & Kenning, C. (2006) Mental health provision for young offenders: Service use and cost. *British Journal of Psychiatry, 188*, 541–546.

Beitchman, J.H., Douglas, L., Wilson, B., Johnson, C., Young, A., Atkinson, L. et al. (1999) Adolescent substance use disorders: Findings from a 14-year follow-up of speech/language impaired and control children. *Journal of Clinical Child Psychology, 28:3*, 312–321.

Beitchman, J.H., Wilson, B., Johnson, C.J., Atkinson, L., Young, A., Adlaf, E. et al. (2001) Fourteen year follow-up of speech/language-impaired and control children: Psychiatric outcome. *Journal of the American Academy of Child and Adolescent Psychiatry, 40*, 75–82.

Bercow, J. (2008) *Bercow review of services for children and young people (0–19) with speech, language and communication needs.* Nottingham, UK: DCSF Publications.

Bor, W., McGee, T.R. & Fagan, A.A. (2004) Early risk factors for adolescent antisocial behaviour: An Australian longitudinal study. *Australian and New Zealand Journal of Psychiatry, 38:5*, 365–372.

Brownlie, E.B., Beitchman, J.H., Escobar, M. Young, A., Atkinson, L., Johnson, C. et al.

(2004) Early language impairment and young adult delinquent and aggressive behavior. *Journal of Abnormal Child Psychology, 32:4*, 453–467.

Bryan, K., Freer, J. & Furlong, C. (2007) Language and communication difficulties in juvenile offenders. *International Journal of Language and Communication Disorders, 42*, 505–520.

Clegg, J., Stackhouse, J., Finch, K., Murphy, C. & Nicholls, S. (2009) Language abilities of secondary age pupils at risk of school exclusion: A preliminary report. *Child Language. Teaching and Therapy, 25:1*, 123–139.

Cohen, N.J., Menna, R., Vallance, D., Im, N. & Horodezky, N. (1998) Language, social cognitive processing, and behavioral characteristics of psychiatrically disturbed children with previously identified language and unsuspected language impairments. *Journal of Child Psychology and Psychiatry, 39*, 853–864.

Gregory, J. & Bryan, K. (2011) Speech and language therapy intervention with a group of persistent and prolific young offenders in a non-custodial setting with previously undiagnosed speech, language and communication difficulties. *International Journal of Language and Communication Disorders. 46:2*, 202–215.

Hammill, D.D., Brown, V.L., Larsen, S.C. & Wiederholt, J.L. (1994) *Test of Adolescent and Adult Language – Third Edition*. Austin, TX: Pro-Ed.

Hartshorne, M. (2006) *The cost to the nation of children's poor communication. I CAN Talk Series – Issue 2*. London: I CAN.

Heckman, P. & Carneiro, J. (2003) *Human capital policy*. Cambridge, MA: National Bureau of Economic Research Working Paper No. 9495.

Joffe, V. (2006) Enhancing language and communication in language-impaired secondary school-aged children. In J. Ginsborg & J. Clegg (Eds), *Language and social disadvantage* (pp. 207–216). London: Wiley Publishers.

Larson, V.L. & McKinley, N. (2003) *Communication solutions for older students: Assessment and intervention strategies*. Eau Claire, WI: Thinking Publications.

McPartland, J.M. & McDill, E.L. (1977) Research on crime in schools. In J. M. McPartland & E.G. McDill (Eds), *Violence in schools* (pp. 3–22). Lexington, MA: D.C. Heath.

Mackie, L. & Law, J. (2010) Pragmatic language and the child with emotional/behavioural difficulties (EBD): A pilot study exploring the interaction between behaviour and communication disability. *International Journal of Language and Communication Disorders, 45:4*, 397–410.

Nippold, M.A. (2007) *Later language development. School-age children, adolescents, and young adults.* (3rd ed). Austin, TX: Pro-Ed.

Ripley, K. & Yuill, N. (2005) Patterns of language impairment and behaviour in boys excluded from school. *British Journal of Psychology, 75*, 37–50.

Sanger, D.D., Creswell, J.W., Dworak, J. & Schultz, L. (2000) Cultural analysis of communication behaviors among juveniles in a correctional facility. *Journal of Communication Disorders, 33*, 31–57.

Sanger, D.D., Moore-Brown, B., Montgomery, J., Rezac, C. & Keller, H. (2003) Female incarcerated adolescents with language problems talk about their own communication behaviors and learning. *Journal of Communication Disorders, 36*, 465–486.

Sanger, D., Deschene, D., Stokely, K. & Belau, D. (2007) Juvenile delinquents' views of teachers' language, classroom instruction, and listening behaviors. *Journal of Women in Educational Leadership, 5:2*, 16–34.

Sanger, D., Moore-Brown, B. & Alt, E. (2000) Advancing the discussion on communication and violence. *Communication Disorders Quarterly, 22:1*, 43–48.

Sanger, D., Ritzman, M., Stremlau, A. & Snow, P. (2010) Juvenile delinquent girls reflect on learning in schools and offer suggestions. *Journal of Ethnographic and Qualitative Research, 5*, 45–54.

Sanger, D., Spilker, A., Scheffler, M., Zobell, A. & Belau, D. (2008) A comparison between juvenile delinquents' and teachers' opinions on metalinguistic and metacognitive skills. *Journal of Correctional Education, 59:2*, 145–171.

Smart, D., Vassallo, S., Sanson, A., Richardson, N., Dussuyer, I., McKendry, W. et al. (2003) *Patterns and precursors of adolescent antisocial behaviour. Types, resiliency and environmental influences.* Melbourne: AIFS.

Snow, P.C. & Powell, M.B. (2008) Oral language competence, social skills, and high risk boys: What are juvenile offenders trying to tell us? *Children and Society, 22*, 16–28.

Snow, P.C., Powell, M.B. & Murphett, R. (2009) Getting the story from child witnesses: Exploring the application of a story grammar framework. *Psychology, Crime and Law, 15:6*, 555–568.

Snow, P.C. & Sanger, D.D. (2011) Restorative Justice Conferencing and the youth offender: Exploring the role of oral language competence. *International Journal of Language and Communication Disorders, 46:3, 324–333*.

15 Using Narrative Inquiry to Explore Identity in Children with Speech, Language and Communication Needs

Rena Lyons

Abstract

This chapter outlines theories relevant to exploring identity in children with speech, language and communication needs. Identity is a relatively new concept in speech and language therapy and is concerned with how we see ourselves in relation to others. Narrative inquiry has been used with adults to explore identity. Research on the narratives of children with speech, language and communication needs has focused primarily on structural rather than conversational dimensions of narratives, and has been deficit-based. We know very little about how these children construct identity. The potential value of narrative inquiry as a means of investigating identity in these children will be explored.

Importance of listening to children's perspectives

Given the predominance of the medical model in speech and language therapy, much of our work with children with speech, language and communication needs has been impairment-based and has excluded the voices of these children. Current models of evidence-based practice may marginalize the voices of individuals who use speech and language therapy services (Kovarsky, 2008). In recent years, the new sociology of childhood has challenged us to change the way we view children. This requires a shift from a narrow focus on what children will *become,* to a view that endeavours to take children seriously as they experience their lives now (Greene & Hill, 2005). Listening to the voices and views of children is one of the most neglected aspects of child developmental research (Greig, Taylor & MacKay, 2007). By the nature of their difficulties, those with communication difficulties are particularly vulnerable to being disempowered, silenced and marginalized within society and research (Lloyd, Gatherer & Kalsy, 2006; Rabiee, Sloper & Beresford, 2005; Wickenden, 2011).

What do we know about children with speech, language and communication needs?

There is evidence that children with speech, language and communication needs may have long-term educational and psychosocial difficulties (Clegg, Hollis, Mawhood & Rutter, 2005; Law, Boyle, Harris, Harkness & Nye, 1998). Although many outcome studies provide evidence on the long-term implications of speech, language and communication impairments, they neglect the perspectives of the children themselves. It is encouraging that researchers are now beginning to ask these children and young people to talk about their personal experiences (Holliday, Harrison & McLeod, 2009; McCormack, McLeod, McAllister & Harrison, 2010; Owen, Hayett & Roulstone, 2004; Simkin & Conti-Ramsden, 2009). However, we still know very little about the effect of speech, language and communication impairments on children's identity.

What is identity and why should we be interested?

Identity is a relatively new concept in speech and language therapy and, although it may seem obvious that identity would be a central issue for therapists, the minimal emphasis on identity may be due the strong influence of the medical model (Hagstrom, 2004; Kathard, 2006). In basic terms, identity refers to how one sees oneself in relation to others (Duchan, 2004). There are two broad conceptualizations of identity construction that reflect psychological and sociological approaches. One view conceptualizes identity construction as a long-term internalized project. Scholars who support this approach believe that we are only able and motivated to construct a life story during adolescence and adulthood (Habermas & Bluck, 2000; Habermas & Paha, 2001; McAdams, Josselson & Lieblich, 2006). The individualized perspective of identity does not acknowledge children's position as 'experts' on their own lives in the here and now. The other view of identity is relational and places more emphasis on the construction and performance of identity in socially situated contexts (Thorne, 2004). This socially situated relational view of identity acknowledges that co-conversationalists construct different portrayals of themselves in conversations. Jenkins (2008) bridges this gap between the individual and the relational theories of identity by differentiating between the self and the person. He defines the self as the individual's private experience of him/ herself and the person as what appears publicly in interactions with others. The sociocultural context, within which these interactions take place, provides resources which shape our sense of what constitutes culturally acceptable selves (Bruner, 1987).

> The individual presents herself to others... that presentation is accepted (or not), becoming part of her identity in the eyes of others (or not)... the responses of others to her presentation feed back to her... reflexively they become incorporated into her self-identity (or not) (Jenkins, 2008, p. 71).

Identity is no longer viewed as fixed or given and there is general agreement that individuals construct who they are and how they want to be known. In our constructions of who we are and how we want to be seen, we account for how others may try to categorize us (Antelius, 2009). Therefore, we may have multiple identities that we perform depending on the situations and people we meet. The notion that identity is performed and constructed in social interactions is based on the work of Goffman (1959, 1963).

> To put it simply, one can't be a 'self' by oneself; rather identities are constructed in 'shows' that persuade (Riessman, 2008, p. 106).

The relational aspect of identity is emphasized in identity construction in children. According to Jenkins (2008), by middle childhood (5-6 years) the child begins to acquire a 'public' face to control how he/she is perceived by others. As the child gets older, the peer group, often divided by gender, begins to replace the family as the primary context in which identity develops (Jenkins, 2008; Maybin, 2006; Meadows, 2010). In addition, skills of self-presentation are acquired and public image and how one comes across to one's peers become more important as children get older and become more concerned about what their peers think. Social interaction and feedback from others, especially peers, help in answering the identity question 'Who am I?' (Kinavey, 2006). Some argue that middle childhood and early adolescence may be particularly important times for children's identity. For example, learning identities may be constructed at this time when children and young people have experiences of being assessed and evaluated, and may have more of a sense of differentiating between the self they are and their ideal self (Burden, 2008; Meadows, 2010). Given that reputation and public image are important, especially for older children, professionals and parents need to be aware that they too have a role in the co-construction of identity. Children with speech, language and communication impairments may stand out as being different from their peers and may not want to be 'seen' as different.

What is narrative inquiry?

Qualitative methodologies, in particular narratives of personal experience, have the potential to provide us with useful frameworks for exploring children's identity. Narrative inquiry is a useful methodology for capturing the detailed experiences of a single life or the lives of a small number of individuals through their personal stories (Clandinin & Connelly, 2000; Polkinghorne, 1988). Instead of locating themes across interviews, narrative approaches respect individual agency and keep a story 'intact' by theorizing from the case rather than from themes across cases (Chase, 2008; Riessman, 2008). Some have argued that we construct our identity in our discourse, and the stories we construct and tell about ourselves define who we are both for ourselves and others (Elliot, 2007; McAdams et al., 2006).

There are two broad approaches to narrative inquiry: structural and conversational. In the structural approach, a minimal narrative is defined as a sequence of two independent clauses that are temporally ordered (Labov & Waletsky, 1967). Labov and Waletsky (1967) developed frameworks for analyzing structural elements of narratives. They viewed narratives as having two functions: a reference function that relates information to the listener and an evaluative function that tells the listener something about what the events meant to the narrator or something about the narrator. Evaluations normally centre around, and may indicate, the high point of the story; that is, the climax of the story and the reason why the story is told (Peterson & McCabe, 1983). Evaluations may be verbal or non-verbal (Grove, 2007). There have been criticisms of the structural approach to narratives. Not all narrative data, particularly data generated in interviews or in conversations, may fit into such a structural approach (Benwell & Stokoe, 2006; Elliot, 2007; Frost, 2009; Norrick, 2000). In addition, this model also neglects the interactional context within which the narratives are constructed (DeFina, 2009; Mishler, 1986). This point is clearly illustrated in a study by Sota, Hartman and Wilkins (2006), who studied the narratives of a child with a physical disability called Heidi. They contended that if they were to use a structural account alone, without considering the contributions of her conversation partners, their findings might indicate that the child showed severe problems on all narrative discourse dimensions. Moreover, they claim that the quality of Heidi's narratives may be as much a reflection on her interlocutor's skills to elicit the narrative as they are of her own skills to produce them.

Scholars who advocate a conversational approach to narrative inquiry argue for a broader dimensional approach to narrative, claiming that personal narrative is so varied that it resists definition in terms of a set of fixed and defining features (Ochs & Capps, 2001). Conversational narratives may not have a neat beginning, middle and end, and conversation partners work often ask questions, seek clarifications and make challenges as they try to make sense of the story. Narrative inquiry is an attempt by both the teller and the listener to co-create meaning (Mishler, 1986; Mossige, Jensen, Gulbrandsen, Reichelt & Tjersland, 2005). Conversational narratives can have a number of dimensions – for example, tellership that includes the degree of involvement of the storyteller and the listener in the process of storytelling; tellability that refers to what stories we choose to tell; embeddedness that refers to whether the narrative is detached or embedded in the conversation; and moral stance that refers to how the narrator evaluates what is good in the world and how we ought to live our lives (Ochs & Capps, 2001).

Research on the narratives of children with speech, language and communication needs has focused predominantly on structural aspects of their stories and has found that these children have specific deficits in their narrative abilities (Botting, 2002; Epstein & Phillips, 2009; Norbury & Bishop, 2008). Very few studies have focused on the conversational narratives of these children. For example, what is the point of their narratives? How do they present themselves and others in their narratives? How are their narratives co-constructed with conversation partners? What kinds of stories do they tell?

Could narrative inquiry be a useful way of exploring identity with children with speech, language and communication needs?

Narrative inquiry has been primarily used with adults who can clearly articulate their stories. However, there are arguments that this methodology can and should be used with people with communication impairments (Antelius, 2009; Atkinson & Walmsley, 1999; Barrow, 2008; Owens, 2007). If one of the criteria for narrative research is that the participants should provide clear verbal descriptions of their experiences, then people with learning and communication impairments may not meet these criteria, and may subsequently be excluded from research. If research is positioned in a disability rights perspective, then excluding people who are unable to provide coherent verbal accounts means that the researcher is replicating the inequalities that may exclude disabled people (Owens, 2007). Therefore the definition of narrative inquiry needs to be broadened so that people with communication impairments can be included (Antelius, 2009; Barrow, 2008; Owens, 2007). Researchers must move outside the boundaries of conventional methodological fields to ensure that the voices of vulnerable groups, including children and adults with disabilities, are heard (Aldridge, 2007; Garth & Aroni, 2003). The particular challenges of analyzing the narratives of a child with a language impairment are not to be underestimated.

> Joseph has complex thoughts about his history and his illness but does not communicate these thoughts easily. In telling his story I try to evoke the frustration with communicating that is part of his day to day life (Blumenreich, 2004, p. 82).

By broadening the criteria of narrative inquiry, we may be able to explore how children with speech, language and communication needs present themselves and others in their personal narratives and how they construct and negotiate their identity. We also need to be aware of the role that we play in the identity formation process.

Acknowledgements

I would like to thank Professor Sue Roulstone and Mr Mat Jones, my PhD supervisors, for their support, guidance and invaluable constructive feedback.

References

Aldridge, J. (2007) Picture this: the use of participatory photographic research methods with people with learning disabilities. *Disability and Society, 22:1*, 1–17.

Antelius, E. (2009) *Different voices – different stories. Communication, identity and meaning in people with acquired brain damage.* Linkoping: Linkoping University.

Atkinson, D. & Walmsley, J. (1999) Using autobiographical approaches with people with learning difficulties. *Disability and Society, 14:2*, 203–216.

Barrow, R. (2008) Listening to the voice of living with aphasia: Anne's story. *International Journal of Language and Communication Disorders, 43*(S1), 30–46.

Benwell, B. & Stokoe, E. (2006) *Discourse and identity.* Edinburgh: Edinburgh University Press.

Blumenreich, M. (2004). Avoiding the pitfalls of 'conventional' narrative research using poststructural theory to guide the creation of narratives of children with HIV. *Qualitative Research, 4*(1), 77-90.

Botting, N. (2002) Narrative as a tool for the assessment of linguistic and pragmatic impairments. *Child Language Teaching and Therapy, 18:1*, 1–21.

Bruner, J. (1987). The transactional self. In J. Bruner & H. Haste (Eds.), *Making sense-the child's construction of the world* (pp. 81-96). Abingdon: Routledge.

Burden, R. (2008) Is dyslexia necessarily associated with negative feelings of self-worth? A review and implications for future research. *Dyslexia, 14*, 188–196.

Chase, S. (2008) Narrative inquiry: Multiple lens, approaches, voices. In N. Denzin & Y. Lincoln (Eds), *Collecting and interpreting qualitative materials* (pp. 57–94). London: Sage.

Clandinin, D.J. & Connelly, F.M. (2000) *Narrative inquiry: Experience and story in qualitative research* San Francisco: Jossey-Bass.

Clegg, J., Hollis, C., Mawhood, L. & Rutter, M. (2005) Developmental language disorders – a follow-up in later life. Cognitive, language and psychosocial outcomes. *Journal of Child Psychology and Psychiatry, 46:2*, 128–149.

DeFina, A. (2009) Narratives in interview. The case of accounts: for an interactional approach to narrative genres. *Narrative Inquiry, 19:2*, 233–258.

Elliot, J. (2007) *Using narrative in social research – qualitative and quantitative approaches.* London: Sage.

Epstein, S.-A. & Phillips, J. (2009) Storytelling skills of children with specific language impairment. *Child Language Teaching and Therapy, 25:3*, 285–300.

Frost, N. (2009) 'Do you know what I mean?': The use of pluralistic narrative analysis approach in the interpretation of an interview. *Qualitative Research, 9:1*, 9–29.

Garth, B. & Aroni, R. (2003) 'I value what you have to say'. Seeking the perspective of children with a disability, not just their parents. *Disability and Society, 18:5*, 561–576.

Goffman, E. (1959) *The presentation of self in everyday life*. London: Penguin Books.

Goffman, E. (1963) *Stigma: Notes on the management of spoiled identity*. London: Penguin.

Greene, S. & Hill, M. (2005) Researching children's experience: Methods and methodological issues. In S. Greene & D. Hogan (Eds), *Researching children's experience – approaches and methods* (pp. 1–21) London: Sage.

Greig, A., Taylor, J. & MacKay, T. (2007) *Doing research with children* (2nd ed.). London: Sage.

Grove, N. (2007) Exploring the absence of high points in story reminiscence with carers of people with profound disabilities. *Journal of Policy and Practice in Intellectual Disabilities 4:4*, 252–260.

Habermas, T. & Bluck, S. (2000) Getting a life: The emergence of the life story in adolescence. *Psychological Bulletin, 126:5*, 748–769.

Habermas, T. & Paha, C. (2001) The development of coherence in adolescents' life narratives. *Narrative Inquiry, 11:1*, 35-54.

Hagstrom, F. (2004) Including identity in clinical practices. *Topics in Language Disorders, 24:3*, 225–238.

Holliday, E., Harrison, L. & McLeod, S. (2009) Listening to children with communication impairment talking through their drawings. *Journal of Early Childhood Research, 7:3*, 244–263.

Jenkins, R. (2008) *Social identity* (3rd ed.). London: Routledge.

Kathard, H. (2006) On becoming someone: Self-identity as able. *Advances in Speech-Language Pathology, 8:2*, 79–91.

Kinavey, C. (2006) Explanatory models of self-understanding in adolescents born with spina bifida. *Qualitative Health Research, 16:8*, 1091–1107.

Kovarsky, D. (2008) Representing voices from the life-world in evidence-based practice. *International Journal of Language and Communication Disorders, 43*(S1), 47–57.

Labov, W. & Waletsky, J. (1967) Narrative analysis: Oral versions of personal experience. In J. Helm (Ed.), *Essays on the Verbal and Visual Arts* (pp. 12–44). Seattle: University of Washington Press.

Law, J., Boyle, J., Harris, F., Harkness, A. & Nye, C. (1998) Screening for primary speech and language delay: A systematic review of the literature. *International Journal of Language and Communication Disorders, 33*(Suppl), 21–23.

Lloyd, V., Gatherer, A. & Kalsy, S. (2006) Conducting qualitative interview research with people with expressive language difficulties *Qualitative Health Research, 16:10*, 1386-1404.

McAdams, D., Josselson, R. & Lieblich, A. (2006) Introduction. In D. McAdams, R. Josselson & A. Lieblich (Eds), *Identity and story: Creating self in narrative* (pp. 3–11). Washington, DC: American Psychological Association.

McCormack, J., McLeod, S., McAllister, L. & Harrison, L. (2010) My speech problem, your listening problem, and my frustration problem: The experience of living with childhood speech impairment. *Language, Speech, and Hearing Services in Schools, 41*, 379–392.

Maybin, J. (2006) *Children's voices: Talk, knowledge and identity.* Basingtonstoke: Palgrave Macmillan.

Meadows, S. (2010) *The child as social person.* London: Routledge.

Mishler, E. (1986) *Research interviewing: Context and narrative* London: Harvard University Press.

Mossige, S., Jensen, T., Gulbrandsen, W., Reichelt, S. & Tjersland, O.A. (2005) Children's narratives of sexual abuse: What characterises them and how do they contribute to meaning-making? *Narrative Inquiry, 15:2*, 377–404.

Norbury, C. & Bishop, D.V.M. (2008) Narrative skills of children with communication impairments. *International Journal of Language and Communication Disorders, 38:3*, 287–313.

Norrick, N. (2000) *Conversational narrative: Storytelling in everyday talk.* Amsterdam: John Benjamins Publishing.

Ochs, E. & Capps, L. (2001) *Living narrative: Creating lives in everyday storytelling.* London: Harvard University Press.

Owen, R., Hayett, L. & Roulstone, S. (2004) Children's views of speech and language therapy in school: Consulting children with communication difficulties. *Child Language Teaching and Therapy, 20:1*, 55–73.

Owens, J. (2007) Liberating voices through narrative methods: The case for an interpretive research approach. *Disability and Society, 22:3*, 299–313.

Peterson, C. & McCabe, A. (1983) *Developmental psycholinguistics: Three ways of looking at a child's narrative.* London: Plenum Press.

Polkinghorne, D. (1988) *Narrative knowing and the human sciences.* Albany: State University of New York Press.

Rabiee, P., Sloper, P. & Beresford, B. (2005) Doing research with children and young people who do not use speech for communication *Children and Society, 19*, 385–396.

Riessman, C. (2008) *Narrative methods for the human sciences.* London: Sage.

Simkin, Z. & Conti-Ramsden, G. (2009) 'I went to a language unit': Adolescents' views on specialist educational provision and their language difficulties. *Child Language Teaching and Therapy, 25:1*, 103–122.

Sota, G., Hartman, E. & Wilkins, D. (2006) Exploring the elements of narrative that emerge in the interactions between an 8-year-old child who uses an AAC device and her teacher *Augmentative and Alternative Communication, 22:4*, 231–241.

Thorne, A. (2004) Putting the person into social identity. *Human Development, 47*, 361–363.

Wickenden, M. (2011) Talking to teenagers: Using anthropological methods to explore identity and the lifeworlds of young people who use AAC. *Communication Disorders Quarterly, 32,* 151–163.

16 Listening to Children with Speech, Language and Communication Needs through Arts-Based Methods

Jane Coad and Helen Hambly

Abstract

This chapter describes how arts-based methods can be applied for use in consultation and research projects with children and young people who have speech, language and communication needs. First, what constitutes an arts-based method and how it might be used in consultation and/or research is explored. Following this, a number of arts-based activities using art tools, collages and mapping techniques are considered. Finally, literature and fieldwork undertaken by the authors is drawn upon to inform critical discussion of using arts-based techniques with children and young people with speech, language and communication needs.

Background

Over the last decade there has been an increased emphasis on the active involvement, participation and consultation of children and young people. However, if listening to children and young people is to be a reality there needs to be a move to participatory methods that are specifically devised to engage children (Christensen & James, 2008). Arts-based methods include techniques and activities that provide a powerful medium through which children and young people across a wide range of the developmental continuum can express their views.

Children and young people, including those who have speech, language and communication needs, can use visual arts-based techniques and activities as they provide a 'child-centred' structure to enable them to describe their needs and environments such as in health and social care settings (NE-CF, 2005; National Network for the Arts in Health, 2005). However, whilst arts-based methods have become more popular there is less critical reflection surrounding their use to facilitate consultation and research with children and young people who have speech, language and communication needs (Holliday, Harrison & McLeod 2009; Owen, Hayett & Roulstone, 2004).

It is worth noting that a common misconception about using arts-based activities in consultation or research is that the facilitator or researcher needs to have well-developed artistic skills. Without doubt, an art training will help, but it is not a prerequisite. This chapter will aim to dispel this myth, outlining, first, what constitutes an arts-based method or activity and, second, how it might be used to help listen to children and young people with speech, language and communication needs. It is hoped that readers will understand more about what works in terms of choosing and developing arts-based techniques in their own projects with children and young people with speech, language and communication needs.

Examples of children using arts methods are demonstrated in Figures 16.1 and 16.2. Additionally, a range of different arts-based methods have been identified in the literature, some of which are set out in the box below.

Range of arts-based methods used with children and young people

- Drawing, painting, colouring
- Collages and picture-making
- Craft materials such as pipe cleaners, feathers, glue, glitter, stickers, textiles
- Shapes such as clouds, speech bubbles
- Concept mapping such as plastic wallets and Post-its®
- Photographs (taking them or viewing them); video, use of IT approaches
- Graffiti and walls to post ideas
- Drama, role play and storytelling
- Creative writing such as letters and poetry
- Craft techniques such as clay, making masks, pottery, woodwork
- Visual diaries, journals and scrapbooks

Sources: Barker and Weller (2003), Bendelow, Williams and Aclu (1996), Clark and Moss (2001), Coad (2007), Coad and Lewis (2005), Coad, Plumridge and Metcalfe (2009), Coates (2002), Lewis and Lindsay (2000), Punch (2002), Save the Children (2000)

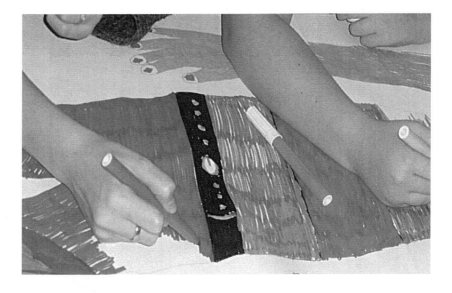

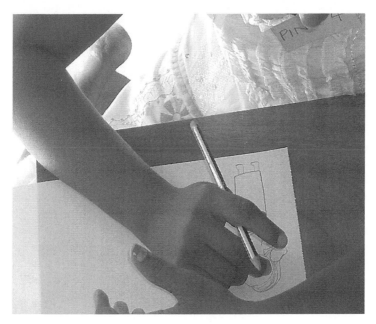

Figures 16.1 and 16.2 Examples of children using art based materials.

At first glance, arts-based methods seem a sensible option, as children and young people can communicate their views and preferences through a safe medium. However, arts-based methods, like any research method, need serious consideration and intense planning (Coad, 2007). Several writers have noted that in using arts-based methods the facilitator or researcher must be clear about which stage the art techniques will be used, such as during warm-up exercises and/or fill-in activities, as the main data collection or at the end whilst waiting for others to finish (Coad, 2007; Kirby, 1999). Decisions need to be made early on where and what will be used and whether other data collection techniques will be undertaken, such as interviews. A practice run-through helps, especially if team members are novices, so that all members are briefed in their roles, but at the same time it is important to make sure that the methods appear fun and spontaneous to the children and young people. Following on, a number of techniques are discussed further in the next section.

Using drawing, arts and craft materials and collage

Drawing techniques have been used with children and young people with variable success (Bendelow et al., 1996; Coates, 2002; Punch, 2002). Children and young people with speech, language and communication needs can have specific academic challenges which may include associated emotional and behavioural difficulties at a much higher rate than children and young people without such needs (Snowling, Bishop, Stothard, Chipcase & Kaplan, 2006; Botting & Conti-Ramsden, 2008; Simonoff, Pickles, Charman, Chandler, Loucas & Baird, 2008; Lindsay, Dockrell & Mackie, 2008).

Creating a drawing or collage and using craft materials may be threatening to some children and young people ('I cannot draw'). Similarly, the activity is so much fun that it is not focused around the task (or aim of the project). To overcome such problems, Coad (2007) suggested ways of using supplementary techniques in conjunction with drawings. One suggestion is to have to hand a range of appropriate craft materials and stickers of expressive faces, food and hobbies. Once a picture is complete, the researcher can spend time with the child or young person, discussing the drawing and adding symbols or written labels to help highlight meanings.

Alternatively, work by the authors and others, have used the creation of posters or collages integrally with the interview event, so in this situation the interview and arts activity are organized in conjunction to one another (Coad et al., 2009; Di Gallo, 2001). In a study with young people with autism, Lingam, Coad, Novak and Emond (2011) supplemented the focus group interviews with arts-based methods when participants appeared to lose interest. At that point they were invited to rate themselves as to whether they felt that they had improved, using a ladder and a set of stars on a wall away from where they were sitting. Moving from one area to another helped interaction and rejuvenated interest. A further example comes from a series of arts-based focus group workshops with children and young people with speech, language and communication needs (see Hambly, Coad, Lindsay & Roulstone, 2011, Chapter 26 in this volume) in which a variety of art tools (pens, pencils, models, glitter glue, stickers, etc.) were provided so that participants had additional and varied choice as to how they would like to express themselves. In both these studies, the adult facilitators did not prompt, but once the children and young people chose items or rated themselves interview, probes were then introduced.

Pulling arts-based methods together

When using arts-based methods it is often helpful to combine the ideas presented by the children or young people. Clark and Moss (2001) developed the use of the *Mosaic Approach* framework for listening to younger children and is described in Press, Bradley, Goodfellow, Harrison, McLeod, Sumsion et al. (2011, Chapter 29 in this volume). Within this framework, Clark and Moss (2001) suggest a two-stage approach that can be applied to listening to children and young people with speech, language and communication needs; the second stage focuses on pulling together or a mapping of children's ideas. In order to use the Clark and Moss (2007) approach, Coad (2007) devised and used a large sheet with plastic pockets (like those to store shoes) and has in several projects hung this on a wall so that children and young people could post items in as they pulled points together.

A different type of mapping involves the use of visual grids. Thomas and O'Kane (1998) invited children aged 8–12 years old to set up their own decision-making chart with two axes on a large sheet of paper: 'What sort of decisions' was the top axis and 'What people' was the side axis. The grid was useful, as it not only facilitated the children's decision-making but it enabled the researchers to explore what the child saw as important decisions. This method draws attention to how children are able to clearly voice their issues given the opportunity to do so. Whilst no evidence could be found of the use of these grids with children and young people with speech, language and communication needs, these types of approaches have strong intuitive appeal and could have potential with this group.

Critical discussion of arts-based methods

There are numerous challenges in using arts-based methods with children and young people with speech, language and communication needs.

Developing the tools

One consideration in the planning phase of arts-based methods is the resources that are available in the project. In the experience of the authors, children and young people with speech, language and communication needs appear to enjoy the spontaneity of using arts-based methods but the materials must be well considered before entering the field. One consideration is that purchase and preparation of art materials always takes more time than originally envisaged and requires careful thought. Further, whilst there is no need to buy the most expensive materials, aspects such as good-quality pens, paper/card and sharp new pencils appear to encourage and value children and young people's participation. Having a range of materials on offer is useful, as what one child or young person enjoys and interacts with may not be engaging to another. Further, it is also worth noting that these are particularly attractive to children and young people if they are different and perhaps more fun than ones they see every day, such as art materials they might use at school.

Consent

Children or young people's consent (or assent) should be ascertained on an ongoing basis in all research. In terms of arts-based techniques with children and young people with speech, language and communication needs, an explanation prior to the activity should occur to clarify the task required, that they can stop when they wish and the time when the activity will finish. Lewis (Coad & Lewis, 2005) used a card technique with children with disabilities where the child was given different-coloured cards to hold up when they wished to stop or change subject. Others have rotated a number of data collection activities to ensure boredom is reduced.

Establishing rapport

Being involved in an arts-based activity with a child or young person can be an effective way of establishing a rapport in a relatively short time, but when the participants have speech, language and communication needs building a relationship of trust requires serious consideration. Several authors provide general guidance about this. For example, Morrow (1999) shared examples of establishing rapport prior to the data collection, such as using drawings to relax the child. One example the authors found successful was a ball or balloon game that was used to help children and young people with speech, language and communication needs introduce themselves at the start of the workshop and also to liven and re-engage children and young people when the group were tiring.

Balancing power

What is most challenging is balancing an arts-based method so that it appears flexible and creative without exercising too much obvious control, but at the same time is useful for meeting the aim of the project. One suggestion is to give the child(ren) the choice of materials that they would like to use; for example, whether they draw or not and what types and coloured pens they use. This also facilitates a more equal power balance (Broome & Richards, 2003). With children and young people with speech, language and communication needs, the facilitator or researcher must have patience in listening and be prepared to wait for the answer rather than answer for the child or young person (Lingam et al., 2011; Mauthner, 1997).

Settings for data collection

Each context where the data collection takes place will bring its own challenges. Arts-based methods can be undertaken in a variety of contexts - such as the classroom, home, youth clubs, hospital rooms – but may require adequate space. If space is limited, such as in the home setting, then the activity may need to be contained. Coad et al. (2009) adapted an art portfolio suitcase so that all arts-based materials could be easily transported, stored and revealed when undertaking a project in family homes about the communication needs of children and young people.

Closure and exit

Children and young people are often proud of their artwork and many are used to writing their name on such pieces. They are also used to keeping the work and taking it to show to their friends and families. In terms of preserving anonymity, one commonly used strategy is to put their name on the back of the paper. Alternatively, some children or young people choose to make up a name and put it on the front of the picture. There remains the issue of keeping or giving back the work to the child or young person participant. This is often dependent on the child preferences and the type of data produced. To overcome such challenges, the authors have included strategies relating to photographing the work produced for analysis, leaving the original with the child or young person. Permission has been sought to use the photographs for subsequent dissemination.

Whilst arts-based techniques give children and young people the opportunity to articulate their feelings through their own visual representations, including those with speech, language and communication needs, a major challenge is understanding what the artwork means to them. Darbyshire, MacDougall and Schiller (2005) suggested that the process of understanding what arts-based methods mean to the child or young person should be considered in terms of interpretation, in which the requirement is to be faithful to the original meaning. However, interpretations need to be appropriate for the cognitive capacity of the child or young person, as well as concise and clear, asking what it is that is produced and the meaning behind it (Holliday et al., 2009).

Feedback and reward are fundamental to valuing the activity and the child or young person. Any reward needs to be considerate to the age/cognitive development, including speech, language and communication needs. At the end of the arts-based activities, children and young people should also be given feedback about what will happen to the work and how it will be used. Strategies commonly used to give feedback include using the artwork in reports or presentations or posters; sending summaries of the findings; and devising a newsletter (Coad, 2007; Darbyshire et al., 2005).

Conclusion

Listening to children and young people with speech, language and communication needs through using arts-based methods can be both challenging and rewarding. Whilst there are numerous arts-based methods that have been used in consultation and/or research, this chapter has only explored a few examples, but has related their use to the context of listening to children and young people with speech, language and communication needs. It is anticipated that in discussing these methods the reader will be able to adapt the principles to other arts-based methods that they may wish to use. This chapter has highlighted throughout that using such methods flexibly can encourage the active participation of children and young people with speech, language and communication needs in order to understand their desires and views. This is important if we are to plan and deliver services that are geared specifically for them.

References

Barker, J. & Weller, S. (2003) 'Is it fun?' Developing children centred methods. *International Journal of Sociology and Social Policy, 23:1*, 33–58.

Bendelow, G., Williams, S.J. & Aclu, A. (1996) It makes you bald: Children's knowledge and beliefs about health and cancer prevention. *Health Education, 3*, 12–19.

Botting, N. & Conti-Ramsden, G. (2008) Social cognition, social behaviour and language in late adolescents with a history of SLI. *British Journal of Developmental Psychology, 26:2*, 281–300.

Broome, M.E. & Richards, D.J. (2003) The influence of relationships on children's and adolescents participation in research. *Nurse Researcher, 52:3*, 191–197.

Christensen, P. & James, A. (Eds) (2008) *Research with children: Perspectives and practices.* London: Falmer.

Clark, A. & Moss, P. (2001) *Listening to young children. The Mosaic approach.* London: Joseph Rowntree Foundation/ National Children's Bureau.

Coad, J. (2007) Using art based techniques in engaging children and young people in health care consultations audit and/or research, *Journal of Research in Nursing, 12:5*, 567–583.

Coad, J. & Lewis, A. (2005) *Engaging children and young people in research: A systematic literature review for* The National Evaluation of The Children's Fund. *Expert papers.* Birmingham University. Online. Retrieved from www.ne-cf.org

Coad, J., Plumridge, G. & Metcalfe, A. (2009) Involving children and young people in the development of art-based research tools. *Nurse Researcher, 16:4*, 56–64.

Coates, E. (2002) 'I forgot the sky!' Children's stories contained within their drawings. *International Journal of Early Years Education, 10:1*, 21–35.

Darbyshire, P., MacDougall, C. & Schiller, W. (2005) Multiple methods in qualitative research. *Qualitative Research, 5:4*, 417–436.

Di Gallo, A. (2001) Drawing as a means of communication at the initial interview with children with cancer. *Journal of Child Psychotherapy, 27:2,* 197–210.

Hambly, H., Coad, J., Lindsay, G. & Roulstone, S. (2011) Listening to children and young people talk about their desired outcomes. In S. Roulstone & S. McLeod (Eds), *Listening to children and young people with speech language and communication needs.* London, UK: J&R Press.

Holliday, E.L., Harrison, L.J. & McLeod, S. (2009) Listening to children with communication impairment talking through their drawings. *Journal of Early Childhood Research, 7:3,* 244–263.

Kirby, P. (1999) *Involving young researchers: How to enable young people to design and conduct research.* York: JRF/Youth Work Press.

Lewis, A. & Lindsay, G.E. (Eds) (2000) *Researching children's perspectives.* Buckingham: Open University Press.

Lindsay, G., Dockrell, J. & Mackie, C. (2008) Vulnerability to bullying and impaired social relationships in children with Specific Language Impairment. *European Journal of Special Educational Needs, 23,* 1–16.

Lingam, R., Coad, J., Novak, C. & Emond, A. (2011, in press) Identity and empowerment: A phenomenological study of teenagers with developmental coordination disorder. Obtain from the 1st author raghu.lingam@bristol.ac.uk

Mauthner, M. (1997) Methodological aspects of collecting data from children: Lessons from three projects. *Children and Society, 11:1,* 16–28.

Morrow, V. (1999) It's cool... 'cos you can't give us detentions and things, can you? In P. Milner & B. Carolin (Eds), *Time to listen to children* (pp. 203–215). London: Routledge.

National Evaluation of the Children's Fund (NE-CF) (2005) *Evaluators' handbook.* Retrieved from www.ne-cf.org

National Network for the Arts in Health (2005) *What is arts in health: Community arts in health.* National Network for the Arts in Health (online). Retrieved from www.nnah.org.uk

Owen, R., Hayett, L. & Roulstone, S. (2004) Children's views of speech and language therapy in school: Consulting children with communication difficulties. *Child Language Teaching and Therapy, 20:1,* 55–73.

Press, F., Bradley, B.S., Goodfellow, J., Harrison, L.J., McLeod, S., Sumsion, J. et al. (2011) Listening to infants about what life is like in childcare: A mosaic approach. In S. Roulstone & S. McLeod (Eds), *Listening to children and young people with speech language and communication needs.* London, UK: J&R Press.

Punch, S. (2002) Interviewing strategies with young people: The secret box, a stimulus material and task-based activities. *Children and Society, 16:1,* 45–56.

Save the Children (2000) *Children and participation: Research, monitoring and evaluation with children and young people.* London: Save the Children.

Simonoff, E., Pickles, A., Charman, T., Chandler, S., Loucas, T. & Baird, G. (2008) Psychiatric disorders in children with autism spectrum disorders: Prevalence, co-morbidity, and associated factors in a population-derived sample. *Journal of the American Academy of Child and Adolescent Psychiatry 47:8*, 921–929.

Snowling, M.J., Bishop, D.V.M., Stothard, S.E., Chipcase, B. & Kaplan, C. (2006) Psychosocial outcomes at 15 years of children with a preschool history of speech-language impairment. *Journal of Child Psychology and Psychiatry and Allied Disciplines, 47*, 759–765.

Thomas, N. & O'Kane, C. (1998) The ethics of participatory research with children. *Children and Society, 12:5*, 336–348.

17 Cognitive and Linguistic Factors in the Interview Process

Julie Dockrell and Geoff Lindsay

Abstract

Speech, language and communication needs raise challenges for interviewer and interviewee alike. In order to provide a range of views in research and practice, specific attention must be paid to the factors which can limit authentic participation or result in unreliable reports. This chapter considers the ways in which studies of memory and language can provide relevant data to help interpret interviews and support the development of techniques. Attention to these details can enhance the reliability, validity and authenticity of participants' responses, which may in turn lead to greater benefits when research is used to drive policy and practice.

The interview process

Giving children and young people with speech, language and communication needs a voice respects their right to participate in research about themselves. The process can be problematic. To do justice to the participants' beliefs and views we need both appropriate methods of elicitation and an accurate means of interpreting responses. The responsibility rests with those carrying out consultations to find appropriate methods of understanding views and experiences (Morris, 2003). A range of methods have been developed to provide all children and young people with the opportunity to make authentic, valid and reliable responses (Lewis, 2002). Both the possible methods used and the ethical dilemmas imposed on the researcher have been the focus of a number of recent reviews (see, for example, Knight, Clark & Petrie, 2006; Nind, 2009). Typically, however, these reviews do not consider the significant demands placed on the respondent's cognitive and linguistic skills. Such demands have implications for interviews with children and young people with speech, language and communication needs.

Studies of memory and language in children and young people can provide relevant data to help interpret interviews and support the development of techniques to enhance the reliability and validity of the information provided. Often when eliciting views participants are asked to provide information about an episode, their feelings or an explanation of why something has happened. All of these tasks involve memory and linguistic skills and the ability to reflect back on the question and the responses provided.

Asking questions

There has been a long history in psychology of examining the ways in which we solicit the views of children and young people. Children's willingness to respond to questions, even when such questions are nonsensical or refer to episodes which have not occurred, raises the important issue of how questions ought to be phrased to elicit the most reliable and, if appropriate, detailed responses. When children are questioned using free recall formats, they can be as accurate as adults, although less information is recalled. More specific questions increase the amount of information provided, but the responses are less accurate and subject to response biases.

There has been less research on the impact of children's cognitive and linguistic development on responding to survey questions, despite the increased use of these methods. Fuchs (2009) designed a set of age-appropriate questions that were administered to a large cohort (n=205) of children aged between 8 and 14. He observed the children's response behaviour directly in the interview by video-recording them and then coding for aspects of verbal and non-verbal behaviour. In addition, data about children's cognitive abilities were collected. He noted the occurrence of problems in responding either explicitly (asks for explanation, provides 'don't know' response) or implicitly (e.g. uncertainty, refusal to answer or inadequate answer). Implicit problems were significantly more frequent (75%) than explicit problems. There were also complex relationships with cognitive skills. As one might predict, increased working memory skills resulted in fewer problems with the questions, but only for boys. In contrast, girls with increased vocabulary skills experienced greater difficulties. Higher general intelligence resulted in fewer problems for girls but increased problems for boys.

The question format

When they don't know the answer to a question both children and adults are more likely to answer yes/no questions than other types of questions, whereas with unanswerable wh- (open-ended) questions, that is questions starting with the words who, what, why, where, when or how, they tend not to provide answers. If closed questions are necessary, then follow-up questions may be required to check that the interviewee is not attempting to answer a question to which they do not know the answer (Waterman et al., 2001). It is of concern that, despite this knowledge, interviewing of children, especially those with developmental difficulties, often involves forced choice or closed questions. Open-ended interviews may yield more accurate information than do focused questions, particularly when questions involve option posing or suggestive prompts (Lamb & Fauchier, 2001). As children and young people with speech, language and communication needs may find open-ended questioning quite difficult, careful consideration of the use of confirmatory data collection is required.

Interview format

Semi-structured interviews allow for the systematic coverage of a range of issues, and if they are related to *specific* incidents can elicit reliable and accurate responses (Ericsson & Simon, 1980). Open-ended interviews allow for more broad-ranging information to be produced but they elicit less systematic information, and the information that is elicited tends to tap generalized reconstructions or perceptions. These two different approaches are subject to different limitations.

The semi-structured approach used by Palikara, Lindsay and Dockrell (2008) was designed to elicit specific issues related to the young people's experience of schooling and the support they received. Therefore there was a need to collect systematic data that covered participants' views on aspects of schooling, family and additional support. In contrast, a study by Magiati, Dockrell and Logetheti (2002) aimed to elicit children's views of differences and diversity using an open-ended approach. Participants were asked to generate ways in which children could differ. Their responses indicated that, in contrast to previous research, even the youngest children were developing rich representations of differences and diversities. The semi-structured approach may force individuals to respond to issues that may not be important for them, while the open-ended approach may miss critical dimensions because they are not probed. Moreover, the open-ended approach does not allow for a systematic comparison of the same dimensions across respondents.

These issues raise particular problems for interviewing children and young people with speech, language and communication needs. First, the interviewer may not know whether the respondent knows the answer to the questions posed or what the correct answer should be. Rephrasing or repeated questioning may lead to fabricated responses. Second, researchers and practitioners often try to 'simplify' the format of questions with the potential result that responses may not reflect the individual's knowledge or beliefs. The possibility of using multiple sources of data collection (triangulation) to construct accurate interpretations should be considered, but is rare in research with children and young people with speech, language and communication needs (see Carroll & Dockrell, 2011, Chapter 25 in this volume; Press et al., 2011, Chapter 29 in this volume).

Memory factors

There is increasing evidence that problems with working memory can impact on more general memory processing, that is, the recall of everyday information (McNamara & Wong, 2003). These difficulties impact on the recall of both the details of particular events (episodic memory) and in the steps required to complete a sequence of activities (procedural memory). Importantly, presenting appropriate neutral cues and prompts for children with speech, language and communication needs can increase recall to match that of typically developing matched peers.

One common component of an interview is to ask a participant to recall an event, which is a situation they have been involved in or a situation they may have witnessed. There is a range of factors that impact on the ways in which events are recalled and an awareness of these factors is important if we are to draw valid conclusions from interview data. These factors include: what is to be recalled; the ways in which questions are asked; how they influence the accuracy of the response; and the gap between the event and when the event is to be recalled. Events which have been witnessed or the respondent had been involved in are recalled well.

Experimental studies have demonstrated that information presented after an event or information that is omitted in a later reconstruction can change an individual's reported memory. Subsequent reports can be inaccurate or fabricated. There are also individual differences that influence reporting. Older children recall significantly more than younger children, but even younger children (3–4 years) can provide detailed accounts of events under some conditions (Poole & Lindsay, 2001). Younger children are more susceptible to false information. Yet typically developing 8-year-old children still report fictitious events in an event recall situation, even when specific checks have been included to minimize errors of recall. Children with mild learning disabilities can perform as well as their age-matched peers on many of these recall tasks, while children with moderate learning disabilities show significantly poorer performance than their age-matched peers (Henry & Gudjonsson, 1999) but children with learning disabilities may change their responses more often to repeated questioning than typically developing children (Henry & Gudjonsson, 2003).

Events are not the only phenomena people are asked to recall. It is not uncommon to ask individuals how they were feeling over a period of time or during a particular experience. Memories associated with events of high importance or strong emotions will endure in a highly detailed form for many years (Conway, 1998). However, less salient events are less well recalled. As an example, children are sometimes asked about their feelings about receiving extra support in class or during an examination. Unfortunately, reporting of the emotions about these situations can be inaccurate and there is also a tendency to overestimate emotional states. Individuals who have coped with a situation recall prior emotional states as more intense. The concerns about the validity of reporting emotional states are so strong that these reports should always be supported with corroborating evidence (Keuler & Safer, 1998).

Although children's autobiographical memory can be highly accurate, this can be greatly influenced by how they are questioned about events (Bruck, Ceci & Hembrooke, 2002). In such situations it is not necessarily a single leading question by the interviewer that affects the accuracy of the children's responses but the overall effect of a 'suggestible' interview. To address these concerns researchers have developed a technique termed the 'cognitive interview', a method of enhancing memory through facilitating the process of recall. Much of this work has been done to increase the reliability of interviews in child abuse cases, but the principles are useful to consider in other contexts (Lamb, Orbach, Hershkowitz, Esplin & Horowitz, 2007). The interview goals should be stated, but perhaps the most important element of the process is to reinstate the context by asking the respondent to imagine the situation and to re-establish specific details.

Linguistic factors

Linguistic features of the interview situation are particularly important for children who are developing their language competence. Language is a medium for accessing representations of events and considering feelings. Formulating the response to a question places cognitive demands on respondents. It appears that language skills, rather than non-verbal ability, are the key factor in encoding and recall (Bishop & Donlan, 2005).

It is also important to establish that the respondent's understanding of the words is the same as the interviewer's. There is no simple mapping between understanding a word and producing it. There is growing evidence that children may have subtly different representations of some words. For example, some people with developmental difficulties include different people in the category 'friend' compared with those typically considered by researchers (Barlow & Kirby, 1991). Children with speech, language and communication needs also experience difficulties in extracting meaning from context such that the 'context' of the interview may not supply the respondents with sufficient structure to access the information required to respond in an authentic manner.

The additional information processing demands that are created by interview situations may reduce an individual's ability to understand grammatical sentences that might be understood in less demanding situations. Acquiescence in interviews may be seen as a response to questions that are too complex either grammatically or in the type of judgement needed. The ability of the interviewee to read the pragmatic demands of the situation also needs consideration and familiarity with the interviewer may be important. Children with communication disorders attain higher test scores with familiar, as opposed to unfamiliar, adults (Fuchs, 1987). Familiarity will also impact on interview performance (Carter et al., 1996).

An experimental study by Johnston, Miller, Curtiss and Tallal (1993) highlights some of the subtle interplay between these factors. These researchers were interested in whether adults' questions were related to children's use of ellipsis. Ellipses are cases where one or more words are left out of a response; these words are needed to express the sense of a situation completely. Johnston et al. provide the following example:

A: It'd be hard to sleep with a walrus, wouldn't it?

C: Because he is so big and fat.

Missing information of this kind may either invalidate an interview or lead the interviewer to draw unwarranted conclusions. Ellipses were first measured in the utterances produced by language-impaired children and typically developing children when they were not being questioned. There were no differences between the groups. The researchers then examined the children's language that was produced in response to questions. They found that for the children with language impairments, but not the typically developing children, there was a marked increase in ellipses in response to questioning. These authors suggest that for the children with language impairment questions may convey implicit messages of expectation and challenge. An elliptical answer may be the wisest course. Questioning also places demands on the children's ability to comprehend language such that more effort is spent in making sense of the situation and less is available for responding. Suggesting that a child or young person has the competence to understand and respond in an 'interview' misses the fact that their performance in the 'interview' may be compromised by a range of factors.

Listening to answers

We have discussed how memorial and linguistic factors may impact on a young person's ability to engage in an interview in the way intended, but also of concern is the respondent's ability to reflect on what they are able to answer. Interviewing is a two-way process which often involves revisiting issues and reflecting on one's own knowledge about the situation. Metacognition is self-awareness about one's cognitive activities and as such provides the basis for analyzing a problematic situation, addressing the problem and monitoring the solution.

Much of the research on metacognition has focused on enhancing or understanding the problems pupils have in learning and developing appropriate teaching strategies (Wong, 1987). Relatively little research has examined these factors for children and young people with speech, language and communication needs and the implications for interviews. Yet comprehension monitoring is central to the interview situation. Some children will know they know, others will think they know, while others know they don't know and some don't know they don't know. Metacognitive skills continue to mature until adolescence and are important both for inter- and intrapersonal communication.

These problems have implications for understanding the ways in which children and young people with speech, language and communication needs respond to materials and questions. Studies of students with learning disabilities have highlighted a lack of awareness of important parts of a text and a difficulty in self-monitoring. Interviewers need to be particularly sensitive to the use of context to support use of metacognitive skills, possibly by the use of probe questions.

Implications

There is growing evidence that children and young people with speech, language and communication needs can reflect meaningfully on their past and current experiences. Language and cognitive factors need to be considered in the design, execution and analyses of interview data. There are specific reasons to expect that certain populations of respondents may have more difficulties and the specific strengths and needs of these groups require systematic consideration. Where appropriate, modifications can be developed. However, these modifications need to be piloted and evaluated in terms of any different or additional demands or biases that are introduced.

Acknowledgements

All the children, families and professionals who have been involved in our research studies. Some of the issues have been raised in:

Dockrell, J.E. (2004) How can studies of memory and language enhance the authenticity, validity and reliability of interviews? *British Journal of Learning Disabilities, 32*, 161–165.

Dockrell, J.E., Lewis, A. & Lindsay, G.A. (1999) Researching children's perspectives: A psychological dimension. In A. Lewis & G.A. Lindsay (Eds), *Researching children's perspectives* (pp. 46–58). Buckingham: Open University Press.

Key references on the topic

Conway, M.A. (1998) *Cognitive models of memory.* London: Psychology Press/Taylor & Francis.

Henry, L.A. (in press) *The development of working memory in children: Typical and atypical perspectives.* Thousand Oaks, CA: Sage.

Sudman, S., Bradburn, N. & Schwarz, N. (1996) *Thinking about answers: The application of cognitive processes to survey methodology.* San Francisco, CA: Jossey-Bass Publishers.

References

Barlow, J. & Kirby, N. (1991) Residential satisfaction of persons with mental retardation living in an institution or the community. *Australia and New Zealand Journal of Developmental Disabilities, 17,* 7–23.

Bishop, D.V.M. & Donlan, C. (2005) The role of syntax in encoding and recall of pictorial narratives: Evidence from specific language impairment. *British Journal of Developmental Psychology, 23,* 25–46.

Bruck, M., Ceci, S.J. & Hembrooke, H. (2002) The nature of children's true and false narratives. *Developmental Review, 22,* 520–554.

Carroll, C., & Dockrell, J. (2011) Listening to the post-16 transition experiences of young people with specific language impairment. In S. Roulstone & S. McLeod (Eds), *Listening to children and young people with speech language and communication needs.* London: J&R Press.

Conway, M.A. (1998) *Cognitive models of memory.* London: Psychology Press/Taylor & Francis.

Ericsson, K.A. & Simon, H.A. (1980) Verbal reports as data. *Psychological Review, 87,* 215–251.

Fuchs, D. (1987) Examiner familiarity effects on test-performance: Implications for training and practice. *Topics in Early Childhood Special Education, 7:3,* 90–104.

Fuchs, M. (2009) *The reliability of children's survey responses: The impact of cognitive functioning on respondent behavior.* Component of Statistics *Canada,* catalogue no. 11-522-X. Retrieved from *www.statcan.gc.ca/pub/11-522-x/2008000/article/10961-eng.pdf*

Henry, L. & Gudjonsson, G.H. (1999) Eyewitness memory and suggestibility in children with mental retardation. *American Journal of Mental Retardation, 104,* 491–508.

Henry, L. & Gudjonsson, G. H. (2003) Eyewitness memory, suggestibility, and repeated recall sessions in children with mild and moderate intellectual disabilities. *Law and Human Behaviour, 27,* 481–505.

Johnston, J., Miller, J., Curtiss, S. & Tallal, P (1993) Conversations with children who are language impaired. *Journal of Speech, Language, and Hearing Research, 36,* 973–978.

Keuler, D. & Safer, M. (1998) Memory bias in the assessment and recall of pre-exam anxiety: How anxious was I. *Applied Cognitive Psychology, 12,* 127–137.

Knight, A., Clark, A. & Petrie, P. (2006) *The views of children and young people with learning disabilities about the support they receive from social services: A review of consultations and methods.* London: Thomas Coram Research Unit, Institute of Education, University of London.

Lamb, M. & Fauchier, A. (2001) The effects of question type on self-contradictions by children in the course of forensic interviews. *Applied Cognitive Psychology, 15,* 483–491.

Lamb, M.E., Orbach, Y., Hershkowitz, I., Esplin, P. & Horowitz, D. (2007) Structured forensic interview protocols improve the quality and informativeness of investigative interviews with children. *Child Abuse and Neglect, 31,* 1201–1231.

Lewis, A. (2002) Accessing through research interviews the views of children with difficulties learning. *Support for Learning, 17,* 110–116.

Magiati, I., Dockrell, J.E. & Logotheti, A. (2002) Young children's understanding of special educational needs. *Journal of Applied Developmental Psychology, 23:4,* 409–430.

McNamara, J.K. & Wong, B. (2003) Memory for everyday information in students with learning disabilities. *Journal of Learning Disabilities, 36:5,* 394–406.

Morris, J. (2003) Including all children: Finding out about the experiences of children with communication and/or cognitive impairments. *Children and Society, 17,* 337–348.

Nind, M. (2009) *Conducting qualitative research with people with learning, communication and other disabilities: Methodological challenges.* National Centre for Research Methods, 24pp. ESRC National Centre for Research Methods Review Paper NCRM/012.

Palikara, O., Lindsay, G. & Dockrell, J. (2009) Voices of young people with a history of specific speech and language difficulties in the first year of post-16 education, *International Journal of Language and Communication Disorders, 44:1,* 56–78.

Poole, D. & Lindsay, D. (2001) Children's eyewitness reports after exposure to misinformation from parents. *Journal of Experimental Psychology Applied, 7,* 27–50.

Press, F., Bradley, B.S., Goodfellow, J., Harrison, L.J., McLeod, S., Sumsion et al. (2011) Listening to infants about what life is like in childcare: A mosaic approach. In S. Roulstone & S. McLeod (Eds), *Listening to children and young people with speech language and communication needs.* London: J&R Press.

Waterman, A., Blades, M. & Spencer, C. (2000) Do children try to answer nonsensical questions? *British Journal of Developmental Psychology, 18,* 211–226.

Waterman, A., Blades, M. & Spencer, C. (2001) Interviewing children and adults: The effect of question format on the tendency to speculate. *Applied Cognitive Psychology, 15,* 521–531.

Wong, B.Y.L. (1987) How do the results of metacognitive research impact on the learning-disabled individual? *Learning Disability Quarterly, 10:3,* 189–195.

Part III Examples

18 Listening to Individuals with Language Impairment
What One Can Learn in 30 Years

Bonnie Brinton and Martin Fujiki

Purpose of the project

Cody, age 24, wants to attend a group discussion on dating held for young adults by a local church group. The first challenge he encounters is getting there. Cody does not know where the activity is being held, so he calls Rob, his roommate, for directions. Rob gives Cody the directions, and Cody starts out in his car. Cody cannot find the activity so he calls his mother to ask for advice. Cody's mother calls Rob's mother. Rob's mother finds Rob and tells him to call Cody's mother. Cody's mother simultaneously talks to Rob on her landline and to Cody on her cell phone. With Rob's help, she 'talks Cody down' to the apartment where the discussion is being held. Once he arrives, Cody wants to interact with the other young people, but this isn't easy for him. Afterwards Cody reports that the discussion went well. Even so, Cody's mother and Rob share an unsettling doubt. They wonder how Cody's peers perceived his interaction at the activity. How did he come off?

There is a reason for their concern. Cody has grown up with language impairment (LI), initially identified when he was 4 years old. Despite his typical non-verbal IQ, his language problems make it difficult for him to keep up with his peers in conversation. Socially, Cody is friendly, outgoing, and anxious to make friends and establish dating relationships. The social landscape is formidable for him, however. He has difficulty reading social cues and understanding the emotional reactions of others. He loves to joke with peers, but he 'hammers' a joke into the ground, talks on about interests others may not share, and sometimes makes insensitive comments. He intends no impertinence, but he conveys disrespect when he is unable to acknowledge opinions other than his own. Despite the fact that he did not perceive any difficulty in the group discussion, Cody's mother and roommate know that he may have interacted in a way to draw negative attention to himself. Listening to Cody teaches us about the impact of LI on the life of a child as he matures. The purpose of this project is to report on principles learned from listening to Cody and other children with LI over the last 30 years.

Children and young people

Cody was initially seen in the Brigham Young University Speech and Language Clinic in the USA at age 4. Treatment has not only involved working directly with him, but also with his family, teachers and peers (Brinton, Fujiki & Robinson, 2005). He is representative of several hundred other individuals with LI seen by the authors in research projects and clinical settings. Most of these children have ranged in age from 3 to 12 years of age.

Investigators

The investigators are speech and language therapists who have worked in school, hospital and university settings.

Methods and procedures

The investigators have studied children in cross-sectional studies as they entered ongoing conversations with peers, worked on collaborative tasks with peers, talked about their social worlds and played outside. Other aspects of this work have involved teacher reports on the social and emotional behaviour of children with LI at school as well as student self-reports about their friendships within the classroom and their peer contacts in activities outside of school.

Findings and outcomes

Listening to children and young people with LI has taught us three major points: LI is pervasive and persistent, LI is isolating, and LI is individualistic.

Language impairment is pervasive and persistent

LI is traditionally considered as a deficit limited to language – hence the term 'specific language impairment'. The more that is learned about LI, however, the more it becomes clear that its tendrils spread wide and deep. As Cody's mother reflected, 'Language impairment affects every aspect of his life.' Cody's early language difficulties undermined his ability to communicate his needs, wants, and feelings to his family. At 5, Cody could not narrate what he had done over the course of a day, and his interactions often consisted of rather frustrating exchanges. His parents posed a series of questions (e.g. 'What did you do? Who did you play with?'), but Cody could not respond in a comprehensible way. He did not enjoy sharing books because the language was not accessible to him. As Cody entered school, he had trouble grasping sound–letter relationships, acquiring new vocabulary, following directions, and processing information. As he made his way through school his LI continued to undermine his academic performance, particularly in subjects with heavy language demands.

Cody's experience was not unusual. The persistent roadblock that LI presents to academic performance is well documented in the literature. These difficulties were painfully evident in a recent study of five young women identified with LI as children (Brinton, Fujiki & Baldridge, 2010). The manifestations of their LI changed somewhat over the years, as did the classification labels used to describe their deficits. Despite special services, language and academic difficulties persisted. One young woman required an alternative high-school setting, three depended on special academic classes, and one was just surviving in regular classes.

The influence of LI spreads well beyond academics. As children with LI recognize their academic problems, their self-esteem may suffer. In addition, many children with LI struggle to establish and maintain positive social relationships, especially with peers. Undoubtedly, their difficulty communicating limits their social interaction. Cody's early difficulty expressing himself hindered his ability to play with other children. At 24, his problems understanding abstract language (e.g. sarcasm and double entendre) continue to interfere with his ability to connect with other young people. Even so, the social difficulties Cody has experienced cannot be totally explained by his language deficit. This is also the case for many other children with LI; the social problems they demonstrate exceed what might be expected considering their language level. These children have difficulty entering ongoing interactions even if they don't need to speak to do so. Once they gain access to an interaction, they tend to contribute less than do their typically developing peers. They do not often extend themselves to help, comfort and share with their peers. They may have difficulty anticipating the emotions that specific situations might elicit, and they do not easily read the emotion cues of others – even cues as basic as facial expression. It has become increasingly clear that language and social and emotional competence are inextricably intertwined, and the social and emotional difficulties associated with LI persist as children mature.

Language impairment is isolating

Children with LI may lack the basic building blocks foundational to forming positive interpersonal relationships. Clearly, weak language processing abilities do not support the sharing of experiences, ideas, and feelings in a way that promotes closeness with peers. In addition, poor social and emotional competence can sabotage peer acceptance and inhibit friendship formation. Many children with LI demonstrate reticent withdrawal. That is, they are anxious and fearful to interact with others or they seem immobilized in the midst of peers who are playing or working. When children with LI work in collaborative groups, their typical peers often ignore or exclude them. When they go out to the schoolyard, they may wander from group to group without being accepted in the play. They may have difficulty making friends and, not surprisingly, they report loneliness in school and fewer peer contacts outside of school (see Brinton & Fujiki, 2009 for review).

The isolation children with LI experience may begin in preschool and extend into adulthood. For example, in elementary school Cody had difficulty making close friends in his neighbourhood. At age 11, he bemoaned, 'I'm like a broken toy. I just get passed from one person to another. Nobody wants to play with a broken toy' (Brinton & Fujiki, 1999, p. 49). By middle school, his isolation led to victimization. Looking back at his middle school experience, he reminisced, 'That was hell… I got bullied, picked on, threatened… I wanted to curl up in a ball and cry… Every day was torture.' At 24, he describes his interactions with peers, 'I'm at a different speed. Everyone's going NASCAR[1] and here's me, eee eee eee eee (pantomiming pedalling a bicycle and waving). You just lapped me ten times' (Cody, personal communication). Even though Cody has an extraordinary level of support (his parents are always available to help him, his older brothers employ and mentor him, his speech and language therapists treat him and his roommate often looks out for him), his isolation persists. He is still working to achieve the peer friendships and romantic relationship he longs for.

---

1   NASCAR, the National Association for Stock Car Auto Racing, is the largest governing body for stock car races in the USA.

Language impairment is individualistic

By definition, children with LI have difficulty with language. Still, each one is unique. Most children with LI have academic problems, but some perform better than others. Most children have social difficulties, but some do not. The manifestations of LI can change as an individual child develops and encounters different contexts. For some children like Cody, social and emotional problems increase as they transition from a supportive elementary school context to a more demanding middle school. Others may improve as they mature.

Children with LI also present with varying levels of impairment, and some adjust to challenges differently than others. For example, some aspects of Cody's deficit are more severe than those of many other individuals with LI. At the same time, he has unexpected strengths. Although many individuals with LI dislike print, Cody is an avid reader of fiction despite the fact that he has difficulty interpreting character motives and understanding abstract references. He is genuinely interested in others, even though he does not readily accommodate them in conversation. Like every person with LI, Cody presents a profile all his own.

Reflection on issues

Listening to children and young people has underscored the complexity of LI and its far-reaching impact on the lives of individuals. Children with LI have deficits with language and academic learning. Just as importantly, they have difficulty with social and emotional competence. As a result, they often have problems establishing and maintaining positive relationships with others, and the resulting loneliness and isolation can be devastating. Those who work with children with LI must be prepared to address the complex nature of their needs. It is not enough to facilitate isolated skills; therapists must support the communicative, academic, social and emotional development of the whole child.

It is difficult to predict the specific trajectory of an individual child's development, so it is necessary to be constantly alert to changing needs. In most cases, it can be expected that LI will persist beyond childhood. At each stage of intervention, it is important to keep a forward vision of what will contribute most to the quality of an individual's life. For example, when Cody was in elementary and secondary school, he needed support managing the demands of his coursework and negotiating the social landscape of his school and neighbourhood. At 24, he is no longer concerned with improving his language for academic potential. Rather, he is vitally interested in learning to interact more effectively with his peers. As his mother explains, 'The social stuff is everything.' As children with LI grow into adulthood, the social and emotional aspects of communication become more and more significant, and it is vitally important to keep this fact in mind when we plan intervention for young children. Only by looking forward can the most effective supports be provided to maximize each child's potential for growth.

References to this project

Brinton, B. & Fujiki, M. (1999) Social interactional behaviors of children with specific language impairment. *Topics in Language Disorders, 19:2,* 49–69.

Brinton, B. & Fujiki, M. (2009) 'The social stuff is everything:' How social differences in development impact treatment for children with language impairment. In A. Weiss (Ed.), *Therapeutic change in communication disorders: Borrowing from developmental knowledge of individual differences* (pp. 7–27). New York: Psychology Press.

Brinton, B., Fujiki, M. & Baldridge, M. (2010) The trajectory of LI into adolescence: What four young women can teach us. *Seminars in Speech and Language, 31,* 122–133.

Brinton, B., Fujiki, M. & Robinson, L. (2005) Life on a tricycle: A case study of language impairment from 4 to 19 years. *Topics in Language Disorders, 25:4,* 338–352.

19 The Stammering Information Programme
Listening to Young People Who Stammer

Elaine Kelman, Ali Berquez and Frances Cook

Purpose of the project

The Stammering Information Programme was a government-funded initiative to raise awareness, knowledge and skills about stammering in educational staff across England, using the voice of young people who stammer.

Children and young people

Children and young people who stammer aged 7 to 18 participated in a Delphi study to determine what they would like education staff to know about stammering. A film was then made of young people who stammer expressing these views, which was disseminated to educational staff across England.

Investigators

The Stammering Information Programme was carried out by three specialist speech and language therapists and a research assistant at the Michael Palin Centre for Stammering Children. The children and young people in the study were on the current or past caseload of the team of 11 specialist therapists at the Centre.

Method and procedures

This chapter will include a brief overview of how a Delphi approach (Goodman, 1987; Keeney, Hasson & McKenna, 2006) was used to determine what groups of experts considered to be the key messages about stammering for those in the educational workforce. The Delphi approach includes a number of iterative stages. The first stage involved facilitating four expert focus groups to generate one question each, which they agreed would produce the most answers from their peers. The groups were:

- educational staff
- parents of children and young people who stammer
- children who stammer aged 7 to 11
- young people who stammer aged 12 to 18.

For the purposes of this chapter, the outcome of the children's and young people's groups only will be discussed.

The children's group agreed the best question would be 'What I wish everyone in my school life would know', while the young people's group's question was 'What do people working in education need to know about stammering?' In stage two, each of these questions was then sent to a larger cohort of 25 children and 27 young people who stammer, asking for their responses. In stage three, the cohort's responses were compiled into a list and returned to participants for rating in order of importance. Once the statements had been rated, they were returned, and those with the greatest consensus were identified. This process produced eight statements from each group, which were then used as the basis for the DVD and resources.

The next step involved 21 children and young people aged 6 to 18 being professionally filmed at the Centre, talking informally to camera without a script about their stammering and how school staff can be helpful. The eight hours of footage were edited by the therapists to select the clips that the Delphi study had identified as being the users' key messages.

A DVD was produced which included a short 10-minute video and a more detailed 20-minute video of the children and young people, as well as some printable resources for educational staff. The DVD and resources were piloted in a range of preschool, primary, secondary and further education settings and the feedback was used to refine the DVD and accompanying resources.

Six thousand copies of the DVD 'Wait, wait I'm not finished yet...' were produced and are being distributed free of charge to educational staff in England through a number of channels. This includes the network of speech and language therapists who provide in-service training to schools; teacher training establishments; the special educational needs coordinators' networks; parents of children who stammer; direct mailings of DVDs to all schools in a number of local authorities; and via education conferences and exhibitions. A number of articles have been published to raise awareness of the issue and the DVD has been placed on the Michael Palin Centre (www.stammeringcentre. org) and British Stammering Association websites (www.stammering.org).

Findings and outcomes

The list of statements which were rated most highly by the two groups can be found in the Appendix. The subsequent DVD reflects these sentiments in the words of the children and young people who stammer. The film opens with Sean (aged 7) saying, 'Having a stammer is hard, so that's why some of us are going to tell you all about it.' Lucas (4) then tells the viewer, 'I talk and I say something, only I can't say it when I'm stuck.' Daniel (16) says, 'if someone said that I'm inferior to someone because of my stammer, because of my talking, then well obviously I disagree because well heck at school I would like to think that I'm one of the bright ones there'. He also describes how 'my English teacher lets me do my oral tasks at lunchtime so I can just feel secure'. Ricky (18) adds, 'the teachers used to give me shortened paragraphs – that was nice of them because it slowly helped to build up my confidence'. Tyrell (16) explains that 'sometimes I want to say something and I can't say a single word, so the people around me won't even know I'm trying to talk and then by the time I get it out they would already have moved on. It's quite frustrating sometimes'. Samuel (10) says, 'it makes me not answer a lot of questions at school when I know lots of them but I just won't answer them'. Tyler (8) tells the viewer, 'I would really like my teachers to come over to me and have a little talk' and Ricky advises staff to 'try to keep eye contact with the pupil'. Daniel (11) says, 'sometimes people finish off my sentences but if they get it wrong I have to start again, which is very frustrating'. These messages expressed by the children and young people are both powerful and informative for the educational staff, as reflected in the feedback described below.

The DVD was launched in October 2009 and copies were distributed across England. Feedback forms were used with the DVD at in-service training sessions and 860 were returned by December 2010. Nearly all of the respondents (99.5%) said they would recommend the DVD to a colleague. A more in-depth analysis of 157 of the forms demonstrated the impact of the DVD on educational staff. The majority of the comments identified the practical skills needed to support pupils who stammer in school. Analysis of these responses indicated that the top three messages taken away from watching the DVD were as follows:

- Asking the pupil who stammers what support they would like: For example, a teacher trainer commented that 'the key message for the teaching assistants I showed it to during a training session was to ask the child what helps! – They tend to know best';

- Giving time to pupils who stammer: For example, a teaching assistant said that she has learned to 'give plenty of time – don't be tempted to rush them', and a class teacher said, 'above all be patient and give the child time to talk';

- Praising/encouraging pupils who stammer and building their confidence. For example, a special educational needs coordinator had learned to 'reassure and make them [pupils who stammer] feel valued and that their speech is important.'

Respondents also commented about a range of information that they had taken away—for example, knowledge about the various forms of stammering, how pupils who stammer feel, that it is not related to intelligence and that it affects each person in different ways.

The Stammering Information Programme has been independently evaluated by a team of researchers at the University of Warwick, who will submit their findings to the UK government in 2011. The DVD has also been viewed on the Michael Palin Centre website by more than 350 people across the world.

Reflection on issues

The Stammering Information Programme was a government-funded initiative to raise awareness, knowledge and skills about stammering in the educational workforce in England. Previous initiatives to achieve this goal have been driven and produced by professionals determining what they thought education staff needed to know, based on their experience of working with young people who stammer. The user's voice was sometimes included, but it did not determine the content, nor did it predominate in the presentation of material.

The final product of the Stammering Information Programme is a DVD, which consists entirely of children and young people talking directly to the viewer about their stammering and how they can be helped at school. They are stammering as they express their feelings and requests. This powerful tool has added validity, as it represents the views not just of the children and young people featured on the video but the wider population of their peers. The Delphi method was an invaluable tool in the process of listening to these young people and determining the consensus views about what should be included on the DVD. The overarching message of *'Wait, wait I'm not finished yet...'* is that the young people are experts about their stammering, they would like to be asked by staff about how they can help them in school, they would like to be given time and encouragement to say what they want to say and they would like to be listened to.

Acknowledgements

The authors would like to thank: the Department for Education (previously the Department for Children, Schools and Families); the children, young people and their families and members of the educational workforce who participated in this project; colleagues at the Michael Palin Centre for Stammering Children; and the speech and language therapists who contributed to the project across England.

References to this project

Berquez, A., Cook, F.M., Millard, S.K. & Jarvis, E. (2011) The Stammering Information Programme. A Delphi study. *Journal of Fluency Disorders*, 36:3, 206–221

Berquez, A., Kelman, E. & Jarvis, E. (2010) Support for stammering. Special issue of *Nasen Magazine* (November), 52.

Berquez, A, Kelman, E. & Jarvis, E. (2010) Wait, wait I'm not finished yet... *Special Children Magazine. Meeting Children's Additional Educational Needs*. October/November, 36–38.

References

Goodman, C.M. (1987) The Delphi technique: A critique. *Journal of Advanced Nursing*, 12, 729–734.

Keeney, S., Hasson, F. & McKenna, H. (2006) Consulting the oracle: Ten lessons from using the Delphi technique in nursing research. *Journal of Advanced Nursing*, 53:2, 205–212.

Appendix

The statements generated by the children and young people in the Delphi study:

Children

- Stammering does NOT reflect or affect intelligence.
- I am not different to anyone else just because I stammer.
- People need to know that I stammer (I find it hard to get my words out).
- They need to know that I can't help stammering (but I try my best to stop).
- People should give me time to think when I'm asked a question.
- People should not tell me what to do; for example, 'spit it out', 'hurry up'.
- People at school should know I have a stammer, so they don't bully me.
- People should not laugh at me or tease me because of my stammer.

Young people

- Being put on the spot in high-pressure situations is difficult.
- Stammering is a very personal and sensitive issue, and being hassled about something that's not your fault can have a demoralizing effect on your confidence.
- Stammering makes people feel embarrassed, frustrated, depressed, nervous, upset, under-confident, annoyed, isolated.
- People who stammer should be treated equally to people who don't stammer.
- Listen to the people who stammer.
- Do not make potentially disheartening remarks, e.g. 'nearly forgot it then', if asking for their name and it takes them a while to answer.
- People who stammer should not be patronized.
- Don't tolerate bullying.

20 'Give me time and I'll tell you'

Using Ethnography to Investigate Aspects of Identity with Teenagers Who Use Alternative and Augmentative Methods of Communication (AAC)

Mary Wickenden

Purpose of the project

The purpose of the study was to explore aspects of identity and the lifeworlds of teenagers who use alternative and augmentative methods of communication (AAC). The research draws on Jenkins' (2004) theoretical approach to identity, which suggests that identity is a constantly evolving concept across the lifespan and consists of two complementary aspects:

- Selfhood – broadly how the person sees themselves

- Personhood – broadly how the person is seen by others

A lifeworlds approach sets out to achieve a rounded picture of a person and their life and highlights their perspectives (Schutz, 1967). It is therefore necessary to ask them about themselves, to see them in a range of contexts and to ask others about them. The research questions were:

1. How do young people with severe physical and communication impairments who use AAC see themselves (selfhood)?

2. How are young people who use AAC seen by others (personhood)?

3. What kinds of social relationships do young people who use AAC have?

4. What role does the body play in the development of selfhood, social relationships and personhood, for young people who use AAC?

5. What kinds of methodologies work best when doing research with young people with severe communication impairments?

Children and young people

The key participants were nine teenagers who use alternative and augmentative communication (AAC) aged 10–15 years. All have four-limb cerebral palsy, typically developing cognitive skills and broadly normal verbal comprehension. Four participants have some natural speech; the others have little or none. All use at least one 'low tech' mode of communication (e.g. signs, symbols, communication book, eye gaze board) in addition to a 'high tech' (computer-aided voice output aid or 'voca') communication aid. Types of voca varied, as did methods of access. All are wheelchair users who need assistance with many daily activities and live at home with their parents and siblings. They attend a range of different schools: six special, two split placements and one mainstream.

Additionally, less in-depth data was collected from 15 other teenage AAC users with similar impairments. Parents, siblings, friends, as well as school and activity club staff, also contributed data through interviews, informal conversations or focus group discussions. Throughout the project three adult AAC users acted as research advisers and provided a valuable sounding board for ideas, including commenting on initial analyses and interpretations of the data. Participants were recruited purposively through contacts with special schools or via 1Voice, a national family support group for children and young people who use AAC.

Investigator

The author is an anthropologist with previous experience as a speech and language therapist (SLT) working with children. This change of discipline was precipitated by the author's increasing dissatisfaction with the rather narrow view of people that a purely clinical role offers and an interest in cultural aspects of childhood and disability (Wickenden, 2011).

This study draws on theoretical influences from three overlapping disciplines: childhood studies, disability studies and anthropology. In combination, these promote the use of participatory, facilitatory and sometimes emancipatory methodologies, such that research is *with* active participants rather than *on* or *about* passive subjects (Christensen & James, 2003; Morris, 2003). Thus both children and disabled people are recognized as 'social actors' or 'agents' who have views about their lives, which they can and should be asked about, and it is the researcher's task to design methods to make this possible. Disabled children, and particularly those with communication disabilities, have generally been excluded from this kind of participatory research (Davis & Watson, 2002; Rabiee, Sloper & Beresford, 2005). Anthropological perspectives view people's lives in social rather than psychological ways, placing more emphasis on both the role of relationships between people and structures in society than on individual aspects alone in affecting how life is experienced (Reeve, 2006). Thomas (2004) argues that research which explores and exposes the real lives of disabled people is 'humanizing' and this was an aim of the study described here.

Thus, the research relationship with the teenage participants was very different from that between a therapist and a client, which is usually much more goal-orientated. The author was more like an older friend than a professional, although of course bound by an awareness of child protection and power issues and respect for the young people's privacy and age differences. Although the researcher's previous professional experience was known to many of the adults, she was keen not to be identified in this way to the young people, as this might affect their responses (either positively or negatively) and limit the ways in which the research relationship might develop. In negotiating a role, the author's clinical experience undoubtedly helped in gaining access to schools, but it was understood by all that she was not working in the role of an SLT. Thus, as an 'interested adult' without a prescribed relationship with the young people (e.g. not a parent, teacher, therapist), the author was able to 'join in' with their lives in ways which were different and more flexible than those of other adults.

Notwithstanding this anthropological approach, having the skills and experience of an SLT were invaluable in communicating flexibly and sensitively with the young people. There was often a sense, though, during initial meetings with the participants, that they were making a careful assessment of this new adult, and her 'user-friendliness', especially as they had not met 'a researcher' before.

Method

The main research method used in anthropology is ethnography and more specifically participant observation. This is a naturalistic qualitative approach, in which the researcher negotiates a role as both an observer of real situations and also simultaneously is immersed as an active member of the community being studied (Hammersley & Atkinson, 1995). The researcher tries to fit in and not to change or disrupt what is going on. This enables them to become 'part of the scene' and to observe and participate in a variety of aspects of the society of interest. In this project the fieldwork was over two years and this (importantly) allowed enough time for the author to get to know the participants' 'language' (or, more broadly, ways of communicating), that is, their very individual ways of talking, using both low- and high-tech AAC. This involves complex and skilled switching between different modes. It took some time to be able to recognize and understand their subtle use of non-verbal communication and their ways of combining low- and high-tech methods to get different types of messages across. The teenagers were seen many times in a variety of settings (school, home, clubs) and doing different activities. This enabled the researcher to see the rich variety of their lives and to talk to them about themselves informally without the time pressure that exists in one-off interviews or questionnaires. It also meant that data was triangulated across time and settings and, by asking a range of people (such as family members, and school or club staff) for their views of their lives, to put the teenagers' perspectives into context. Thus data on the teenagers' selfhood and personhood was gradually built up.

Participant observations took place mainly in the teenagers' homes and schools, as well as at activity clubs and holiday schemes as appropriate. The researcher spent 60–80 hours with each key participant during the fieldwork period. In school she had a role similar to a classroom assistant, joining in with whatever the teenagers were doing throughout the school day. This included a full range of subject classes, sports, drama, residential field trips and outings, therapy sessions and, in some cases, helping with care tasks such as feeding, toileting and changing for swimming. At home she joined in like a close family friend with activities the teenager suggested, including: shopping trips, family outings, meals, computer games and Wii, chatting, playing with siblings, going on a guided tour around their village, etc. The teenagers always had control and choice over what the researcher was involved with, and at times they suggested extra activities that they thought she should come to (guides, bowling trip, house hunting, watersports club, athletics competition). They denied access to activities on only a very few occasions.

As well as participant observation in the main settings where the teenagers spent time, the author had a series of (10–20) individual 'extended narrative conversations' with the participants spread over the period of the study. Often AAC users do not have the opportunity to tell stories, because of the time constraints imposed by their means of communication, so this was unusual for them. The narrative conversations focused on a range of pre-planned topics (see Appendix A) and were audio-recorded in addition to the author drawing mindmaps of the conversations as they proceeded (Appendix B) .

All the data collected were qualitative and consisted of: field notes made during participant observation, transcripts from narrative conversations, interviews and focus group discussions, written work by teenagers, photos taken by the researcher and by participants (photo-voice task) and a video made by teenage members of 1Voice. These data were uploaded to NVivo (QSR, 2006) and were coded and analyzed thematically in an iterative process. Analysis started during the fieldwork, so as themes emerged interpretations and analysis were regularly presented back to the teenagers, the research advisers and to parents. Thus respondent validation of, and commentary on, the analysis was an integral and ongoing part of the process.

Findings and outcomes

Five major themes emerged and these were given names that the teenagers could relate to:

- Whose voice is that? (communication issues as they relate to identity)

- Being a family person and being a teenager (selfhood)

- Me myself I (selfhood: autonomous and disabled selves)

- Don't just see the chair! (the body, physical aspects of identity and the role of the kit)

- My family and others (personhood: the views of others and social relations)

In summary, the findings were that teenagers who use AAC view themselves first and foremost as family people and as normal teenagers. They had the same interests and concerns as their siblings and peers; for example, wanting to be seen as competent and social people, as cool, funny, sporty, clever, sexy, caring, etc. They had essentially pragmatic and accepting attitudes to their impairments and wanted to have the best, most reliable 'kit' (power wheelchairs and vocas) possible. They saw their bodies as 'normal for them' (Watson, 2002). They wanted opportunities to do the same things as other teenagers and were frustrated and angered when they were excluded from these or were pathologized or patronized. Most had strong ideas about what teenagers should be doing (going out independently to shops, cinemas, clubs and pubs, being moody, having fun, having friends, making their own decisions). They also had clear ideas about what they would like to do as adults, including studying and or working, living alone although with assistance and having active social lives and close relationships.

They were clear that it was possible to be both disabled and normal. This view was echoed by their families who insisted that they were 'normal' families. There was no hint that this use of the word 'normal' might in itself be problematic. Despite their generally positive view of themselves, the teenagers reported a range of negative experiences, especially in relation to making friends and social relationships outside the family. They had reduced social networks compared with their peers and siblings and were aware to varying extents that their visible physical and communication disabilities sometimes formed a barrier between them and others. They wanted to be seen as socially competent people and for who they *are* rather than what they can *do*. This echoes the findings of previous research about the lives and perceptions of adults with disabilities (Thomas, 2004).

Implications for practice

It is argued that ethnography provides a more holistic and less pathologizing view of its participants than many research methods. It is particularly suited to AAC users, since their slow speed of communication makes rapid methods unworkable and frustrating for them. Ethnography enables the researcher to reveal the views and voices of a group who are often excluded from being active participants in research. This group of approaches is useful because they provide detailed and contextual information, and have the ability to analyze the social being not just the psychological being. The person is thus seen within the natural contexts of family, friends and school and it is their own perspectives which are highlighted. The method aims for depth rather than breadth of investigation. The author learned much more about the participants and their lives than would ever be possible through meeting them on a limited number of times in one setting. Through becoming a 'fly on the wall', she had the privilege and advantage of seeing their many different 'selves'. However, of course it is a highly time- and resource-expensive method, which is rarely possible for busy practitioners. Nonetheless some aspects of the approach maybe useful in promoting more holistic and social views of disabled people.

The multiple sites and long-term nature of the study provided insight into how young AAC users experience their worlds similarly to other teenagers, as well as to their differences. Their disabilities became less important and their individual interests and perspectives emerged strongly. This resonates with much of the literature on disability and identity which suggests that disabled people generally have positive self-identities and that these are not necessarily primarily linked to their disabled status (Watson, 2002). These insider views captured through ethnography of what it is like to be a young person with a complex communication disability can be used to inform policy and service provision, which might then be a better match with the teenagers' own priorities. The study shows that young people who use AAC are more interested in the ways that they are like others of their age than in the ways that they are different, and that they identify themselves most importantly as family people and sociable teenagers rather than as disabled. Thus their interest is in policies and services which facilitate mainstream and inclusive practices as far as possible and which change attitudes. They particularly dislike being left out of things that other teenagers do and the negative attitudes of people who focus on their differences from, rather than their similarities to, their peers. The participants' verdicts on the process and purpose of the project were: 'it's fab', 'I love it', 'you should tell the schools what we say' and 'it's good to ask us!'

Reflection on issues

Very clearly in this type of qualitative research the researcher is part of, and not outside, the process of researching. There is a continuous reflexive process during which the researcher considers her own skills, her relationships with participants and responses to what she sees. This is included as part of the picture, rather than being eliminated. Although observations and interpretations are indeed subjective, they have been validated over time by looking for similar evidence on multiple occasions and in several settings, and by asking participants and parents for their feedback on possible interpretations of the data. In general the author found that the teenagers, families and research advisers agreed with her suggested interpretations, although they were not afraid to tweak them for accuracy on occasions. The ethnographic process of using relationships which develop 'in the field' was highly effective in finding out more about this 'hard-to-research' group.

Ethics and consent

Ethical approval was granted from the University of Sheffield prior to the start of the study. Ethical considerations throughout the study were given special attention, especially as disabled young people without speech are recognized as a particularly vulnerable group who are at risk of coercion, and their wishes can easily be and often are overruled. Consent was regarded as on ongoing process, which was revisited frequently both with the teenagers and their parents, particularly when an unusual or ethically sensitive issue such as feeding or personal care arose. This process-orientated approach to ethics was especially important, because the nature of ethnography means that the researcher and the participants become very familiar with each other over the extended period of the study. The ethnographer may then become regarded as a friend and thus refusal to allow particular types of involvement might be difficult if the explicit research aim of the study was not regularly reiterated.

Acknowledgements

Many thanks to the teenagers, their families and friends, the school and club staff and the research advisers for welcoming me into their worlds and giving me so much of their time and of themselves, and to my PhD supervisors for their encouragement and constructively critical support. Thanks also to the funders: an ESRC/MRC studentship and the Harold Hyam Wingate Foundation.

References to this project

Wickenden, M. (2011) Talking to teenagers: Using anthropological methods to explore identity and the lifeworlds of young people who use AAC. *Communication Disorders Quarterly*, 32, 151–163.

Wickenden, M. (2010) Teenage worlds, different voices: An ethnographic study of identity and the lifeworlds of disabled teenagers who use Augmentative and Alternative

Communication. Unpublished PhD thesis. University of Sheffield. Available online from http://etheses.whiterose/ac/uk/860

Wickenden, M. (2010) Talk to me as a teenage girl: An anthropological study of identity and lifeworlds with teenage AAC users. *Communication Matters, 24:3,* 4–8.

Wickenden, M. (2011) 'Talk to me as a teenage girl': Experiences of friendship for disabled teenagers who have little or no speech. *Childhoods Today,*5,1.

Wickenden, M.(2011) Listen to Us Too! Booklet available online at http://cscy.group.sehf. ac.uk.knowledge/indec/html, and http://1voice.info/links.html

Wickenden, M. (2011, in press). Whose voice is that?: Issues of representation arising in an ethnographic study of the lives of teenagers who use Augmentative and Alternative Communication. *Disability Studies Quarterly* special edition.

Websites about this project

1Voice: http://www.1voice.info

1Voice video made by 12 teenagers over a weekend: http://www.youtube.com/ IVoice:Listen to me

References

Christensen, P. & James, A. (2003) *Research with children: Perspectives and practices.* London: RoutledgeFalmer.

Davis, J.M., & Watson, N. (2002) Countering stereotypes of disability: Disabled children and resistance. In M. Corker & T. Shakespeare (Eds), *Disability/postmodernity: Embodying disability theory* (pp. 159–175). London. Continuum International Publishing.

Hammersley, M. & Atkinson P. (1995) *Ethnography.* London: Routledge.

James, A. (1999) Learning to be friends: Participant observation amongst English school-children (the Midlands, England). In C.W. Watson (Ed.), *Being there: Fieldwork in anthropology* (pp. 98–120). London: Pluto Press.

James, A. (2007) Giving voice to children's voices: Practices and problems, pitfalls and potentials. *American Anthropologist, 109:2,* 261–272.

Jenkins, R. (2004) *Social identity.* London: Routledge.

Morris, J. (2003) Including all children: Finding out about the experiences of children with communication and/or cognitive impairments. *Children and Society, 17:5,* 337–348.

QSR. (2006) *NVivo Version 7.0.* QSR International Pty Ltd.

Rabiee, P., Sloper, P. & Beresford, B. (2005) Doing research with children and young people who do not use speech for communication. *Children and Society, 19,* 385–396.

Reeve, D. (2006) Towards a psychology of disability: the emotional effects of living in a disabling society. In D. Goodley & R. Lawthorn (Eds), *Disability and psychology: Critical introductions and reflections* (pp. 94–107). London: Palgrave.

Schutz, A. (1967) *The phenomenology of the social world.* Evanston, IL: Northwestern University Press.

Thomas, C. (2004) Developing the social relational in the social model of disability: A theoretical agenda. In C. Barnes & G. Mercer (Eds), *Implementing the social model of disability: Theory and research* (pp. 32_47). Leeds: The Disability Press.

Watson, N. (2002) Well I know this is going to sound very strange to you but I don't see myself as a disabled person: Identity and disability. *Disability and Society, 17:5,* 509–527.

Appendices

Appendix A Main topics for extended narrative conversations

- my important people

- I am (self-description)

- my life story

- things I love and hate

- me and friends

- my treasure box (favourite stuff)

- people who help me

- my ways of talking

- my dreams for the future

- four vignettes about dilemmas a teenager using AAC might have

Appendix B Example of mindmap: Josie (15). Topic: making a new friend at school.

Josie was asked, 'If a new girl joined your class, what would you think about when making friends with her?' The conversation took about one hour. Josie has no speech and used a complex idiosyncratic system of non-verbal communication and an e-tran eye gaze system in preference to her high-tech voca on this occasion. In brackets are additional contributions added later in the conversation.

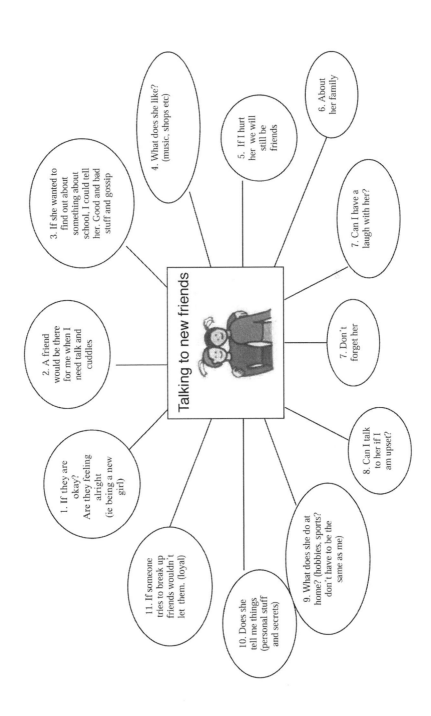

Talking to new friends

1. If they are okay? Are they feeling alright (ie being a new girl)

2. A friend would be there for me when I need talk and cuddles

3. If she wanted to find out about something about school, I could tell her. Good and bad stuff and gossip

4. What does she like? (music, shops etc)

5. If I hurt her we will still be friends

6. About her family

7. Can I have a laugh with her?

7. Don't forget her

8. Can I talk to her if I am upset?

9. What does she do at home? (hobbies, sports? don't have to be the same as me)

10. Does she tell me things (personal stuff and secrets)

11. If someone tries to break up friends wouldn't let them. (loyal)

21 Listening to 4- to 5-Year-Old Children with Speech Impairment Using Drawings, Interviews and Questionnaires

Sharynne McLeod, Jane McCormack, Lindy McAllister, Linda J. Harrison and Erin Holliday

Purpose of the project

This chapter describes a project that aimed to listen to preschool children with speech impairment (speech sound disorders). The children took part in the Sound Effects Study, part of a larger project which was investigating the prevalence and severity of speech impairment in Australian preschool children, as well as the impact of speech impairment on children's development, and their families' wellbeing (McLeod, Harrison & McAllister, 2007–2009). The project was unique in considering the views of preschool children with speech impairment alongside the views of their adult communication partners and in using a multi-method approach in order to elicit and appreciate children's views. This chapter describes the methods used in the Sound Effects Study to listen to children's views about their talking and, specifically, to address the following research question: How do 4- to 5-year-old children describe and understand the experience of living with speech impairment?

Children and young people

The Sound Effects Study involved 143 children (aged 47 to 70 months) who had been identified by parents and/or teachers with concerns about how they 'talk and make speech sounds'. The children, 96 (67.1%) males and 47 (32.9%) females, were recruited after screening of 1097 children from 33 early childhood centres (e.g. preschools, long-day care centres) in rural, regional and metropolitan areas of Australia. All spoke English as their first language, and none had been diagnosed with cognitive difficulties or other developmental disorders. That is, the children's speech impairment was of unknown origin, and was their primary area of difficulty. Their mean percentage of consonants correct (PCC) was 68.09 (SD = 14.31, range = 17.9–96.4). Most children had moderate–severe speech impairment.

Thirteen preschool children were purposefully selected from the larger sample of children (n=143) to be interviewed. These children were selected in order to represent both sexes and a range of ages, severities (as measured by percentage of consonants correct), involvement in speech and language therapy intervention, family characteristics and living locations. The children were interviewed along with 21 significant others identified by the children's parents (including the children's friends, siblings, parents and teachers). The focus of this chapter is on insights gained from the children, triangulated with data from significant others primarily as reported in McCormack, McLeod, McAllister and Harrison (2010). Parents' perspectives of access to and participating in speech and language therapy is explored in McAllister, McCormack, McLeod and Harrison (2011), but not described in this chapter.

Investigators

Three of the investigators in this project were speech and language therapists (McLeod, McCormack and McAllister), one an early childhood educator (Harrison) and the other a teacher education student (Holliday). Three of the investigators also were university professors (McLeod, Harrison, McAllister) with longstanding research backgrounds in working with children; the others undertook higher degrees as part of the project. The second author (McCormack), a qualified speech and language therapist, was the project officer for the Sound Effects Study and collected data with the children and their families.

Method and procedures

The Sound Effects Study was multifaceted, encompassing both quantitative and qualitative tools and analyses to describe and understand children's views about talking. Parents and teachers identified the children because they had concerns about the children's ability to 'talk and make speech sounds'. Parents provided consent for their children to participate in assessments and interviews. Each child was invited to participate in the project and a child-friendly information sheet was read to them. They were then asked to give verbal assent to participate in the tasks. Children were able to request an end to the assessment and/or interview at any time and their request was respected. As part of the data coding, each child was given a pseudonym to protect their identity and this was used in presentations and publications.

Children were interviewed by people not connected to their daily life, to reduce issues of power discrepancy or coercion. All of the assessments and interviews were conducted face to face in a location that was familiar to the child (e.g. home or early childhood centre), with a familiar person (typically the mother) nearby. The comprehensive communication assessments incorporated an evaluation of their speech, receptive and expressive language, hearing, oromusculature, non-word repetition, pre-literacy skills, voice and fluency to answer other goals of the broader research project. Following the assessments and interviews, the children were asked to draw themselves talking to someone and were asked about their talking using the techniques outlined below.

The *Kiddy-Communication Attitude Test* (KiddyCAT; Vanryckeghem & Brutten, 2007) investigates children's perceptions of their speech ability and difficulties they have with talking. The KiddyCAT is a standardized assessment that provides normative data for children aged 3–6 years. The test comprises 12 *yes/no* questions, including 'Is talking hard for you?' and 'Do you think that people need to help you talk?'

Child drawings of themselves talking to somebody, and their descriptions of their drawings in response to prompt questions (e.g. 'Who is in the drawing?', 'Do you like talking to this person?'), were analyzed using a meaning-making approach to understand how children perceive their communication. Holliday, Harrison and McLeod (2009) identified six potential key features or focal points that may be present in the drawings of children with communication impairment. These included: Talking and listening, Accentuated body features (mouth, eyes, ears), Facial expressions, Colour and vitality, Sense of self and Negativity (e.g. no conversational partner, scribbling). These focal points were noted in the drawings completed by children in this study (see Figures 21.1 and 21.2 for examples of accentuated body features).

The Speech Participation and Activity Assessment – Children (SPAA-C) questions for children (McLeod, 2004) investigates children's feelings about the way they talk, and how they feel when talking in specific contexts (e.g. to parents, siblings, friends and teachers). Children are provided with visual prompts (e.g. faces showing a range of emotions – happy, sad, in-the-middle expressions, a blank face for other feelings and a question mark signifying 'don't know') to assist in answering. For example, children were asked, 'How do you feel about the way you talk?' and could select from the following options: ☺☺☹○ ?

Communication assessments of the 143 children lasted approximately 1–1½ hours and took place over one or two sessions, depending on the child's concentration during the tasks. Interviews of the 13 children were conducted by the same speech and language therapist who had conducted the communication assessments, typically within eight weeks of the assessment. The remaining interview was conducted by a teacher with special education training.

Interpretivism (Liamputtong & Ezzy, 2005) was used as the theoretical framework in order to gain a richer understanding of children's lives, and data were analyzed from a meaning-making perspective. Techniques used to ensure rigour in the data analysis included immersion in the data (e.g. rereading of transcripts), constant comparative analysis (e.g. checking analysis of one transcript with another) and triangulation of methods (e.g. comparing data obtained from assessments with drawings, observations and verbal responses during interviews).

Figure 21.1 Tim (on the left; 4 years 3 months old) talking to his sister. He spoke about 'listening' and emphasized their ears. Copyright © 2011 by S. McLeod, L. McAllister, L.J. Harrison and J. McCormack. Reprinted with permission.

Figure 21.2 Nelson (on the right; 5 years 8 months old) talking to his friend about 'watching telly [TV] and eating chocolate frogs'. Notice the large ears of his friend, particularly the ear closest to Nelson. Copyright © 2011 by S. McLeod, L. McAllister, L.J. Harrison and J. McCormack. Reprinted with permission.

Findings and outcomes

The Sound Effects Study showed that preschool children with speech impairment have views about their speech, and can express those views when data collection methods are selected which facilitate their involvement; that is, when methods incorporate non-verbal activities (drawings) and verbal activities with scaffolding/cues (*yes/no* questions, interviews with visual prompts). In the Sound Effects Study, analysis across the range of data collection methods revealed common themes. First, most of the children were happy about talking and about the way they talked. Their use of colour and happy facial expressions in their drawings of themselves talking, and positive responses to interview and the KiddyCAT questions, reflected this perspective. Second, most of the children did not perceive themselves as having a 'speech problem'. Their depiction of themselves as similar to their conversation partners (in their drawings) and their reports on the KiddyCAT that talking was not 'hard' for them reflected this positive sense of self. Furthermore, children showed an awareness of the need for *listening*, as well as *speaking* when 'talking to someone'. Their drawings featured mouths *and* ears (see Figures 21.1 and 21.2), and their responses to interview questions revealed their perspective that sometimes it is the listener (not the speaker) who has a problem when communication breaks down. Thus, while parents and teachers had identified these children as having difficulty talking – and this was confirmed on the formal speech assessment data – the children revealed a different perspective focusing more on the problems of the listener.

Understanding the different perspective of children may have implications for speech and language therapy, which has traditionally focused on 'correcting' speech skills (Van Riper & Erickson, 1996). As McCormack, McLeod, Harrison, McAllister and Holliday (2010, p. 14) suggested, 'young children who do not perceive a problem with their speech skills (but rather with their communication partner's listening),… may be reluctant to participate in intervention that focuses on themselves as the speaker'. Furthermore, simply making children aware of the speech problem will not guarantee their motivation to participate in speech and language therapy. For instance, in the Sound Effects Study, two children who identified talking as 'hard' (indicating some awareness of difficulty talking) still did not think people needed to help them talk. Such children (and their families) might benefit from a holistic intervention approach, which could incorporate strategies that enabled others to listen better and minimized child frustration (e.g. creating and using available cues such as a diary to share knowledge of events, or a list of child's typical productions of words), alongside strategies that aimed to improve the child's speech (McCormack, McLeod, McAllister & Harrison, 2010).

Reflection on issues

Using a multi-method approach provided rich data for considering children's views about their talking and their experience of living with speech impairment. Using a range of methods was important in order for the research to reflect the range of perspectives that children wished to share. The findings showed that children not only have different perspectives to adults, but that the perspectives of individual children develop and change, and are influenced at all times by contextual factors (Daniel & McLeod, 2006). For instance, at times an individual child's response on one task appeared inconsistent with their response on another (e.g. responding positively to *yes/no* questions about talking, but identifying they felt 'sad' about their talking). However, the authors determined that different data obtained from the same children should be considered valid, and interpretations should acknowledge children's changing perspectives, 'rather than seeking "one truthful perspective" from children' (Dockett & Perry, 2007, p. 49).

Acknowledgements

The authors wish to thank the children, their families and teachers who participated in the Sound Effects Study for sharing their experiences, and Jacqui Barr, for assisting with data collection. This research was supported by Australian Research Council Discovery Project Grant DP0773978.

References to this project

Holliday, E.L., Harrison, L.J. & McLeod, S. (2009) Listening to children with communication impairment talking through their drawings. *Journal of Early Childhood Research, 7:3*, 244–263.

McAllister, L., McCormack, J., McLeod, S. & Harrison, L.J. (2011) Expectations and experiences of accessing and participating in services for childhood speech impairment. *International Journal of Speech-Language Pathology, 13:3*, 251–267.

McCormack, J., McLeod, S., Harrison, L.J. & McAllister, L. (2010) The impact of speech impairment in early childhood: Investigating parents' and speech-language pathologists' perspectives using the ICF-CY. *Journal of Communication Disorders, 43:5*, 378–396.

McCormack, J., McLeod, S., McAllister, L. & Harrison, L.J. (2010) My speech problem, your listening problem, and my frustration: The experience of living with childhood speech impairment. *Language, Speech, and Hearing Services in Schools, 41*, 379–392.

McCormack, J., McLeod, S., Harrison, L.J., McAllister, L. & Holliday, E.L. (2010) A different view of talking: How children with speech impairment picture their speech. *ACQuiring Knowledge in Speech, Language, and Hearing, 12:1*, 10–15.

McLeod, S., Harrison, L. J., McAllister, L., McCormack, J. (2011) *Speech sound disorders in a community sample of preschool children*. Manuscript in submission.

More information about the Sound Effects Study can be found at http://www.csu.edu.au/research/speech-impairment/index.html

References

Daniel, G. & McLeod, S. (2006) Listening to the voice of children with a communication impairment. In G. Whiteford (Ed.), *Voice, identity and reflexivity* (pp. 187–200). Albury, NSW: Charles Sturt University.

Dockett, S. & Perry, B. (2007) Trusting children's accounts in research. *Journal of Early Childhood Research, 5:1*, 47–63.

Liamputtong, P. & Ezzy, D. (2005) *Qualitative research methods* (2nd ed.). Melbourne: Oxford University Press.

McLeod, S. (2004) Speech pathologists' application of the ICF to children with speech impairment. *International Journal of Speech-Language Pathology, 6:1*, 75–81.

McLeod, S., Harrison, L.J. & McAllister, L. (2007–2009) Children with speech impairment: A population study of prevalence, severity, impact and service provision. Australian Research Council Discovery Project Grant DP0773978.

Van Riper, C. & Erickson, R.L. (1996) *Speech correction* (9th ed.). Needham Heights, MA: Allyn and Bacon.

Vanryckeghem, M. & Brutten, G.J. (2007) *KiddyCAT: Communication Attitude Test for Preschool and Kindergarten Children who Stutter*. San Diego, CA: Plural Publishing.

22 Listening to Children with Cleft Lip and Palate in Germany

Sandra Neumann

Purpose and questions of the project

The data for this chapter were gathered as part of the development of the first German speech assessment for cleft palate speech (CPS) called *LKGSF komplex* (*CPS-complex*) (Neumann, 2011). *LKGSF komplex* is based on the framework of the *International Classification of Functioning, Disability and Health* (ICF/ ICF-CY, WHO, 2001, 2007) and implements the *Speech Participation and Activity Assessment – Children* questionnaire (SPAA-C, McLeod, 2004), which facilitates listening to children, their parents, siblings and friends. So the aim, relevant for the present chapter, was to understand the perceptions of children and young people with cleft lip and palate and speech, language and communication needs concerning their communication.

Demographic of children and young people

Ten children and young people with cleft lip and palate and speech, language and communication needs were interviewed using questions from the SPAA-C, Part A that had been translated into German (McLeod, 2004). Children's age ranged from 6;1 to 9;10 years, with a mean age of 8;3 years. There was the same number of boys (n=5, age range 6;7–9;10, mean age 8;1) and girls (n=5, age range 6;1–9;3, mean age: 8;4). Only one language (German) was spoken at home. Every child had a repaired cleft lip and palate (eight unilateral CL/P, two bilateral CL/P) and were in speech and language therapy at the time of the interview. Their speech, language and communication needs were characterized by moderate to severe hypernasality, nasal emission, nasal turbulence (for four children), orofacial dysfunctions and articulatory cleft type characteristics (CTCs), such as backing, pharyngeal realizations and/or glottal stops, and slightly or moderately reduced intelligibility in all of the cases.

Investigator

The investigator and author of the present chapter is a speech and language therapist and researcher at the University of Cologne in Germany. She analyzed the *CPS-complex* data from the SPAA-C questionnaires. The data collectors were 60 speech and language therapists from Germany, Austria and Switzerland with experience in working with children with cleft palate speech (Heck, 2010).

Method and procedures

The children and young people with cleft palate speech were interviewed by their well-known speech and language therapist in clinical practice or in hospital by a speech and language therapist of the cleft palate-craniofacial team. All parents of the interviewed children give their agreement to use the data anonymously for research and publication.

To listen to the children and young people with cleft palate speech, the *Speech Participation and Activity of Children* questionnaire, version 2.0 (SPAA-C, McLeod, 2004) was translated into German. The original English version of the SPAA-C was developed by considering the Activity and Participation construct of the *ICF* (WHO, 2001) in a two-stage process (development and revision) by Australian speech and language therapists (see McLeod, 2004 for a description). The aim of the SPAA-C is to listen to children with speech, language and communication needs concerning 'the impact of speech difficulties on children's lives' (McLeod, 2004, p. 79). The questionnaire contains 6 parts: questions for (A) the child, (B) friends, (C) siblings, (D) parents, (E) teachers and (F) significant others, which could be used flexibly as interview (verbal or written) or in a role play using puppets for small children. The information the speech and language therapist or educator gained can be used to set cooperative therapy goals, which have an impact on the child's whole life (McLeod, 2004).

For the present study, the data collectors were asked to use the *LKGSF complex* material and the SPAA-C questionnaires in clinical practice and send it back. Because of the heterogeneity of which parts of the questionnaire were used, the following findings and outcomes only reflect the analysis of Part A: questions for the child for the group of children aged 6;0–9;11 years. These questions for the child are summarized into four sections: Who you are (5 items; for example, 'What are you good at?'), Your friends (1 item; 'Who do you like to play with?'), School/preschool (4 items; for example, 'What is hard for you at school/preschool?') and Your talking (17 items; for example, 'Do you think your talking is different from other children's?') including a 10-question Likert scale for indicating children's feelings about their talking in different situations. In the German adaptation of the SPAA-C, there were two additional questions in the 'Your talking' section: 'How do you feel when you talk to other children?' and 'How do you feel when others talk for you?' The children were asked about their speech activity and participation without any triangulation of researchers or methods.

The method used was a general qualitative and phenomenological analysis of interview transcripts of children and young people with cleft palate speech.

Findings and outcomes

Who are you?

Both boys and girls described age-appropriate interests and social and interpersonal processes in social play and friendship (Harrison, 2007) for early (4–7 years) or middle school age (7–10 years). The girls preferred playing with Barbie˙, puppets or Nintendo˙, swimming, reading, riding a bike, crayoning or playing badminton. The boys liked to play with cars, Playmobil˙, Nintendo˙, PC, swimming, playing football or basketball and playing outside.

Your friends

All of the children and young people indicated that they had friends and best friends in their school or neighbourhood. They like spending a lot of time together.

Kindergarten/school

The questions in Section 3 highlighted that the interviewed children most liked swimming and sports, mathematics and arts. Of the five boys, only one did not find anything difficult in school. The others indicated that they had some problems with German (reading and writing) and concentrating, and being seated for a long time. The girls liked crafts and gymnastics and playing in the school playground. Three girls did not indicate difficulties in school, one mentioned problems with calculating and the other indicated she had difficulties speaking to the teachers. Three girls indicated that they were teased at school; the other two said that they were not teased.

Your talking

Each of the children, regardless of gender, indicated that they were concerned about their manner of speaking. They all liked to talk to their family members and friends, but some did not like to speak with strangers or teachers. Only two girls did not think that they spoke in a different way. The other children indicated that they say words (n=2), or 'letters' (n=1), in a wrong way. One boy indicated that he felt like he has a different voice and misses out some 'letters' while speaking; one girl said she was inarticulate; and three children could not indicate what was different in their speech.

Four of the five children pointed out that they were teased because of their talking. One boy said that other children called him 'crooked nose'.

One question asked, 'Do people often ask you to say things again? How does this make you feel?' Eight of the children indicated that they were asked to say things again and that they either felt angry (n=4) or sad (n=4). If other children or strangers did not understand the children, they indicated different ways to cope with this: five children (four girls, one boy) said the words or phrases again and tried to speak more intelligibly, while three of the remaining four boys preferred to react in an aggressive way. One boy said he repeated the sentence three times and then he became angry and shouted out loud. Another boy said he goes overboard and starts to beat the person who did not understand. The third boy said he thinks about getting angry and then asks his brother or friend to speak for him. Similar responses can also be seen in the results of the Likert-scale questions – the children felt sad (n=7) or angry (n=1) when people didn't understand what they say.

In summary most of the children (n=8) felt OK about the way they talk, happy when talking to friends (n=9) or to their parents (n=8), and happy or 'in the middle' talking to their siblings (n=4/n=6), to other children (n=2/ n=8) or their [pre]school teachers (n=3/n=6). They felt happy playing with children in [pre]school (n=7) and sad playing alone (n=7). Three children did not like talking in front of the whole class and felt sad (n=7) or angry (n=1) when others talked for them (for detailed data, see Table 22.1).

Table 22.1 Results of Likert scale about feelings about their speaking of children with cleft lip and palate in Germany using the German adaptation of the SPAA-C.

	Happy		In the middle		Sad		Another feeling		Don't know	
	girls	boys	girls	boys	girls	boys	girls	boys	girls	boys
15. How do you feel about the way you talk?	2		8							
	2		3	5						
16. How do you feel when you talk to your best friend?	9		1							
	4	5	1							
17. How do you feel when you talk to your [brothers and sisters]?	4		6							
	2	2	3	3						
18. How do you feel when you talk to your [mum and dad]?	8		2							
	4	4	1	1						
19. How do you feel when you talk to your [pre]school teachers?	3		6						1	
	2	1	3	3						1*
20. How do you feel when your teachers ask you a question?	1		9							
	1		4	5						
21. How do you feel when you talk to the whole class?	1		6		2		1			
	1		4	2		2		1*		
22. How do you feel when you play with the children in [pre]school?	7		3							
	4	3	1	2						
23. How do you feel when you play on your own?			3		7					
			2	1	3	4				
24. How do you feel when people don't understand what you say?			1		7				2	
				1	3	4			2	
Additional questions to SPAA-C										
25. How do you feel when you talk to other children?	2		8							
	2		3	5						
26. How do you feel when others talk for you?			1		7				2	
				1	3	4			2[1,2]	

* depends on the teacher, + feels bad and unpleasant, is embarrassed, starts to tremble, [1] I speak for myself, [2] angry

Implications for practice

This small study listened to children with cleft lip and palate about their subjective experiences in individual speech activities and participation. The study was orientated by the ICF-CY. It was able to give first impressions of children's problems with communication in their developmental environment and allows speech and language therapists to plan intervention and goal-setting in a broader biopsychosocial way in cooperation with the child and family. This takes speech and language therapy beyond eliminating hypernasality and improving children's articulation – it puts an emphasis on the interactional level, on communicative barriers and on the feeling of not being integrated. To listen to the child allows the speech and language therapist to set individual goals together with the child with speech, language and communication needs. It expands the traditional and medical way of child-centred intervention to a therapy model, which focuses on activity, participation and the child's environment.

Reflection on issues

The results only allow a preliminary impression of children's level of speech activity and participation and of their individual feelings concerning their speech. Future research with a larger sample size, different age groups and a differentiation between the type of cleft, time of primary surgery and manner of speech and language therapy would be useful. This might help to determine the special problems in activity and participation relating to barriers and/or facilitators in environment of children with cleft palate speech to optimize speech and language interventions.

Acknowledgements

The author wishes to thank the children and their families who participated in research for assisting in the second evaluation of the *CPS complex*. Special thanks go to all the participating speech and language therapists and Nina Heck for assisting with data collection.

References

Harrison, L.J. (2007) Speech acquisition in a social context. In McLeod, S. (Ed.), *The international guide to speech acquisition* (pp. 78–85). Clifton Park, NY: Thomson Delmar Learning.

Heck, N. (2010) Formative Evaluation des Diagnostik- und Dokumentationsinventars‚LKGSF komplex': Diagnostik für Menschen mit LKGS-Fehlbildungen – ein Beitrag zur Prozessqualität in der Sprachtherapie [Formative evaluation of CPS complex – a contribution to process quality in speech language therapy]. Unpublished bachelor thesis, University of Cologne/ Germany.

McLeod, S. (2004) Speech pathologists' application of the ICF to children with speech impairment. *International Journal of Speech-Language Pathology, 6:1,* 75–81.

Neumann, S. (2011) *LKGSF komplex – Sprachtherapeutisches Diagnostik- und Dokumentationsinventar für Menschen mit LKGS-Fehlbildung [CPS complex –Speech assessment and documentation material for clients with cleft lip and palate].* München: Ernst Reinhardt Verlag.

23 'I can't say words much'
Listening to School-Aged Children's Experiences of Speech Impairment

Graham Daniel and Sharynne McLeod

Purpose of the project

To have communication impairment as a child can impact one's entire life. As a child this impact can include being bullied or withdrawing from peers in the playground (Fujiki, Brinton, Isaacson, & Summers, 2001; Knox & Conti-Ramsden, 2003), and having lower academic attainment (Harrison, McLeod, Berthelsen & Walker, 2009). The effects of having a communication impairment can also extend into adult life, with links to social, emotional and occupational outcomes that are less advantageous than for individuals without a communication impairment (McCormack, McLeod, McAllister & Harrison, 2009, 2010). This project set out to develop an understanding of the impact of speech impairment (or speech sound disorder) on the everyday lives of children in order to inform health practitioners, educators and other caregivers about ways of providing a more holistic approach to working with these children, and those who are within their worlds.

Children and young people

The participants for this research were identified using purposive sampling, where individuals with experience of the phenomenon under study, or 'information-rich cases' (Patton, 2002, p. 242), are identified and invited to participate in the research. The research focused around the lives of six primary-school-aged school children with speech impairment, who served as the primary source of data. Participants were identified through personal networks, an information leaflet placed in practising speech and language therapist waiting rooms and information in local media.

There were five male and one female focus children, from 5 to 8 years of age. All of the focus children had speech impairment of unknown origin, with no reported cognitive or hearing difficulties. Their speech impairment was of varying severity, ranging from mild to severe (childhood apraxia of speech). One child also had a co-occurring language impairment. The research also included interviews with those in a close relationship with the focus child, including parents, siblings and teachers, and others of significance in their lives, such as grandparents, close friends and sports and music coaches. In total, 34 interviews were completed.

Investigators

The authors were both researchers who worked in a large rural university in Australia. The first author is an experienced primary school teacher and lecturer in child development and educational psychology; and the second, an experienced speech and language therapist, and professor of speech and language acquisition. This experience of working with children and young people, and of speech and language therapy, enabled the researchers to sensitively investigate these children's experiences. The second author's experience in speech and language also enabled understanding and a more fluent conversation with the children who had less intelligible speech. The authors' experience and expertise also enabled implications to be developed across these professional fields.

Method and procedures

The research was interpretivist in design, employing qualitative methods of data gathering and analysis. Qualitative research aims to build a deep understanding of the human dimension of experience, and develop professional practice that takes these needs and interests into account. Rather than relying on information from a large, statistically significant sample participant group, qualitative research uses multiple sources and methods of data collection to develop a rich description of what the experience of the phenomenon under study is like (Patton, 2002). The use of multiple methods of data gathering is also recognized as an inclusive way of enabling children and young people from diverse backgrounds to express themselves and contribute their insights into research of significance to them (Smith, 2005). The collection of data from a range of sources employing a variety of methods is also referred to as a Mosaic approach (Clark & Moss, 2001).

Semi-structured interviews with participants were based around relevant questions from the *Speech Participation and Activity Assessment – Children* (SPAA-C) (McLeod, 2004). The SPAA-C was developed in response to the *International Classification of Functioning, Disability and Health* (ICF), which takes into account a person's Body Structures, Body Function, Activity and Participation, Personal and Environmental Factors in order to understand the complexity of health and wellness (World Health Organization, 2001) and includes questions for children, friends, siblings, parents, teachers and others in the child's life. The focus children also completed drawings, which were used as the basis for further discussion (McLeod, Daniel & Barr, 2006). A copy of a recent speech and language therapy assessment report was also requested to assist the researchers' understanding of the children's speech and language status.

The participants' experiences and the meanings they attribute to these experiences, and in particular how they related to the child's speech impairment, became the basis for an interpretive analysis. Interpretive analysis is an inductive form of analysis that uses patterns in the data to generate theory. Initially, this process involved identifying the key statements (Maxwell, 2005) within the data that revealed significant elements of the child's experiences of the phenomenon. Multiple source data allowed the investigators to corroborate, authenticate or establish the uniqueness of the data provide, a process referred to as triangulation (Bogdan & Biklin, 2006).

These key statements were then brought together to form a dataset for analysis. In this process, the researchers looked for 'recurring regularities' (Guba, 1978, p. 53), and significant or poignant experiences that provided insights into the phenomenon of speech impairment. In developing these categories, the researchers referred back to the original transcripts to ensure these meanings reflected the child's statements and experiences, and to other sources of data, again triangulating the analysis. These triangulation processes provided a method to give strength and validity in this interpretive research (Mertler, 2006; Yin, 2009).

Findings and outcomes

The children's interviews, drawings and questionnaires revealed their awareness of their speech and its impact on their relationships with others, and the consequences of these impacts for these children in their daily lives. Of particular significance were the children's experiences of safe and unsafe contexts, and the different responses these contexts created.

All the focus children indicated that they enjoyed many of the activities associated with children of their age, including playing with friends, sporting activities, computer games, drawing and family-based activities. The focus children's siblings, friends and families confirmed that the child's speech was rarely a problem within these favoured activities (Barr, McLeod & Daniel, 2008). Siblings, friends and families of the focus child also indicated that the children were more relaxed about their speech in these familiar or emotionally safe situations.

Although their speech appeared to create few concerns in the home environment or when interacting with close friends, the focus children were aware of their speech and the ways in which their speaking affected their relationships with others. James described himself as having 'a different voice, of course'. Another reported that he 'talked differently' to his friend, and another noted, 'I can't say words much'. Only the youngest child indicated being happy about his speech. When placed in contexts where others were not easily able to understand these children's speech, the impact of speech impairment on a child's life became more apparent.

The focus children reported being teased about their speech, and some were excluded by others. With awareness that others sometimes had difficulty understanding them, these children used a number of strategies to communicate and meet their needs. One of these strategies was to use gestures. Another common strategy was to involve (by invitation or by necessity) a family member or friend to act as an interpreter and mediator in order for the child to fully communicate with others. Often, it was a sibling who played an important role in the child's life, interpreting and advocating on their brother's or sister's behalf (Barr & McLeod, 2010; Barr et al., 2008).

These children also expressed frustration when their communications were not understood. In the absence of understanding, or an 'interpreter', these children would sometimes give up. Luke's grandmother, for example, reported, 'he just looked up at me after about six times of getting it wrong and said, "It doesn't matter Nanna." ' This frustration was also sometimes expressed physically, in crying or tantrums, or other inappropriate behaviour. Luke's teacher reported that 'He'll tend to thump and then talk later.'

Children also withdrew from the context, either by seeking out an emotionally safe place or trusted person in order to protect themselves. Siblings again played a role here (Barr et al., 2008). These experiences of marginalization and withdrawal reflect previous findings by Brinton, Fujiki and Robinson (2005, p. 151), who identified that 'children with language problems frequently experience social difficulty'.

Reflection on issues

Working with children and young people presents a number of ethical and methodological issues that need to be addressed in order to provide meaningful information without negatively interrupting the participants' lives. With young children often wanting to please the interviewer (Ceci & Bruck, 1998), and being socialized to follow adults' requirements and requests (Hurley & Underwood, 2002), issues relating to the veracity of these children's recollections of events, and the influence of the power imbalance between adult and child, needed to be carefully addressed. In this research, it was also important that the child participants were comfortable being interviewed, and that existing understandings and knowledges, and relationships between participants, were not disrupted. With its aim of developing an understanding of aspects of the lives of these children, child-friendly research methodologies and procedures were therefore employed.

Interviews with the children were conducted in the child's home, with at least one parent present to promote a less threatening interview environment. Preliminary discussions with parents, and the provision of the questions to be asked in advance, allowed the researchers to adjust the interview in response to any relevant issues identified by the family. These questions were also designed with an awareness of not disturbing the relationships between participants, and their own views and awareness of each other. Specific questions about the speech impairment were kept to a minimum.

Consent was gained from the parents for the interviews to take place in advance, and then reconfirmed on the day of the interview. Parents explained the context of the researchers' presence to the children and that we would like to talk with them about the child's interests and experiences and their speech. After an opportunity for the child to ask questions, their verbal assent was gained indicating they were happy to talk with us and do some drawings for us to keep.

Although children and young people's voices are seen as representing a valid voice in reporting on their worlds (MacNaughton, Smith & Lawrence, 2004), it was acknowledged that children may hold alternative understandings of events, which may be less accurate or detailed than adults, and that their memories and understandings of events may change with time and as children grow and develop (Dockett & Perry, 2007, p. 49). The involvement of a range of interviewees from different aspects of the child's life enabled the researchers to develop a richer understanding of the child's world from a number of perspectives, and to corroborate these through the qualitative methodology of triangulation of data sources. The use of multiple methods of data gathering also allowed the child to express their ideas in non-verbal forms, as well as acting to guide and stimulate dialogue as part of the interviewing process. The researchers also kept field notes to augment the information.

With these child-friendly processes, and methodologies of collecting and validating data, a richer understanding of these children's lives was developed. The implications for professional practice are considered within a number of publications emerging from this research (see, for example, Barr & McLeod, 2010; Barr et al., 2008; Daniel & McLeod, 2006), all of which support the importance of listening to children's perspectives.

References to this project

Daniel, G. & McLeod, S. (2006) Listening to the voice of children with a communication impairment. In G. Whiteford (Ed.), *Voice, identity and reflexivity* (pp. 187–200). Albury, NSW: Charles Sturt University.

McLeod, S., Daniel, G. & Barr, J. (2006) Using children's drawings to listen to how children feel about their speech. In C. Heine & L. Brown (Eds), *Proceedings of the 2006 Speech Pathology Australia National Conference* (pp. 38–45). Melbourne: Speech Pathology Australia.

References

Barr, J., & McLeod, S. (2010) They never see how hard it is to be me: Siblings' observations of strangers, peers, and family. *International Journal of Speech-Language Pathology, 12:2*, 162–171.

Barr, J., McLeod, S. & Daniel, G. (2008) Siblings of children with speech impairments: Cavalry on the hill. *Language, Speech, and Hearing Services in Schools, 39*, 21–32.

Bogdan, R.C. & Biklen, S.K. (2006) *Qualitative research for education: An introduction to theories and methods* (5th ed.). Boston: Pearson Education Group.

Brinton, B., Fujiki, M. & Robinson, L. (2005) Life on a tricycle: A case study of language impairment from 4–19 years. *Topics in Language Disorders, 25:4*, 338–352.

Ceci, S.J. & Bruck, M. (1998) Children's testimony: Applied and basic issues. In W. Damon (Ed.), *Handbook of child psychology* (Vol. 4, pp. 713–774). New York: Wiley.

Clark, A. & Moss, P. (2001) *Listening to young children: The Mosaic approach*. London: National Children's Bureau.

Daniel, G., & McLeod, S. (2006) Listening to the voice of children with a communication impairment. In G. Whiteford (Ed.), *Voice, identity and reflexivity* (pp. 187–200). Albury, NSW: Charles Sturt University.

Dockett, S. & Perry, B. (2007) Trusting children's accounts in research. *Journal of Early Childhood Research, 5:1*, 47–63.

Fujiki, M., Brinton, B., Isaacson, T. & Summers, C. (2001) Social behaviours of children with language impairment on the playground: A pilot study. *Language, Speech, and Hearing Services in Schools, 32*, 101–113.

Guba, Y. (1978) *Towards a methodology of naturalistic inquiry in educational evaluation*. Monograph 8. Los Angeles, CA: UCLA Centre for the Study of Evaluation.

Harrison, L. J., McLeod, S., Berthelsen, D. & Walker, S. (2009) Literacy, numeracy and learning in school-aged children identified as having speech and language impairment in early childhood. *International Journal of Speech-Language Pathology, 11:5*, 392–403.

Hurley, J.C. & Underwood, M.K. (2002) Children's understanding of their research rights before and after debriefing: Informed assent, confidentiality and stopping participation. *Child Development, 73*, 132–143.

Knox, E. & Conti-Ramsden, G. (2003) Bullying risks of 11-year-old children with specific language impairment (SLI): Does school placement matter? *International Journal of Language and Communication Disorders, 38:1*, 1–12.

McCormack, J., McLeod, S., McAllister, L. & Harrison, L. J. (2009) A systematic review of the association between childhood speech impairment and participation across the lifespan. *International Journal of Speech-Language Pathology, 11:2*, 155–170.

McCormack, J., McLeod, S., McAllister, L. & Harrison, L.J. (2010) My speech problem, your listening problem, and my frustration: The experience of living with childhood speech impairment. *Language, Speech, and Hearing Services in Schools, 41*, 379–392.

McLeod, S. (2004) Speech pathologists' application of the ICF to children with speech impairment. *International Journal of Speech-Language Pathology, 6:1*, 75–81.

McLeod, S., Daniel, G. & Barr, J. (2006) Using children's drawings to listen to how children feel about their speech. In C. Heine & L. Brown (Eds), *Proceedings of the 2006 Speech Pathology Australia National Conference* (pp. 38–45). Melbourne: Speech Pathology Australia.

MacNaughton, G., Smith, K. & Lawrence, H. (2004) Hearing young children's voices: ACT children's strategy. *Consulting with children birth to eight years of age*. Canberra: Children's Services Branch, ACT Department of Education, Youth and Family Services.

Maxwell, J.A. (2005) *Qualitative research design: An interactive approach*. Thousand Oaks, CA: Sage.

Mertler, C.A. (2006) *Action research: Teachers as researchers in the classroom*. Thousand Oaks, CA: Sage.

Patton, M.Q. (2002) *Qualitative research and evaluation methods* (3rd ed.). Thousand Oaks, CA: Sage.

Smith, K. (2005, June) Children's voices in pedagogy and policy making. Paper presented at the *Centre for Equity and Innovation in Early Childhood Conference*, Melbourne.

World Health Organization (2001) *ICF: International classification of functioning, disability and health*. Geneva: Author.

Yin, R.K. (2009) *Case study research: Design and methods* (4th ed.). Thousand Oaks, CA: Sage.

24 Listening to Adolescents after Traumatic Brain Injury

Lucie Shanahan, Lindy McAllister and Michael Curtin

Purpose of the project

The purpose of our study was to explore the perception that young people with traumatic brain injury (TBI) held about their executive functioning skills, compared with their parents' perception, to determine effective rehabilitation approaches for children and young people.

Children and young people

Two adolescent males and their mothers participated in this study. Both adolescents, Harry and Jack,[1] had acquired a severe TBI in childhood: Harry at 4 years; 10 months (4;10) and Jack at 6 years; 9 months (6;9). At the time of participating in this study, Harry was 18;5 years, completing his final year of high school, and was employed part-time with the Australian Defence Force Reserves. Jack was 16;8 years and had just commenced a full-time bricklaying apprenticeship, combined with part-time attendance at a technical college. He left school the previous year after achieving his Year 10 School Certificate. Neither Harry nor Jack had been engaged with rehabilitation services for over 12 months at the time of participating in the study.

Both young people had average intellectual abilities, as measured by the *Weschler Intelligence Scale for Children, Fourth Edition – Australian Adaptation* (Weschler, 2003), and spoke English as their first language. Harry demonstrated significantly impaired expressive verbal language skills but intact auditory comprehension skills. Jack presented with moderately reduced expressive verbal language skills, but also had intact auditory comprehension skills. A standardized assessment of executive functioning skills, the *Test of Problem Solving 2 – Adolescent edition* (Bowers, Huisingh & LoGiudice, 2007), indicated that Harry showed a mild reduction in skills, while Jack's skills were within the

---

1 Not the participants' real names.

average range. Interestingly, an ecological assessment of executive functioning, using the *Party Planning Task* (Chalmers & Lawrence, 1993), showed Harry's skills to be superior to Jack's, although both were within the range expected for young people with severe TBI. This discrepancy between standardized and ecological assessment was typical of assessment outcomes in the TBI population, with standardized assessment often failing to reflect a person's cognitive and self-regulatory skills present in real-life and everyday activities (Levin & Hanten, 2005).

Investigator

The primary author (Shanahan) is a speech and language therapist within a specialized, community-based paediatric brain injury rehabilitation service in rural Australia. This service supports children and young people with TBI, their families and school staff using a collaborative, contextualized approach. The second author (McAllister) is a qualified speech and language therapist and university professor, while the third author (Curtin) is a qualified occupational therapist and a university professor. McAllister and Curtin both have research backgrounds in working with children and young people and provided academic guidance for this project.

Method and procedures

The study adopted a mixed-methods approach, incorporating qualitative plus quantitative methods (Creswell & Plano Clark, 2007), to explore young people's perceptions of their executive functioning skills. The nature of the approach being used for this study and the questions being asked meant that data was best obtained through in-depth investigation of a small number of participants. As such, purposive sampling was used. Adolescent participants were recruited from the caseload of the multi-disciplinary rehabilitation service with which the first author was employed. Adolescents who were eligible for inclusion in the study were those who had acquired a TBI, had an average IQ as determined by neuropsychological assessment, no co-morbidity of Attention-Deficit Disorder, documented executive functioning deficits post-injury and were aged between 15 and 19 years. Adolescents who had been engaged in speech and language therapy with the primary author were considered to be eligible for inclusion in this study, so long as this author had not also acted as the adolescent's case manager/rehabilitation coordinator. This criterion was included due to the close and intense relationship often built between a family and case manager, and so to avoid the possibility of coercion jeopardizing the ethical integrity of the study.

Members of the multi-disciplinary team, other than the first author, identified potential participants from the team's client list. Harry and Jack were specifically selected to participate in the study because, in addition to meeting the inclusion criteria, their families had been extensively involved in, and supportive throughout, the rehabilitation process. Harry and Jack were also considered appropriate candidates for participation in the research, as both of them had shown insight into their cognitive difficulties during previous therapy sessions, had received multi-disciplinary rehabilitation services across multiple contexts (e.g. school, home, community, vocational) and had trialled and adopted various compensatory cognitive strategies post-injury.

An information pack that included study information sheets and an expression of interest (EOI) form was mailed to Harry and Jack's families. Upon return of the EOI form, the primary investigator met with families to discuss the study and answer any questions; consent forms were signed at this meeting. Harry and Jack's mothers were also interviewed for this research.

Data collection occurred in a manner considerate of each participant, with sessions conducted at a venue of the participant's choice. As is expected in mixed-methods research, our study used a variety of tools to collect quantitative and qualitative data; however, as the focus of this chapter is on the in-depth interview data collected, only methods pertaining to that phase are presented here. Details of other data collection methods are presented elsewhere (see, for example, Shanahan, McAllister & Curtin, 2011).

An individual, face-to-face interview occurred with Harry, Jack and their mothers, to explore their perceptions of their or their sons' executive functioning skills, including how competent Harry and Jack felt in applying these skills to everyday tasks and contexts. By applying a recursive method to interviews, respondents were encouraged to offer information through a conversational approach and all efforts were made to maintain a typical conversational interaction during the interviews (Minichiello, Madison, Hays & Parmenter, 2004). The aim of in-depth, unstructured interviews is to gain 'richly textured, person-centred information' (Minichiello et al., 2004, p. 412), and the pre-existing therapeutic relationships the primary author held with each informant facilitated this approach. Each interview lasted approximately 60 minutes and was audio-recorded with the participants' consent. Field notes were also recorded immediately following each interview, to supplement audio material, note informant's emotional and behavioural state and any prominent topics or features of the interview.

Interviews were transcribed verbatim and analyzed using interpretative phenomenological analysis (IPA) (Smith, Flowers & Larkin, 2009). IPA has been shown to be a complementary approach to clinically based research through its explicit acknowledgement of the importance of the researcher's interpretation and that, at times, researchers are unable to divorce themselves from acquired knowledge and clinical experience (Dean, Smith & Payne, 2006). The process shown in Table 24.1 is informed by Smith et al. (2009) and outlines the process undertaken in this study.

Table 24.1 Steps taken in analyzing interview.

Step	Researcher activities
Transcription	• Verbatim transcription of Harry's, then Jack's, then parental interviews
Reading/rereading transcripts	• Immersion in transcribed interviews – commenced initial noting and documenting reactions to data
Developing emerging themes	• Developed document that recorded related comments from each transcript side-by-side to facilitate interpretation across data sets
Searching for connections across emergent themes	• Concurrent development of thematic maps for each participant
Looking for patterns across cases	• Compared theme maps • Identified superordinate themes in individual cases and higher-order concepts represented across cases
Data verification	• Participant checked transcripts and themes • Blind peer coding of transcript samples to ensure rigour of themes • Debriefing of analysis process with research team

Findings and implications

Five key themes emerged from the interview data and these are listed in Table 24.2 alongside a quote from Harry or Jack's interview transcript to illustrate the content of each.

Table 24.2 Key themes and illustrative quotes.

1. Development of self (identity and role development; individuation and family differentiation)	'In the Army I feel more where I want to be…they see me in the ways that I show, the real side of me, *me*… it's where I fit…' (Harry)
2. Bond (a secure relational basis with a non-parental adult; a role within a team)	'And I want to do it because I look up to my Boss …he makes me realize like, what happens in this situation and that… And when I make a mistake he always sits… and he always shows me' (Jack)
3. Task relevance (personally relevant tasks of optimal challenge)	'Some of the schoolwork we do here is not even relevant… what I do in the army I'm gonna be using in like five minutes time' (Harry)
4. Motivation and engagement (interest, autonomy and active participation)	'When it come to assignments [at high school] there's no way I could've done it myself… But now I reckon I could do [my technical college] assignments by myself' (Jack)
5. Confidence and competence (self-esteem)	'I feel pretty confident [in my planning and organizing skills] in the army actually. More confident than anywhere else' (Harry)

The focus in this chapter is on two implications of these findings that have direct relevance to the ways clinicians listen to children and young people with TBI throughout their rehabilitation. Implication 1 directly links to theme 5 listed in the table, but implication 2 represents the convergence of all themes.

Implication 1: Rehabilitation needs to build confidence

The adolescents and parents had different expectations of the outcomes of rehabilitation. Adolescents were primarily seeking *confidence* in their skill base, while parents were seeking to observe repeated examples of *competent* skill use by their sons in order for parents to develop a sense of confidence in their children's abilities. By listening to Harry and Jack throughout this study, it became apparent that their primary need to develop confidence in their skills, rather than competence, creates a mandate for clinicians to work with adolescents in ways that promote confidence in their skills first. From this, adolescents will consequently desire a sense of competence. However, within the practice of outcomes-driven rehabilitation, altering the focus from a 'competency'-driven framework to an 'efficacy'-driven framework will require individual clinicians to continually listen to their clients and ask themselves where their focus lies.

Implication 2: Factors needed to engage young people in rehabilitation

The second key implication of this study was the elucidations of contextual factors that facilitate young people's engagement in rehabilitation. Contexts supporting the needs of identity development, autonomy, relatedness and self-efficacy enable adolescents to hold positive perceptions of their executive functioning skills. This implication highlights the importance of considering the normal developmental processes of adolescence and the influence of these on children and young people participating in rehabilitation. The findings from this study suggest that contexts that meet typical developmental needs create the impetus for engaging in rehabilitation and, as a result, make adolescents 'ripe for rehabilitation'.

Reflection on issues

The methods adopted in this study allowed for a rich exploration of adolescents' and parents' perceptions of executive functioning skills following childhood-acquired TBI. Importantly, Harry and Jack both commented on the experience of having their opinion heard, and the confidence they garnered from doing the 'telling' rather than 'being told'. However, the depth of information obtained was achieved, in part, as a result of the previous therapeutic relationships between the first author and participants.

Whilst the power issues inherent in this relationship were acknowledged, the collaborative foundations on which these relationships were built proved facilitative to the data collection, and interview process in particular. The approach used by the first author in providing rehabilitation services of establishing collaborative relationships within community contexts in which the child or young person, parent, teacher or other team member is a respected contributor to the rehabilitation programme was central to the level of trust that occurred within the interview process. The rapport that had been built between the first author and young people in particular facilitated the breadth and depth of disclosure. Similarly, the first author's knowledge and understanding of the adolescents' language and communication needs meant that she was able to support and scaffold their participation in the interview. Having this level of understanding was particularly important in knowing when, for example, to facilitate word-finding, refrain from talking to allow auditory processing and language generation, or rephrase a question or comment to prevent communication breakdown and loss of momentum in the interview. It would appear from the results of this study that establishing supportive and collaborative relationships with young people, and understanding their communication abilities and needs, is imperative to engaging them in research processes and ensuring that their opinions are truly heard.

Acknowledgements

Many thanks to Harry, Jack and their mothers for participating in this study and willingly sharing their experiences and perceptions.

References to this project

Shanahan, L., McAllister, L. & Curtin, M. (in press) '…This is worth it to me now…' Building identity to build executive functioning skills. In J. Contole (Ed.), *Proceedings of the 2010 Victorian Brain Injury Recovery Association 10ᵗʰ Annual Forum.* Melbourne: Victorian Brain Injury Recovery Association.

Shanahan, L., McAllister, L. & Curtin, M. (2011) The Party Planning Task: A useful tool in the functional assessment of planning skills in adolescents with TBI. *Brain Injury, 25:11,* 1080-1090.

References

Bowers, L., Huisingh, R. & LoGiudice, C. (2007) *Test of Problem Solving 2 – Adolescent: Examiner's manual.* East Moline, IL: LinguiSystems.

Chalmers, D. & Lawrence, J. (1993) Investigating the effects of planning aids on adults' and adolescents' organisation of a complex task. *International Journal of Behavioural Development, 16:2,* 191–214.

Creswell, J.W. & Plano Clark, V. L. (2007) *Designing and conducting mixed methods research.* Thousand Oaks, CA: Sage.

Dean, S.G., Smith, J.A. & Payne, S. (2006) Low back pain: Exploring the meaning of exercise management through interpretative phenomenological analysis (IPA). In L. Finlay & C. Ballinger (Eds), *Qualitative research for allied health professionals: Challenging choices.* (pp. 139–155). Chichester: John Wiley & Sons.

Levin, H.S. & Hanten, G. (2005) Executive functions after traumatic brain injury in children. *Pediatric Neurology, 33:2,* 79–93.

Minichiello, V., Madison, J., Hays, T. & Parmenter, G. (2004). Doing qualitative in-depth interviews. In V. Minichiello, G. Sullivan, K. Greenwood & R. Axford (Eds), *Handbook of research methods for nursing and health science* (pp. 411–446). Frenchs Forest: Prentice Hall Health.

Smith, J.A., Flowers, P. & Larkin, M. (2009) *Interpretative phenomenological analysis: Theory, methods and research.* London: Sage Publications.

Weschler, D. (2003) *Weschler Intelligence Scale for Children – Fourth edition: Administraton and scoring manual:* Marrickville, Australia: Harcourt Assessment.

25 Listening to the Post-16 Transition Experiences of Young People with Specific Language Impairment

Catherine Carroll and Julie Dockrell

Purpose of the project

Investigations of the post-16 experiences of young people with a history of specific language impairment are limited in number and scope in the United Kingdom. This chapter reports how a group of young people were able to describe their transition experiences based on a mixed-methods approach. The first of the two research questions focused on their transition outcomes and experiences in relation to education, employment, social activities and independence. The second question examined factors that had facilitated and inhibited the post-16 transition of the young people from their perspective.

Young people

Sixty young people (12 female and 48 male) with a history of specific language impairment ranging between 17 and 22 years of age (average age was 19) completed a telephone survey to investigate their transition experiences since leaving school (Carroll & Dockrell, 2009). Two years later, 19 (4 female and 15 male) of the original cohort were purposively sampled and interviewed face to face to explore their views on what had facilitated and hindered their transition experiences to date. The participants at this stage ranged 19 to 24 years of age, with an average age of 21. All of the young people had attended the same special residential school for pupils with speech, language and communication needs in the southeast of England.

Investigators

The lead investigator had been a teacher at the school – the young people were known to the author and many had been taught by her. The investigation was part of a PhD undertaken by the first author and supervised by the second author, who was a consultant educational psychologist to the school.

Method and procedures

Young adults with specific language impairment are much underresearched in terms of their transition, but also in respect to the research methods that might best capture this experience. It was known anecdotally to the lead investigator that many of the participants were in further education and that some had moved on to higher education as well as employment. It was important not to underestimate their capacity to participate whilst acknowledging potential difficulties with elements of the research process because of the history of their language needs.

A mixed-methods sequential purposive design, involving quantitative and qualitative data collection methods, was adopted. Data was collected from the survey on a range of variables relating to the transition of the young people and almost two years later from the semi-structured interviews on the views of the young people that examined the factors that had helped and hindered their transition. A sequential, in preference to a simultaneous, research design was used for three reasons. The first reason was in response to the needs of the two research questions and, second, to allow for purposive sampling for the interview stage. The third consideration was that any form of interview which attempted to address both research questions in any depth might have been too long for the participants. The study used two main analytic techniques: quantitative analysis of the survey interviews and thematic analysis of the face-to-face interviews.

Behavioural and cognitive factors associated with language difficulties had to be considered when choosing the research instruments. Studies have shown that for language and literacy these young people continue to fall behind in respect to their peers during adolescence (Conti-Ramsden, Durkin, Simkin & Knox, 2009; Dockrell, Lindsay, Palikara & Cullen, 2007; Snowling, Adams, Bishop & Stothard, 2001). At a cognitive level, possible difficulties with auditory processing, working memory, attention, executive functioning, phonology, morphology, syntax, semantics and pragmatic language were all potential concerns in the research process for this group of young people. The use of a postal questionnaire was rejected on a number of grounds. These have poorer response rates compared to other methods, are heavily reliant on literacy levels and do not permit the exploration of novel themes and ideas. In terms of conducting an interview, whether face to face or by telephone, the particular concerns were with accessibility of language, auditory processing, working memory and social interaction demands. However, unlike a postal questionnaire, the investigators believed that it was possible in the research design to make sufficient accommodations in these areas in order to ensure that a more 'authentic' voice on the part of the young person was heard.

A range of accommodations were made and these are summarized in Table 25.1, with the main emphasis on the use of accessible language (established in the pilot phases of the investigation) and sufficient allocation of time at key points in the investigation. The survey and interview instruments included questions that went from the general to the specific to reduce the cognitive demands on the participant at the start of the interview. Both schedules needed to take account of the fact that the participants might have required longer to answer the questions and this was an additional influence on the number of questions that could be included in the schedules. The final consideration was the role of the young people in the project beyond that of participants in the survey and interviews. For this project, their involvement was primarily through the feedback provided in the pilots of the survey and interview schedules. For example, the pilot participants were asked to give feedback on the language levels, length of schedules, relevancy of content and whether the prompt sheet had been helpful. For the second phase, the young people were able to exercise choice as to where they wished to be interviewed – for example, their home, home town or old school – in order to ensure that they felt as comfortable as possible during the interview. Although it did not happen for this investigation, it would be a recommendation for future research in this field that the young people be represented right from the start of the process with their contributions included in the research aims and design.

Table 25.1 Accommodations in the research process.

	Communication and contact before the survey/interviews	Research instruments	Conducting the interview
Language (accessibility)	•Accessible language in correspondence with young person and family •Prompt sheet with interview topics	•Accessible language •Content of questions moves from general to the specific	•Prompt sheet with interview topics
Time (processing)	•Follow-up phone calls to invitations to explain in more depth •Possible further phone call to allow for more considered consent on the part of the young person	•Balancing the aims of the research with the length of interview schedule	•Greater time for asking questions •Time for processing meaning of questions and formulating a response •Repetition/rephrasing of questions •Rest breaks during the interview
Participation of young person	•Position on the research group to inform aims, content and outcomes of the research	•Participation in a pilot to test accessibility of language	•Exercise choice over the venue

Initially, 79 young people were contacted by letter requesting their participation in the study. For those below 18 years of age, letters were sent to parents to ensure their consent to talk with the young person. The letter was followed up by a telephone call to discuss the project further and, if the young person had indicated that they were willing to take part, to arrange a convenient time for the telephone call to conduct the survey. Those participants selected as a result of the sequential sampling process following the survey were contacted by letter and a telephone call and invited to take part in a face-to-face interview. As previously stated, the young people were offered a selection of venues for the semi-structured interview 10 of the 19 participants choosing to be interviewed at the special school they had attended. Both the survey and the interviews were recorded manually and using a dictaphone.

Findings and outcomes

This investigation showed, that despite a history of specific language impairment, the young people were able to engage meaningfully in the research process, which is a finding supported by interview research with a similar group of young people (Palikara, Lindsay & Dockrell, 2009). The telephone survey demonstrated that the participants were able to report their experiences and progress across many aspects of their lives since leaving school. The analysis revealed that the young people were following many different routes, which included further study, training and employment. As a result of further study the majority had increased their level of qualifications, including, for some young people, commencement on degree-level courses. For those participants in employment, retail, manual and the service sectors were the most common career paths. Most of the young people were participating in a range of social and leisure activities and were enjoying spending time with friends socially. Although the majority were still living at home, they experienced greater levels of confidence and independence since leaving school. This breadth of data was complemented by the depth and richness of the interview, which demonstrated the ability of the young people to assess the relative contributions that they and other people and institutions had played in their transition experiences. The most common finding from the interviews highlighted that the young people viewed themselves as the main driving force in their transition, with support from their families.

The level of participation for both phases of the study was high, again demonstrating the strengths of the research methods. A total of 60 young people, out of a possible 79 who had left the special school between 2000 and 2004, agreed to take part in the telephone survey – a high return rate of 76%. For the interview, all of the young people who were invited to take part as a result of the purposive sampling agreed to do so. The length and quality of the responses of the young people for both phases of the study (the interviews ranged from 90 minutes to three hours) revealed just how much they were experts in their own lives.

Reflections on issues

The transition experience of young people with disabilities and learning difficulties has been described as both similar to and different from that of all young people (Dee, 2006). A similar description could be used to describe how young people with a history of specific language impairment participate and experience the research process. It is different, in that greater consideration needs to be given to issues of language and time, and yet the same, in that standard research methods such as the telephone survey and semi-structured interview can be appropriate and effective means of gathering rich data and listening to the voices of this particular group of young people.

Acknowledgements

The authors wish to thank the young people who participated in the project and their families for supporting the young people in the process.

References to this project

Carroll, C. & Dockrell, J. (2009) Leaving special school: Post-16 outcomes of young people with specific language impairment. *European Journal of Special Needs Education, 25*, 131–147.

References

Conti-Ramsden, G., Durkin, K., Simkin, Z. & Knox, E. (2009) Specific language impairment and school outcomes. I: Identifying and explaining variability at the end of compulsory education. *International Journal of Language and Communication Disorders, 44:1*, 15–35.

Dee, L. (2006) *Improving transition planning.* Maidenhead: Open University Press.

Dockrell, J., Lindsay, G., Palikara, O. & Cullen, M.-A. (2007) *Raising the achievements of children and young people with specific speech and language difficulties and other special educational needs through school to work and college.* Nottingham: Department of Education and Skills.

Palikara, O., Lindsay, G. & Dockrell, J. E. (2009) Voices of young people with a history of specific language impairment (SLI) in the first year of post-16 education. *International Journal of Language and Communication Disorders, 44:1*, 56–78.

Snowling, M., Adams, J., Bishop, D. & Stothard, S. (2001) Educational attainments of school leavers with prehistory of SLI. *International Journal of Language and Communication Disorders, 36:2*, 173–183.

26 Listening to Children Talk about Their Desired Outcomes

Helen Hambly, Jane Coad, Geoff Lindsay and Sue Roulstone

Purpose of the project

This chapter describes a project that aimed to listen to children and young people with speech, language and communication needs using arts-based research methods, such as those described by Coad and Hambly (2011, Chapter 16 in this volume). As well as listening to children and young people's everyday experiences, the project also aimed to listen to their ideas and views about outcomes that they value. The project was part of the Better Communication Research Programme (BCRP; Lindsay, Dockrell, Law, Roulstone & Vignoles, 2010), commissioned by the Department for Education in the UK to investigate best practice and cost-effectiveness of services for children with speech, language and communication needs.

Children and young people

The participating children and young people were attending special schools or receiving additional support at mainstream schools for their speech, language and communication needs. In total, 37 children and young people between 8 and 16 years took part in workshops – 26 boys and 11 girls. The majority were of white British background. They had a diverse range of speech, language and communication needs, including primary language impairment, Landau Kleffner syndrome, autistic spectrum disorder, hearing impairment and childhood apraxia of speech. Overall, three children and young people relied mainly on sign language.

Investigators

Three researchers designed and facilitated the participatory workshops: a speech and language therapist (Roulstone); a children's nurse with expertise in arts-based research methods (Coad); and a health psychologist and research student (Hambly). The fourth investigator (Lindsay) managed the Better Communication Research Programme as a whole.

Method and procedures

Seven workshops were organized to take place in five schools in the UK. Each workshop included four to six children and young people and was facilitated by at least two researchers. The groups were organized according to locality (the children's schools) and according to age group (8–11 years and 12–16 years). The workshops lasted approximately an hour and were split into three separate activities, each lasting 10 to 20 minutes. Consent was obtained from parents prior to the workshop and then, at the start of each one, time was spent explaining the purpose of the research and obtaining assent from the children and young people. This was time well spent, as some children and young people were not aware that they had been asked to take part in a research project.

The philosophy of Appreciative Inquiry underpinned the interview schedule. Appreciative Inquiry is a way of asking questions that builds on the positive aspects of a person rather than focusing on their inadequacies. At its heart is a desire to find out what works well and why it works well and the idea that, by appreciating the good in someone or something, one is more likely to discover more of what is good (Coad, Plumridge & Metcalfe, 2009; Cooperrider & Whitney, 1999). Arts-based activities were designed around three key questions: What's good? What could be better (now)? What could be better (future)? Facilitators probed children and young people about their lives and experiences whilst they were engaged in arts activities.

Some of the activities that children and young people engaged with are also described in Coad and Hambly (2011, Chapter 16 in this volume). Eight- to 11-year-olds drew themselves and their families (see Figure 26.1) and used pictures of walls and mountains to illustrate their achievements and struggles and clouds to illustrate their aspirations. Twelve- to 16-year-olds were encouraged to graffiti a large wall and talk about a good, bad and perfect day (see Figure 26.2). Stations were also set up in corners of the room, with each station representing a different aspect of young people's lives, such as 'talking', 'feeling happy' or 'funny' and 'feeling sad' or 'frustrated'. Young people were encouraged to write, draw and talk about these topics. Throughout all the workshops, a large sheet with plastic pockets was hung on a wall so that children and young people could post things that they did not want to share with the rest of the group (see Coad, 2007). A ball game also helped bring the group together when children and young people were tiring.

The workshops were audio-recorded and all children and young people's artwork was photographed. Facilitators wrote detailed field notes immediately after the workshops, based on their memories, the audio recordings and the children and young people's artwork. Audio recordings were not transcribed in full due to the challenges of transcribing children and young people's cross-talk, but key quotes were transcribed verbatim. Field notes were then coded and analyzed thematically by the first author and cross-checked by the other authors. All codes and emerging themes were also checked against children and young people's artwork.

Findings and outcomes

What's good?

Children and young people were very aware of who they were and what they liked about themselves and their lives. They talked with animation about their parents and siblings, their favourite hobbies and their pets, and they valued the relationships they had with their family and friends and the help and support that they received from them. Having fun and laughing was also very important for children and young people of all ages, and particularly for older boys. This was often related to having fun with friends and family, but was also talked about in relation to schoolteachers.

> Boy, 8–11 years: I couldn't say little normal words like cat and stuff... it did help but it was like my Mum and Dad helped me a lot and then it came into my head.

> Boy, 8–11 years: He's funny [Dad]. He does silly things to make me laugh.

> Boy 12–16 years: [Why has this school helped you speak better?] I get a lot more help. I prefer them [teachers]. They are nice to me, joke with me.

Figure 26.1 Listening to a 10-year-old boy about what's good.

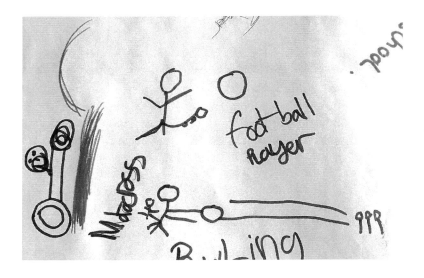

Figure 26.2 Listening to 12- to 16-year-olds about a good day.

What could be better?

Other people. Despite valuing the help and support they receive from key individuals in their lives, many children and young people talked about how other people could listen more and help more. Being understood by other people was felt to be one of the biggest challenges that the children and young people faced in their day-to-day lives. Children and young people found it difficult to articulate exactly what they wanted in terms of help and being listened to, but it was clear that for some the 'help' provided was not enough for them and they were not being understood by their teachers or parents.

> Girl, 8–11 years: People say to me, 'I can't hear you.' I hate this. 'I don't understand you'; they shout at me questions but I can hear them but they shout. They shout at me. I want them to talk to me but they shout.

> Girl, 8–11 years: People just listening to me would help.

Boy, 8–11 years: Teachers don't do anything – they say, 'Oh dear'.

Boy, 8–11 years: When I speak to my mum and dad they interrupt me.

Anger and frustration. Some children and young people also talked about friends and siblings teasing them and the difficulties they have with their friendships. The actions of others interrupting, shouting and teasing appeared to lead to increased feelings of frustration and anger. This was especially notable in the older children and young people. Alongside feelings of anger and frustration towards other people, children and young people also expressed anger and frustration at themselves and their abilities.

Boy, 12–16 years: Some of my friends say, 'Shut up and stop talking.' [How does it make you feel?] A bit sad and a bit angry at the same time. It makes me want to hit them but they're my friends so I wouldn't want to do that.

Boy, 8–11 years: My speaking has not got better. I get cross with myself. Just myself... that I can't do it.

Boy, 12–16 years: I am not good at talking. I get frustrated and angry.

Girl, 8–11 years: [What makes you sad?] I'm always talking too much. I interrupt when the teachers are talking.

My abilities. Many children and young people mentioned areas that they struggled with in school: academically, socially and in sports. Difficulties with learning, listening, reading, concentration, memory, organization and behaviour were talked about as well as specific difficulties with speaking, being understood and 'getting muddled'. For others, wider learning problems were not a concern and they largely viewed their problem as an isolated speech, language or communication issue.

Girl, 8–11 years: I'd like to be a faster talker and be good at listening.

Girl, 8–11 years: I'd like to understand jokes much better – I think the jokes are about me.

Boy, 8–11 years: I'd like to stop arguing with my friends.

Future aspirations

Younger children aged 8 to 11 years spoke less about their future aspirations, but those older than 12 years spoke about their futures with optimism. They had very individual aspirations such as: joining a rugby team, doing well in maths and science, working in a horse stables, being an architect, being a farmer and writing for a newspaper.

Implications for practice

Three themes emerged from listening to children and young people talk about their desired outcomes that have important implications for practice. Firstly, the high value children and young people placed on laughing and joking with friends, family and teachers should be a central consideration by professionals and researchers working with children and young people with speech, language and communication needs. Second, the frequent disclosure by older children and young people about their feelings of anger and frustration either towards themselves or other people is an important area for professional support and further research. And finally, children and young people talked about other people causing them distress or frustration through interrupting or not listening or shouting, rather than their own speech, language or communication difficulties. Their experiences highlight the importance of understanding children and young people's perspectives when working with them to improve communication.

Reflection on issues

Overall, the arts-based research activities worked well as an engaging method to listen to the views of the children and young people. They enabled an informal research environment where children and young people could contribute to conversations as much or little as they wished whilst they engaged with non-verbal activities. One challenge for the facilitators was listening to individuals at the same time as managing the group. Often a child or young person would express something that the facilitator wished to follow up, but the facilitator would be distracted by another child or young person and so opportunities were lost. Despite the challenges of listening to a group of children and young people, the group dynamic enabled a more social, fun, research environment where children and young people could bounce ideas and experiences off each other. Within the group context, the number of facilitators to children was important to ensure participation for these children and a ratio of at least one facilitator per two children and young people was necessary to assist listening to individual voices.

Acknowledgements

The authors wish to thank all children and young people who took part in the workshops, the teaching staff who helped organize the workshops and the Department for Education for funding the project.

References to other projects and write-ups of this project

Coad, J. & Hambly, H. (2011) Listening to children and young people with speech, language and communication needs through arts-based methods. In S. Roulstone & S. McLeod (Eds), *Listening to children and young people with speech, language and communication needs*. London: J&R Press.

Lindsay, G., Dockrell, J.E., Law, J., Roulstone, S. & Vignoles, A. (2010) *Better communication research programme first interim report*. London: Department for Education. http://publications.education.gov.uk/eOrderingDownload/DFE-RR070.pdf

References

Coad, J. (2007) Using art based techniques in engaging children and young people in health care consultations audit and/or research, *Journal of Research in Nursing, 12:5*, 567–583.

Coad, J., Plumridge, G. & Metcalfe, A. (2009) Involving children and young people in the development of art-based research tools. *Nurse Researcher, 16:4*, 56–64.

Cooperrider, D.L. & Whitney, D. (1999) *Collaborating for change: Appreciative inquiry*. San Francisco, CA: Berrett-Koehler Publishers.

27 'Everything is easier 'cos they get it…'

Listening to Young People's Views about People Who Work with Them

Wendy Lee

Purpose of the project

The Communication Trust (www.thecommunicationtrust.org.uk) believes a workforce confident in their knowledge of speech, language and communication is crucial in ensuring children and young people are supported to develop these essential skills. The Trust aims to deliver a programme of work built on a foundation of best practice and contingent with the views of young people with speech, language and communication needs. Consultations were completed to gather these views focusing on desired skills, knowledge and behaviour of the children's workforce.

Children and young people

Children and young people were recruited predominantly from the Communication Trust membership organizations. Eighty-five children and young people with speech, language and communication needs (age range 7 to 24) were consulted. There was a geographical spread, with a mix of gender and ethnic origin. Young people had a range of speech, language and communication needs, including: moderate speech or language delays (though the majority had more persistent needs); specific language impairment; those linked to moderate or severe learning difficulties, sensory or physical impairments. Some children and young people had additional behaviour needs. Some participants used alternative and augmentative systems of communication, including simple signs and symbols and electronic voice output communication aids.

The consultations occurred during eleven sessions that took place over a 12-month period, which included 5 individual interviews and 10-group sessions; the smallest group was with 3 young people, and the largest with 17. The sessions lasted between 30 and 50 minutes, depending on numbers and ages and abilities of the young people involved.

Children and young people were consulted predominantly within their own settings, which included mainstream, special and specialist schools, youth groups, charity groups and a pupil referral unit. Additionally, a participation conference was held at a specialist school, attended by pupils from this, and other, schools.

Investigator

Two investigators ran the project. The first was a speech and language therapist, experienced in working with children and young people across the age range with speech, language and communication needs and a member of the Communication Trust core team. The second investigator was a senior development officer for participation of young people with disabilities for the Council for Disabled Children (CDC), experienced in working directly with young people with disabilities. There was no direct relationship between investigators and participants.

Method and procedures

Consultations were to inform the UK's national agenda around the children's workforce. Some were also part of a project for the Children's Workforce Development Council (CWDC) to feed the views of children and young people with special educational needs and disabilities into national workforce drivers.

Consultations were with individuals or in groups. A semi-structured approach enabled participants to comment and discuss in whatever way they chose. They were encouraged to think of specific scenarios, situations and people to help consider the issues.

A range of methodologies and approaches were available to ensure that all young people were able to contribute (Clark, Quail & Moss, 2003) and that information was sought from different perspectives to ensure consistency of response. Methodologies included use of pictures, photos, symbols and interactive activities, such as drawing round participants and adding comments to create a 'good' worker. Stars and stickers were used to highlight important features with rating scales or diamond ranking activities. Activities were fun and interactive. Participants' understanding of information and tasks and investigators' understanding of their views were checked. Sometimes participants chose to discuss issues freely, with few activities. Where possible, sessions were audio- or video-recorded with field notes and photos of activities taken. Staff from the children and young people's settings were generally involved in consultation sessions. Although this presented a potential conflict, it was deemed useful to ensure that children were comfortable, communication methods for all individuals were facilitated, additional needs were met and consultation techniques were shared. In individual interviews with older and more able young people, attendance of staff was optional. The children and young people were seen only once. However, it was felt that additional follow-up time would have enhanced the consultation cycle, allowed us to work with staff and young people to consider next steps, how best to use the information gained and to make future plans around participation.

Reflection on issues

Ethical issues were taken into account throughout (Alderson & Morrow, 2004). The aim was to capture opinions within a good practice framework of consulting (Clark et al., 2003) and research with children (Tisdall, Davis & Gallagher, 2009). Careful account was taken of children's cognitive and language levels.

Consultations were opportunities to include the voices of young people with special educational needs and disability in national policy development. However, for many participants, these national issues were both difficult to understand and hard to see as relevant, which challenged consensual issues.

The process was made clear to children and young people, as was information about how their views would be shared. Careful checking ensured that children and young people understood that their responses would be shared with people around them and with the wider context.

Participants were given the opportunity to opt out at any time and reminded that they did not have to respond or join in, though encouragement to participate was given, as appropriate. The investigators' skills and experience in working with children with speech, language and communication and learning needs was key to enabling this.

Despite difficulties with understanding the wider context, children and young people commented positively on the experience and benefits were reported by staff in sharing the views of young people within their settings. In some, staff reported that the opportunity to reflect on comments of participants was beneficial. Techniques used were also seen as useful tools for them to consult more regularly with young people. In some settings, the process was very much a partnership between investigators and staff, though a careful balance was maintained so that staff did not direct the route of consultations and children were given appropriate freedom of voice.

Findings and outcomes

Consultation data was transcribed and analyzed to identify recurring themes, issues and ideas, supported by direct quotations from young people. For some, their initial focus was on narrow details of their lives, finding it difficult to generalize – for example, 'Bob (our "good worker") should like fish' – though it was often possible to clarify their meaning, in this case, about having workers with shared interests.

How young people might view different workers and whether different professionals needed different skill sets was of interest in the project. For many children and young people, though, the profession or designation of the people who worked with them was irrelevant.

Although the investigators aimed to gather information about knowledge, skills and behaviours, children and young people focused very much on *personal qualities*. It was important for them to have workers who cared about them, had a positive attitude and spent time listening, talking and getting to know them: 'They need to listen', 'Yeh, friendly', 'Be caring', 'Be kind to me'. When asked to expand, communication skills featured prominently – the ability to listen and talk with them was important, both generally and at an appropriate level for them to understand and engage: 'They need skills in knowing and communicating at the right level'

Participants valued workers who helped them with their *communication skills*: 'They [teachers, speech and language therapists, support and care staff] help me with my communication and socialize and what words mean'; and commented on the frustrations of being misunderstood or not listened to: 'I just felt like screaming and shouting at her face [teacher]'.

Alongside communication was a key theme of *independence*. Participants repeatedly reported the need for support and encouragement to develop skills to do tasks themselves, not having tasks done for them. They were clear that they all had different needs and their workers needed to be aware and prepared to get to know them as individuals: 'I like that I can do it myself – I want to do things myself', 'Also I find things difficult and sometimes I do need a bit of help.' Participants highlighted the importance of staff consistency and the challenges when this didn't happen: '[I had]… three different people in one day… it was sad.'

For many, it was especially important that workers *understood their underlying difficulty and its potential impact*, particularly for those with 'hidden' speech, language and communication needs who felt they were often misunderstood: 'People think I am bad', 'The best people, they understand the nature of my condition – I'd say that was the most important thing.' They also highlighted clearly the impact on them when this didn't happen: 'They couldn't understand me and I couldn't trust them.'

Balanced against specific skills, young people commented on *wider skills and attributes* that they appreciated: 'I like the instructors, they're jokey and say stuff that I've only heard teenagers saying – it's funny.'

Children and young people were also asked to consider what the workforce should know. They were very clear that whoever worked with them should have the *appropriate professional knowledge*. This was seen as a necessity and very much an expectation: 'They need the right knowledge for the job if that makes sense', 'like if you see a doctor, you expect them to know about illness and stuff'.

The children and young people spoke passionately about those people who made a difference in their daily lives, with all participants reporting positive experiences. They felt it was very easy to recognize those who had passion for their job and wanted to make a difference. They also spoke about negative impacts when people working with them did not have the skills they believed important: 'because she didn't believe me I kept saying I didn't do it but she sent me outside anyway. Do you know where you get to a certain point and you're there when your temper gets to a certain height and you can't even see straight.'

Although discussions focused on workers who had regular contact with children and young people, those who had less contact were highlighted as important, with the potential to have a significant impact, both positive and negative, dependent on their knowledge, skills and attitudes.

Young people were asked how it would affect their lives if the workforce fulfilled their ideas of a 'good worker'. Without exception, young people described how it would make their life easier: 'There would be less stress, more advice. We would always have that time, we can have a laugh.'

Children and young people are clear about what they want from the workforce: positive personal qualities, workers who take time to get to know them, with a solid knowledge of their skills and areas of need. Most importantly, young people emphasized the need for a workforce that could effectively listen and communicate with them.

Unanimously, children and young people felt positive workforce behaviour would make life easier, enable development of their skills and prevent other issues. Many children and young people described positive experiences, with enormous impacts: 'I used to be quiet and on my own, now I talk and am sociable and make new friends'; 'Everything is easier 'cos they get it.'

Acknowledgements

Thanks go to the children and young people who generously gave their time, voices and insight.

References to this project

The Communication Trust (2009) Children and young people's views: What do children and young people think about speech, language and communication skills? Retrieved from http://www.thecommunicationtrust.org.uk/~/media/Communication%20Trust/Documents/Childrens%20Consultation%20FINAL%20Oct%202009.ashx

The Communication Trust (no date) The speech, language and communication framework (SLCF). Retrieved from http://www.thecommunicationtrust.org.uk/~/media/Communication%20Trust/Documents/SLCF%20%20%20Final%20Version.ashx

References

Alderson, P. & Morrow, V. (2004) *Ethics, social research and consulting with children and young people*. Ilford: Barnardo's.

Clark, A., Quail, S. & Moss, P. (2003) *Exploring the field of listening to and consulting with young children*. London: Thomas Coram Research Unit/DfES.

Tisdall, E.K.M., Davis, J.M. & Gallaher, M. (Eds) (2009) *Research with children and young people: Research design, methods and analysis*. London: Sage.

28 Designing a Measure to Explore the Quality of Life for Children with Speech, Language and Communication Needs

Chris Markham

Purpose of the project

This project was part of a larger piece of research that developed a quality of life (QoL) measure for children with speech, language and communication needs. QoL is a growing area of research in speech and language therapy and an excellent opportunity for clinicians and carers to include children's priorities in their own care and management. This chapter focuses on one particular project within the research programme. The project aimed to understand the experience of daily life for children and young people with communication difficulties. The study presented here is based on the idea that communication needs impact on children's QoL and, in order to understand and measure this in research and clinical settings, it is necessary to elicit the views of children and young people first.

Previous work on the QoL for children with speech, language and communication needs had been conducted with parents and carers, but none directly with children and young people themselves. Most definitions of QoL, particularly in chronic and cognitive conditions, agree that it can only be fully understood from an individual's perspective and consequently this project was committed to understanding it from the voices of children themselves. The challenge for the project, though, was to elicit the responses of children and young people with communication needs about something as complex as QoL. This chapter describes how the project achieved this, by answering the question, What is the quality of life experience for children and young people with speech language and communication needs?

Children and young people

The study aimed to provide a rich description of QoL from as many children's perspectives as possible, within the boundaries of a qualitative methodology. As a result, children and young people were purposefully sampled and recruited into the study from speech and language therapy caseloads across a variety of clinical and school settings. To be eligible and able to participate in the research, the children and young people were:

- Aged between 6 and 18 years.
- Attended full-time education within a mainstream educational setting, language unit or special school.
- Had a diagnosed speech, language and communication need, but with sufficient receptive and expressive language skills to participate in the research with minimal support from others. These skills were determined by participants' speech and language therapists, who were independent of the study.

Using these guidelines, the study recruited a total of 29 children and young people aged between 6 and 18 years. The children represented a range of speech, language and communication needs, including dysfluency, expressive and receptive language impairments, phonological delay and disorder and children with pragmatic needs. These speech, language and communication needs were distributed across both the age range and genders. Reflecting the gender distribution of communication needs, 22 males and 7 females were recruited into the study. The children and young people attended mainstream schools, language units within mainstream schools or were from a school for children and young people with specific language impairment.

Investigator

The investigator is a qualified and experienced speech and language therapist, now working as a university lecturer, with a background and passion for research and evidence-based practice.

Method and procedures

This project was part of a larger programme of research that used mixed methodologies to develop a QoL measure for children and young people with speech, language and communication needs. This particular project used a qualitative approach to describing children and young people's perspectives of their QoL. Qualitative research focuses on the beliefs, experiences and interpretations of participants themselves, which was a crucial design element in this study's aim to reveal the perceptions of young people. Qualitative research encourages participants to use the richness of their own words to explore and describe their experiences and consequently ensured children and young people's direct participation in describing their own life experiences in relation to the research question. Qualitative methods are also well suited to research with people who have communication needs, because these methods are able to include a range of creative data collection techniques.

Indeed, this study was designed with the children and young people's needs in mind and therefore aimed to provide a supportive platform for children and young people to talk. For this reason, seven focus group interviews were conducted with groups of four to five children and young people, organized according to their key stage of schooling. Focus group interviews (FGIs) provided the children and young people with a research environment that was sensitive to their needs. FGIs were particularly useful, as participants were familiar with small group work within therapy and education settings and therefore it provided both a naturally occurring and supportive social setting (Heary & Hennessey, 2002; Lewis & Lindsay, 2000).

More importantly to the aim of the study, FGIs provided a facilitated environment for children to talk about themselves. One of the powerful characteristics of FGIs, in this sense, is that they are able to include the use of enabling activities. Enabling activities are used by researchers as alternative methods of asking questions and encouraging responses to them. The enabling activities used in this study were based on a set of playing cards designed for the groups and are shown in the Appendix. These cards included pictorial representations (visual supports) of different areas of children's lives, relevant to their QoL, for example, happiness, school, friends, home, play, etc.

Enabling activities involved using these picture cards in games suitable to the group's average age, to facilitate discussions amongst themselves about their communication needs and their daily lives. For example, in younger groups children played a fishing game to catch the pictures and talk about them (see

Figure 28.1), whereas in older groups young people would pair similar or opposite pictures and then use these to talk about themselves in relation to them. In order to preserve the children's perspectives, facilitation of the FGIs was non-directive and involved minimal prompting and comment. All of the FGIs were held in settings aimed to maximize children's comfort, including meeting and small group teaching spaces in their schools.

Figure 28.1 Children using the enabling resources in a fishing game. Photograph used with permission from children and parent.

This method provided a rich set of data grounded in the perspectives of children and young people themselves. There came a point when data saturation was reached (i.e. no new information was being discussed during interviews), so data collection ended and analysis started.

Findings and outcomes

Across all of the FGIs there were eight themes in what children and young people said about their lives. These are shown in Table 28.1, alongside all of the different codes the researcher used to highlight the relevant comments of the children and young people.

Table 28.1 Themes and codes representing the perspectives of children.

THEME	CODES
Achievement	achievement
Emotions	anxiety, confidence, frustration
Independence	awareness, confidence, independence, life skills, strategies
Individual needs	awareness, intelligibility, specific difficulties, understanding
Relationships	bullying, family, friendships, integration, communicating, lonely, normality, relationships
Relaxation	hobbies and play, relaxation, home
School	achievement, homework, teachers, bullying, achievement, noise, holism, confidence, teachers, understanding, friendships
Support	awareness, home, help, reactions, parents, therapy, understanding, teachers

In summary, these themes and codes illuminate some of the life experiences of children and young people when they have speech, language and communication needs. The eight themes range from comments children and young people made about things within themselves to some that were outside of their control, such as their social and learning environments. For example, internal factors included children and young people's comments about their own self-help skills, emotional needs, specific communication needs and the value they placed on having to relax, play and pursue their own interests and hobbies. Things outside of their control that were discussed in groups included their desire for opportunities to achieve, and to coexist in caring relationships and supportive environments, both at home and at school. Indeed, within all of the focus group discussions, friendships, relaxation and school life were themes that were core to the experience of quality of life. It is important to note that, although some of the themes would be found in comments of typically developing children and young people, the specific detail in their comments and the relative importance given to 'individual needs', 'supportive relationships and environments' help us to understand the experiences of children and young people with speech, language and communication needs.

The following quotes from children and young people with speech, language and communication needs who participated in this research best illuminate their experience of living with a communication difficulty. The themes which these quotes relate to are shown in italics, before each quotation.

Male, 15:   *School.* 'Umm, I was in school and there's a lot of instructions, Yeah and I can't always remember them all. If I watch the others you know that helps. When I am at school I worry about the other students [being] noisy and loud.'

Male, 8:   *School.* 'Listening to the teachers, because when they are talking and I can't listen very much.'

Male, 12:   *School.* 'Well, when I have a lesson they say oh no lesson changed, and I go, I'm confused. Just leave the lessons where they are.'

Male, 7:   *Individual needs.* 'I find it hard when I am not sure what to do. It's like when we're going to play again and we're not sure, what to do we say "pass"?'

Male, 13:   *Individual needs.* 'You can't understand everything. I've learnt that now but, I don't understand a lot you know like in art they do primary colours in the second week other colours and all that art things and I just say no to some things and I just get left behind.'

Male, 17:   *Individual needs.* 'It is hard sometimes with certain work you have got to do and you have problems with your speech so you understand what they mean but cannot make them understand what you mean so you can't do the work and that is hard.'

Male, 18:   *Emotions.* 'With some people I have to say things a few times and that gets me annoyed.'

Female, 8:   *Independence.* 'It makes my life better when I do all my work and nobody helps me.'

Male, 12:   *Achievement.* 'What makes my life better is being proud of myself.'

Reflection on issues

These findings were shown to two groups of six children and young people who had participated in the FGIs. All of the children shown the findings agreed that they represented the things they had said and that there was nothing they wanted to add. This was a particularly important part of the research, because it provided some evidence that the findings had indeed revealed the voices of children themselves. Subsequent validation, involving other researchers, analyzing the same data, also showed the consistency of these findings between the recordings of FGI conversations and the results shown here. These validated findings were then used as the basis for the design and question items of a new QoL measure for children and young people with communication needs (Markham, 2008).

Acknowledgements

The author thanks all of the children, young people, their families, therapists and teachers for participating in and supporting this study. The research was funded by the National Institute for Health Research Grant RDA 01/05.

References to this project

Markham, C. (2007) Exploring children's quality of life: Experiences of a clinical researcher. *RCSLT Bulletin, 667*, 12–13.

Markham, C., van Laar, D., Gibbard, D. & Dean, T. (2008) Children with speech, language and communication needs: Their perceptions of their quality of life. *International Journal of Disorders of Language and Communication, 43*, 1–21.

References

Heary, C.M. & Hennessey, E. (2002) The use of focus group interviews in pediatric health care research. *Journal of Pediatric Psychology, 27*, 47–57.

Lewis, A. & Lindsay, G. (2000) *Researching children's perspectives.* Buckingham: Open University Press.

Markham, C. (2008) The development and validation of a Quality of Life measure for children with speech language and communication needs. Unpublished doctoral thesis, University of Portsmouth, Portsmouth.

Appendix

Enabling resources

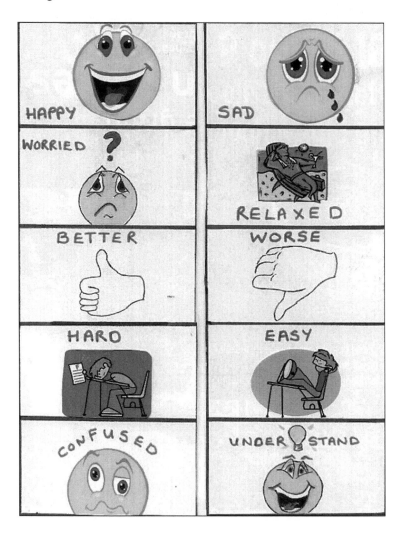

Reprinted with permission from the artist.

29 Listening to Infants about What Life is Like in Childcare

A Mosaic approach

Frances Press, Ben S. Bradley, Joy Goodfellow,
Linda J. Harrison, Sharynne McLeod, Jennifer Sumsion,
Sheena Elwick and Tina Stratigos

Purpose and questions of the project

The research project 'What's life like for infants in childcare?' is concerned with understanding infants' lived experience in centre-based and home-based childcare by ascertaining, as closely as possible, the perspectives[1] of infants themselves. Understanding infants' perspectives of their experiences has necessitated developing tools and skills to listen attentively to prelinguistic infants.

Much current commentary on infants in childcare emanates from the perspective of adults. Recently greater attention been paid to the experience of childcare from the infants' perspective (Clark, Kjørholt & Moss, 2005). By purposively seeking out infants' own perspectives, it is hoped that this study contributes to the development of nuanced and comprehensive understandings of infants' lives in childcare and, as a consequence, provides an empirical basis for enhancing their quality of life in childcare. It is anticipated that the results of the project will provide new insights into infants' capacities, capabilities and perspectives; extend current conceptualizations of early childhood programme quality; expand our understanding of responsive infant childcare and how it can be achieved; and assist Australia to better meet its responsibilities

---

1 While the term 'perspective' is commonly used, it is acknowledged that this is a contested term and it may not be possible to come to an understanding of infants' perspectives (Elwick, Bradley & Sumsion, 2011).

concerning children's rights, particularly the participation rights of very young children.

Children and young people

The project focuses upon prelinguistic infants in home-based and centre-based childcare settings (family day-care homes (FDC) and long day-care centres (LDC) respectively). By attentively listening to infants we hope to give them a voice about their childcare experiences. For the purpose of this project, infants are considered to be aged between birth and 18 months.

The project, at the time of writing, involves two LDC settings and six FDC homes in New South Wales (NSW), Australia. Taken together, these represent a mix of urban and regional locations and diverse socioeconomic/cultural demographics. Of the 36 children currently participating in the study, 24 are in LDC centres (14 girls and 10 boys), and 12 are from FDC homes (5 girls and 7 boys). Over the ensuing 12 months, it is anticipated that additional children will be recruited from additional FDC homes and LDC centres.

Listening to babies who have no or limited verbal language (in the form of words) involves obvious challenges. Infants' utterances and physical cues may be overlooked, poorly understood, misunderstood or inconsistently understood. In the day-to-day environment, adults may be unused to paying close attention to the minutiae of infants' cues and/or adult perspectives may be considered as having greater legitimacy to that of infants. Hitherto, much research concerning infants within early childhood education and care services has focused on issues such as the nature of the environment in which infants are placed, the interactions of caregivers with infants or the outcomes of infant care. Shifting the lens to focus upon the infants themselves to determine their viewpoint requires a continual destabilization of habituated positions.

Investigators

Led by a team from Charles Sturt University and supported by Family Day Care Australia (FDCA) and KU Children's Services (KU), and an Australian Research Council (ARC) Linkage grant, the study brings together researchers from the disciplines of early childhood education, policy, psychology, child development, communication and speech and language therapy. Data are gathered within each type of early childhood programme (family day-care homes and infants' rooms in centre-based long day care) by doctoral students and research assistants with backgrounds in early childhood education.

Method and procedures

Infants' experiences and quality of life in childcare are affected by their parents, carers, other children, the physical environment, resources, the internal policies of the childcare service and the external policy environment. Childcare contexts are complex; thus our approach emphasizes the value of multiple perspectives in generating new insights into the phenomena of infants' childcare experiences. The Mosaic approach, which involves the 'bringing together of different pieces or perspectives in order to create an image of children's worlds' (Clark 2005, p. 31), provides the framework for the research methodology. This entails seeking the insights of carers, older children and parents to help uncover each infant's viewpoint. Additionally, we have extended the conceptualization and application of Mosaic methodology to incorporate dialogue between diverse theoretical approaches, with each researcher bringing to the project their own theoretical and disciplinary lens. Figure 29.1 illustrates the multiplicity of sources, contexts and perspectives utilized in the project.

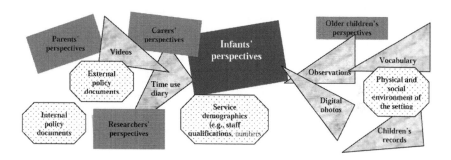

Figure 29.1 Mosaic for understanding infants' experiences: sources, contexts and perspectives. The *marbled triangles* represent key sources of data gathered by the doctoral students and research assistants. The *grey rectangles* represent the range of perspectives and the *dotted octagons* represent contextual information key to shaping infants' childcare environments. Reprinted with permission from Sumsion, J., Harrison, L., Press, F., McLeod, S., Goodfellow, J., & Bradley, B. (2011). Researching infants' experiences of early childhood education and care. In D. Harcourt, B. Perry & T. Waller (Eds), *Researching young children's perspectives: Debating the ethics and dilemmas of educational research with children* (pp.113–127). London: Routledge.

Comprising a significant subset of the data sources shown in Figure 29.1 are the tools the researchers use to 'listen' to infants. The drawing together of a range of data, often derived through observation tools (video, photographs, written records of directed observations), enables the researchers to become more attuned to the infants themselves and to edge closer to each infant's own viewpoint.

The researchers have been conscious of the need to continuously dislodge themselves from their own perspectives as adults and the lenses of their own expertise to get closer to infants' own perspectives. Active, open and challenging dialogue between different theoretical, philosophical and disciplinary bases and individual perceptions is an integral part of the dislodgement process and helps the research team move from assumed knowledge to more subtle understandings – to better listen.

Research design and sample

The study entails fine-grained observations and analyses using a wide range of data sources. Only those aspects relevant to the project of listening to infants will be elucidated here. These predominantly revolve around the gathering and analysis of case study data.

Two types of case studies are being conducted: short-term case studies of infants in groups and longitudinal case studies of individual infants. The short-term group case studies provide a rich picture of infants as social actors within a group and the longitudinal individual case studies enable insights into infants' experiences over time.

Data is collected through regular (weekly or twice-weekly) half-day visits to each site. The short-term group studies involve visits for up to two months in the FDC homes and for up to six months in the LDC settings. Longitudinal individual case studies commence when infants are 3-4 months old, with data collected for one half-day every two to three weeks for up to 18 months. Data collection focuses on critical times in the childcare day (e.g. arrival, departure, mealtimes) and critical moments (e.g. in skill mastery; conflict with peers/ carers). Decisions about data collection in each setting are made in consultation with carers, with the emphasis on: understanding infants' sense of wellbeing, belonging and scope for agency; engagement; interactions and relationships; and the physical environment.

Digital video footage is gathered in two ways (see Appendix): via: 'babycam' (a miniature camera attached to hat or headband and then worn by the infant) to obtain footage from the physical perspective of infants; and a tripod-mounted video camera focusing on infants' movements, gestures, interactions, attention, emotional states, facial expressions and explorations. *Digital photography* is used by older children and toddlers to identify infants' most/least favourite places, activities, events and interactions, and is supplemented by their descriptions and explanations. A time use diary, developed by the authors specifically for the project, records infants' activities and interactions for five-minute intervals on designated days. The *McArthur Bates Communicative Inventory* (Fenson, Marchman, Thal, Dale, Reznick & Bates, 2007) is filled out by parents and carers to compile a list of words produced by infants in the childcare setting and home. In addition, the doctoral students and research assistants make *observations and field notes* of infants. This information is supplemented by the *children's portfolios* and *developmental records* kept by each service.

Data analysis

Data analysis proceeds iteratively with data collection. Collaborative, multiple interpretations of data are elicited by inviting carers, service managers, parents and, where appropriate, older children, to reflect on and discuss edited videos of key segments. This enables access to carers' practical wisdom, parents' deep familiarity with their infant and children's perspectives on what the infant is saying about their experiences. The co-construction of insights is facilitated by 'seeing and guessing' (Dolby, 2007) – that is, 'saying what you see', 'guessing what it might mean', seeking reactions to the guess and then coming to an agreed understanding about the meaning.

An array of sensitizing concepts/questions and heuristic tools, drawn from different theoretical perspectives, is used to inform interpretations of data, and feedback is sought on those interpretations. For example, from *interpretivist perspectives*: What is important to these infants? Why is this important? What do they enjoy, and what bothers them? How do they manage living a life in two places? From *child development perspectives*: How do these infants manage their attachment needs when separating from the parent and engaging with another? From *critical theory perspectives*: How are these infants enculturated into the childcare setting? What strategies of resistance do they use/encounter? What power relations do they engage in/are they subjected to? From *phenomenological perspectives*: What do these infants direct their (conscious) behaviour/actions towards? What do their bodily actions tell us about their intent? From *intersubjectivity* perspectives: Are these infants affected by relationships between others in their group? What conversations take place amongst them? From *communication* perspectives: What do their first words tell us about the experiences most significant to them? From *sociocultural perspectives*: How are these infants involved in co-constructing the culture in the setting? What culture is being constructed?

Video-viewing and co-construction sessions are videoed and transcribed to assist further analysis. In addition, frame-by-frame viewing of video extracts enables a detailed view of infants' interactions and responses (Sumsion & Goodfellow, in press).

Findings and outcomes

The project is still in progress and much data is still to be collected and analyzed. However, the data collected to date have underscored that each infant's experience is highly individual, even within the same setting. Much of our learning has centred on the process of listening to infants. We have found that hearing and understanding what infants are 'saying' about their time in childcare involves acute observation and fine-grained analysis. This has been facilitated by multiple data sources but it has also required an openness to look beyond the expected and to consciously and continually shift our research gaze from adult reactions and responses back to the infants themselves.

Reflections

Both babycam and frame-by-frame video analysis have been particularly illuminating in enabling our appreciation of those things that are important to infants (see Appendix). When viewing visual data, particularly video, we have needed to constantly remind ourselves to focus on the infant rather than the responses of adults. We are conscious of the role of carers and parents as adept interpreters of infants' signals and the responsibility adults have to the infants in their care. However, focusing on the responses and actions of adults can shift attention from infants' own agency.

Rigour

Rigour is achieved through triangulation of data sources (multiple data collection strategies) and interpretations (multiple perspectives of carers/parents/service managers/older children/researchers and, where possible, infants).

Ethical issues

Although consent is obtained from parents and carers, infants cannot give informed consent. We have also relied on their 'assent' (Hurley & Underwood, 2002), and monitor them closely for any sign of reluctance or distress. We have tried to adopt a reflexive stance, continually asking ourselves questions such as: What right do we have to presume to know what infants are experiencing? How can we ensure that listening to infants does not invade their privacy? Are we respecting their right to be silent (Lewis, 2008)? Reciprocity, humility and the development of a participatory community (of researchers, carers, parents and children) have been important elements of our quest to listen (Sumsion, 2003).

Acknowledgements

The project reported in this chapter is funded by the Australian Research Council (LP0883913) and Industry Partners, Family Day Care Australia and KU Children's Services. We thank the children, parents, carers and services that are contributing so generously their time and insights. Thanks also to Belinda Davis (research assistant) and Sandra Cheeseman (doctoral student) for their work and expertise.

References to this project

Elwick, S., Bradley, B.S. & Sumsion, J. (2011) *Infants as others: Uncertainties, difficulties, and (im)possibilities in researching infants' lives*. Manuscript in submission.

Goodfellow, J., Elwick, S., Stratigos, T., Sumison,,J., Press, F., Harrison, L., McLeod, S. & Bradley, B. (2011, in press) Infants' lives in childcare: Crafting research evidence. The First Years Nga Tau Tuatahi. *Journal of Infant Toddler Education*.

Goodfellow, J., Harrison, L.J. & Bradley, B. (2010, July) Living a life (with peers): Reflections on what life is like for infants in group care. *Infant Mental Health Journal* (Suppl) *32:3*, 88–89.

Sumsion, J., Harrison, L., Press, F., McLeod, S., Goodfellow, J. & Bradley, B. (2011) Researching infants' experiences of early childhood education and care. In D. Harcourt, B. Perry & T. Waller (Eds), *Researching young children's perspectives: Debating the ethics and dilemmas of educational research with children* (pp. 113–127). London: Routledge.

Sumsion, J. & Goodfellow, J. (in press) 'Looking' and 'listening-in': Generating insights into infants' experiences of early childhood education and care settings. *European Journal of Early Childhood Research.*

References

Clark, A. (2005) Ways of seeing: Using the Mosaic approach to listen to young children's perspectives. In A. Clark, A. Kjørholt & P. Moss (Eds), *Beyond listening: Children's perspectives on early childhood services* (p. 29). Bristol: Policy Press.

Dolby, R. (2007). *The circle of security: Roadmap to building supportive relationships. Early Childhood Australia, Research in Practice Series, 14(4).*

Elwick, S., Bradley, B.S. & Sumsion, J. (2011) *Infants as others: Uncertainties, difficulties, and (im)possibilities in researching infants' lives.* Manuscript in submission.

Fenson, L., Marchman, V.A., Thal, D., Dale, P., Reznick, J.S. & Bates, E. (2007) *The MacArthur-Bates Communicative Development Inventories: User's Guide and Technical Manual* (2nd ed.). Baltimore, MD: Paul H. Brookes.

Hurley, J.C. & Underwood, M. K. (2002) Children's understanding of their research rights before and after debriefing: Informed assent, confidentiality, and stopping participation. *Child Development, 73,* 132–143.

Lewis, A. (2008) Silence in the context of child voice. *Children and Society. 24,* 14–23.

Moss, P., Clark, A. & Kjørholt, A., (2005) Introduction. In A. Clark, A. Kjørholt & P. Moss (Eds.), *Beyond listening: Children's perspectives on early childhood services.* Bristol: Policy Press.

Sumsion, J., Harrison, L., Press, F., McLeod, S., Goodfellow, J. & Bradley, B. (2011) Researching infants' experiences of early childhood education and care. In D. Harcourt, B. Perry & T. Waller (Eds), *Researching young children's perspectives: Debating the ethics and dilemmas of educational research with children* (pp. 113–127). London: Routledge.

Appendix

Contrasting the baby's and carer's views of the world.

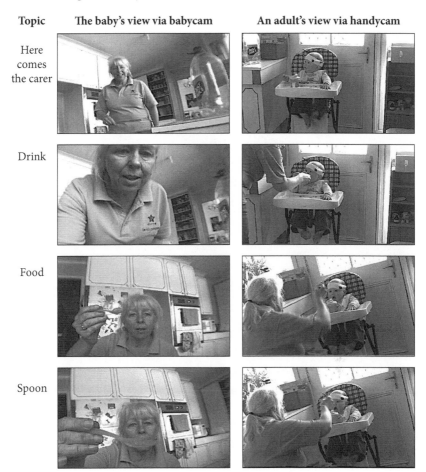

Reproduced with permission from the participants.
© 2011 by Infants Lives in Childcare project research team.

30 Listening to the Views of Children in Longitudinal Population-Based Studies

Linda J. Harrison and Jane McCormack

Purpose of the project

This chapter describes the methods that were developed and used to listen to children in the *Longitudinal Study of Australian Children* (LSAC; Australian Institute of Family Studies, 2009), a population-based study investigating the development of Australian children and the contexts in which they are raised. During the early waves of data collection for LSAC, the main sources of information were adults: the parents and teachers of children participating in the project. However, as the study progressed and the children grew older, measures were introduced to access children's own reports of their experiences and perspectives on their personal, social and learning environments. This chapter reviews the ways that children have been included in the data collection and provides an example of how data obtained from children were used to examine a specific research question: What is the relationship between speech, language and communication needs in early childhood (4–5 years) and children's sense of self-esteem and social interactions at school (7–9 years)?

Children and young people

The LSAC project commenced in 2004 (Wave 1) with the recruitment of two nationally representative cohorts: 5000 babies (aged 6–12 months) and 5000 children (aged 4.5–5 years). This chapter focuses on the older cohort, and specifically Wave 3, when children were aged 7–9 years. At Wave 3, the sample comprised 4329 children (51.1% boys, 48.9% girls) with a mean age of 8.26 years (SD = 0.44). The children had been recruited from every state and territory in Australia, and sample characteristics (e.g. sex, cultural background and socioeconomic status) were broadly representative of the population (Gray & Smart, 2008).

In Wave 1, children with speech, language and communication difficulties were identified by the parent, who was asked to respond in an interview to a series of questions from the *Parents' Evaluation of Developmental Status* (PEDS; Glascoe, 2000), a screener for identifying developmental delays in young children. Children whose parents answered 'yes' or 'a little' to the question 'Do you have concerns about how [child] talks and makes speech sounds?' were identified as having communication difficulty. Of the children who subsequently participated in Wave 3, there were 1041 (24.0%) who had been identified as having speech, language and communication difficulty at 4–5 years, and 3288 (76.0%) who had not been identified.

Investigators

The first author (Harrison) is an associate professor of early childhood education and a founding member of the LSAC Research Consortium, which has been responsible for designing the LSAC project. The second author (McCormack) is a qualified speech and language therapist, who accessed and analyzed data collected from LSAC as part of her doctoral research.

Method and procedures

Within LSAC, the primary methods of data collection were via parent and teacher reports and assessments of each child's physical and cognitive development. However, from Wave 2 onwards, data collection with children, rather than about children, also took place. At Waves 2 and 3, child-reported data were collected via trained interviewers. At Wave 4, new technologies were designed to assist data collection, including a child-completed time use diary (TUD) and an audio computer-assisted self-administered interview (ACASI).

Face-to-face interviews

The content of the child interview was carefully vetted. Criteria for selection of items were that it was only obtainable from the child, discrepant from information provided by teachers or parents, reliable and meaningful, able to provide for a trajectory over future waves and provided in a format that was engaging and enjoyable for the child (AIFS, 2009). As children aged, more items were added to the child self-report component of LSAC. The content in Wave 3 included questions that asked children to rate how they felt about school and schoolwork, their teachers, the other children at school, including experiences of being bullied, and their sense of self-esteem. Response options for the rated scales were shown in a booklet so that the children could pick their answers to each question by pointing, reading the number beside it or reading out the answer.

Time use diary (TUD)

The introduction of the child-completed TUD in Wave 4 saw a change from asking parents to complete a 24-hour diary to asking the child to record their activities from before they woke up in the morning to when they fell asleep at night. The child TUD provided a more accurate coverage of the hours in the day when parents weren't able to report what their children were doing, where they were or who they were with. Children were asked to complete a paper diary on the day before the interview, and were sent a pen and stickers and a letter explaining what to do. The interviewer then sat with the child to review the time and each type of activity for the previous day, prompting the child if there was insufficient written information, and entered the information into a computer version of the TUD.

Audio computer-assisted self-administered interview (ACASI)

The ACASI enabled the 10- to 11-year-old children to answer questions on their own using a laptop computer and headphones, to hear as well as read the question on the screen. This method catered for children of all reading levels. The content areas included questions that asked them to rate how they felt about schoolwork and learning, their teachers, friends, family and themselves, including items about health, enjoyment of physical activities, and sense of self-esteem. The ACASI also included *yes/no* questions about experiences of being bullied by other children.

Findings and outcomes

In this section of the chapter, we report on our analyses of questions administered during Wave 3 to investigate the longitudinal effects of having speech, language and communication difficulty on children's perceptions of their self-esteem and social interactions at school (these data also have been reported in McCormack, Harrison, McLeod & McAllister, 2011). Of interest were children's responses to: the *Marsh Self-Description Questionnaire* (MSDQ; Marsh, 1992) relating to self-esteem; a Bullying Scale adapted from the *Perceptions of Peer Support Scale* (Kochenderfer & Ladd, 1997; Ladd, Kochenderfer & Coleman, 1996), relating to the frequency of bullying incidents (peer victimization) that they had experienced; and the School Liking subscale of the *School Sentiment Inventory* (Ladd & Price, 1987), relating to enjoyment of school. Each of these measures employed a Likert scale for response options. Analyses revealed that the majority of children (both those identified with speech, language and communication needs at 4 to 5 years and those not identified) perceived their self-esteem and social interactions at school in a positive manner (within normal limits). However, there were children whose scores placed them outside the normal range for these skills (i.e. greater than 1SD (standard deviation) from the mean). Within these groups, the proportion of children with a history of speech, language and communication needs was consistently higher than the proportion of children in the group with no such history.

Approximately one fifth (20.1%) of children identified at 4 to 5 years with speech, language and communication difficulties reported bullying at 7 to 9 years. This was significantly higher than in the group of children who had not been identified (13.9%). Children identified with early childhood speech, language and communication difficulties were also more likely to score below the normal range on ratings of self-esteem (MSDQ) (19.2%, compared to 16.2% of children in the group not identified) and to report poorer attitudes to school (23.0% – outside the normal range – compared to 17.4%).

Previous research has shown that children identified with speech, language and communication needs are more likely to have difficulty with social interactions than other children (e.g. Fujiki, Brinton & Todd, 1996; Lindsay & Dockrell, 2000). Oftentimes, these reports are based on parent or teacher perceptions. In the present study, the association between speech, language and communication needs and social difficulties (bullying and less ease in making friends) was demonstrated by reports from the children themselves. Similarly, reports from the children indicated that they have less enjoyment of school than their peers. These findings suggest the need to improve school experiences for children with communication impairment and to target the children's environment as well as the speech, language or communication difficulty they experience.

Reflection on issues

Large-scale, longitudinal, population-based studies such as LSAC bring a number of unique challenges, particularly that of participant retention, cost (home interviews with a large and geographically dispersed sample), the time commitment expected of participants (families and children) and the demand for high-quality data across many domains of development. In LSAC, interest in the research was maintained by using new and efficient ways to collect data, especially with children. A highly innovative feature of LSAC was the cooperative design and production of a television series, *Life at One, Life at Three, Life at Five, Life at Seven,* that has followed 11 (non-study) children and their families from birth. LSAC has required participants to make a long-term commitment (currently estimated at 16 years: 8 biennial waves). Their interest and engagement have been maintained by regular communication with families, through gifts, newsletters with information about the study findings, cards, calendars and invitations to contribute drawings for the annual production of an LSAC calendar. An example of a newsletter created for the 10- to 11-year-old children is included in the Appendix. Strict time limits have been placed on data collection in the home (a total of 90 minutes for all procedures), to reduce the risk of over-burdening participants. The challenges of balancing content demands against time constraints were heightened in Wave 4, when children were expected to complete the ACASI, TUD and physical/cognitive assessments during the home visit. Priority has been given to ensuring that children are interested and engaged in the activities and, as they get older, in the findings of the study. As LSAC plans for future waves, children will be invited to be part of a reference group to contribute their ideas about important issues for young people that should be addressed in this study.

Like other large-scale studies, LSAC has its limitations. As Australia's first nationally representative longitudinal study of children, the breadth of data domains (health, family functioning, education, childcare) addressed by LSAC has meant that there have been limited opportunities for in-depth focus on any one developmental area or particular group of children. For example, children with communication needs were assessed by a parent-report screening measure, and it may be that some identified children would not be diagnosed by a professional assessment or that some non-identified children would be. The broad scope of LSAC, however, has meant that many areas of potential research interest, including areas of particular relevance to government policy, are included.

Acknowledgements

The authors would like to thank the Australian Government Department of Families, Housing, Community Services and Indigenous Affairs (FaHCSIA) for making the *Hello!* 2010 newsletter available to be reproduced in this chapter and acknowledge the design roles of the Australian Institute of Family Studies and the members of the Longitudinal Study of Australian Children (LSAC) Research Consortium: John Ainley, Donna Berthelsen, Michael Bittman, Bruce Bradbury, Linda Harrison, Jan Nicholson, Bryan Rodgers, Ann Sanson, Michael Sawyer, Sven Silburn, Lyndall Strazdins, Judy Ungerer, Graham Vimpani, Melissa Wake and Stephen Zubrick.

References to this project

Harrison, L.J. & McLeod, S. (2010) Risk and protective factors associated with speech and language impairment in a nationally representative sample of 4- to 5-year-old children. *Journal of Speech, Language, and Hearing Research, 53:2*, 508–529.

Harrison, L.J., McLeod, S., Berthelsen, D. & Walker, S. (2009) Literacy, numeracy, and learning in school-aged children identified as having speech and language impairment in early childhood. *International Journal of Speech-Language Pathology, 11:5*, 392–403.

McCormack, J., Harrison, L.J., McLeod, S. & McAllister, L. (2011, in press) A nationally representative study of parents', teachers' and children's perceptions of the impact of early childhood communication impairment at school age. *Journal of Speech, Language, and Hearing Research, 54:5*, 1328–1348.

McLeod, S. & Harrison, L.J. (2009) Epidemiology of speech and language impairment in a nationally representative sample of 4- to 5-year-old children. *Journal of Speech, Language, and Hearing Research, 52:5*, 1213–1229.

References

Australian Institute of Family Studies (AIFS) (2009) *Growing up in Australia: The longitudinal study of Australian children.* Retrieved from http://www.aifs.gov.au/growingup/

Fujiki, M., Brinton, B. & Todd, C.M. (1996) Social skills of children with specific language impairment. *Language, Speech, and Hearing Services in Schools, 27*, 195–202.

Glascoe, F.P. (2000) *Parents' Evaluation of Developmental Status (PEDS): Authorized Australian Version.* Parkville, Victoria: Centre for Community Child Health.

Gray, M., & Smart, D. (2008) Growing up in Australia: The Longitudinal Study of Australian Children is now walking and talking. *Family Matters, 79*, 5–13.

Kochenderfer, B.J. & Ladd, G.W. (1997) Victimized children's responses to peers' aggression: Behaviors associated with reduced versus continued victimization. *Development and Psychopathology, 9,* 59–73.

Ladd, G.W., Kochenderfer, B.J. & Coleman, G. (1996) Friendship quality as a predictor of young children's early school adjustment. *Child Development, 67,* 1103–1118.

Ladd, G.W. & Price, J.M. (1987) Predicting children's social and school adjustment following the transition from preschool to kindergarten. *Child Development, 58,* 1168–1189.

Lindsay, G. & Dockrell, J. (2000) The behaviour and self-esteem of children with specific speech and language difficulties. *British Journal of Educational Psychology, 70:4,* 583–601.

Marsh, H.W. (1992) *Self-Description Questionnaire III: Manual.* Sydney, Australia: University of Western Sydney.

Appendix

Longitudinal Study of Australian Children (LSAC) *Hello!* 2010 newsletter for 10- to 11-year-olds.

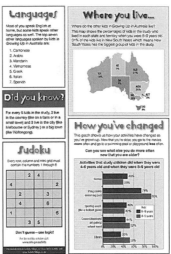

Reprinted with permission and available from: http://www.aifs.gov.au/growingup/pubs/newsletter/participants/helloknewsletter201012.pdf

31 Finding Ways to Listen to Young People in Youth Projects
The Afasic Youth Project

Abigail Beverly and Clare Davies-Jones

Purpose of the project

Afasic is a UK charity supporting parents, children and young people with speech and language difficulties (www.afasic.org.uk). This project arose from listening to the request of some teenage boys with speech, language and communication needs for 'somewhere to go with people like us on Friday night'. A club was set up on Friday nights, during term time, 7–9pm, to enable young people with such needs to meet and socialize in a friendly, supportive setting, to promote their personal and social development through a range of leisure activities and, most importantly, for them to have fun and form friendships. It also expressly aimed to *learn from members* what provision and support they would need as they grew up and to help them achieve independence and be included in society as they reached adulthood.

Young people

The mixed-gender project caters for 35 young people aged 11–19 years who have a primary speech, language and communication need, not generally coupled with another disability. Most have some level of difficulty with social communication, whether as a primary need (e.g. high-functioning autism or Asperger's Syndrome) or as a result of social isolation caused by their speech and language needs. It has a considerably greater proportion of boys, reflecting the higher prevalence of identified communication needs in boys than girls. Members must want to cooperate in social and group activities with appropriate support and encouragement – at a baseline level of 1:8 adults to members.

Adults working with the young people

Regular staffing comprises three sessionally employed staff (two youth-work professionals and a speech and language therapist) supported by a rolling team of volunteers who are mostly students or would-be students of speech and language therapy. The Afasic Project Manager frequently attends, and another youth worker is employed in the off-site programme, particularly for residential weekends. The project benefits greatly from personal experience of speech and language needs brought by Abigail Beverly, who describes in practical terms in the next section how she works with members' diversity of communication needs. The combination of offering different channels of communication and *observing* what suits whom, as well as listening to *verbally expressed* preferences, is a strong thread in the project as a whole. A half-hour debrief after each session draws on observations and feedback from all staff and volunteers to share learning and discuss strategies for activities and members.

Methods and procedures

To listen to young people we needed first to create a *listening environment,* through attention to the detail of communication at every level of the organization. This commitment should be reflected in the attitudes of staff and volunteers as well as in the club's standard procedures. For example, although parents usually make the first approach, once decided a young person is potentially eligible, a letter of welcome to visit is always sent to the young person themselves, with any further information for their parents enclosed to hand on. Also a small cash subscription, paid by each member on arrival, ensures an exchange of greeting and checking in on how their week has been – which increasingly leads to further conversation as they get established. From the outset the message to the young people is that this is *their place*, despite the fact that the actual building is a sessionally rented space with limited possibility to customize beyond having one allocated noticeboard.

The programme overall is strongly influenced by members' choices and reflects the gamut of any good, general youth provision. Its specialism lies in coupling the ethos and best practice of youth work, which starts from where each individual is at and their equal rights to participation, with the knowledge and understanding brought by the speech and language therapist to ensure delivery is accessible to all. The atmosphere is entirely non-clinical and is not problem-focused. The activities include cooking, sports and games, arts, quizzes, trips out to the cinema, bowling, restaurants and travel challenges around London. The activities are all used to develop functional and communication skills in a fun way and to raise confidence and self-esteem.

Findings and outcomes

Abigail Beverly is a volunteer with Afasic Youth Project who runs art workshops designed to encourage members to develop their language skills via creative activities. In the section below, she illustrates both the model of the communication-friendly environment and particular ways of listening to the young people.

My work with Afasic Youth Project: Abigail Beverly

I am a volunteer worker with The Afasic Youth Project. I first heard about the project from Clare Davies-Jones, who knew about my speech and language difficulties but had also found out that I had a great interest in art. Clare told me about the project and the members and asked if I would help out with her art session. That was in 1999 and Afasic has been a very big part of my life ever since.

Part of my work involves me running regular art and crafts sessions. Because I am so aware of the problems these young people can have, I always try to break tasks down into manageable chunks. You have to allow for the fact that different people have different learning styles. At first, because I was a visual learner, I thought *everyone* with speech and language needs was a visual learner.

In fact, I discovered some young people prefer to have things written down in printed text, so they can refer to it and see what comes next, so I try to cover all the different learning styles and use visual, tactile and whatever other methods I can to help understanding. And, of course, I always make sure there is a practical demonstration and that everyone has a chance to ask questions! I do this preparation for a lot of my art projects – so the young people can see what the finished project could look like (for example, kite-making from a plastic bag) to help the members visualize what they are going to create. I hope that I have learned something from my own experiences that helps others.

Another important point is to try to give young people ways of increasing their confidence. If you have a speech and language difficulty you have to be prepared to deal with all the negativity that you can come up against. Some people treat you differently when they hear you have a disability; they almost expect you to fail. Those people never look at the whole person – what you *can* do. They just focus on what you *can't* do.

So, in the sessions, I always try to encourage members to be creative and explore their *own* ideas (see Figure 31.1). I really push some activities because there can be a sense of low expectation for the members. Some people are too quick to say, 'Oh, he can't do that' or 'Give it here. I'll do it for him.'

Figure 31.1 Abby and Michael at the sewing machine. Reprinted with permission.

The Afasic Youth Project is brilliant because it gives members the opportunity to have a go at something new and it helps them to gain the confidence to become more independent. A lot of what it does is about helping the young people gain confidence in communicating. We had one member who joined who was really quiet and barely said a word to us. We encouraged her to be part of the activity, so, even though she wasn't speaking, we gave her the options so she could choose for herself what she wanted to do. It wasn't just saying, 'Oh, that's nice,' but really giving positive encouragement – explaining *why* it was good (good choice of fabrics, liking her use of colours, 'You've really thought about it', etc.) – which helped her confidence grow so that she really opened up.

This doesn't happen overnight. It can take a long time. But she became really talkative, chatting away in a very relaxed way. After a while other members started asking, her, 'How did you do that?' and she was able to explain to them how to do things. It's really great when members are supporting each other.

I think our art sessions work well because the young people get so involved with their projects that they forget they are using lots of words and it's a very social environment with lots of interaction. It's then not about learning 'words' or how to communicate – it's just about having fun and being with other people, so they feel relaxed and are not self-conscious about their difficulty.

In Figure 31.2 we see an example of some of the Afasic members' creative work in the portfolio, which forms a record and an evaluation of the trips and activities they have done. This portfolio was needed as evidence of how the Project is developing and how funders' money is being used, but it also gives members the chance to show what they've done, what they've enjoyed, what they've achieved. It's another way of 'listening' that encourages them to express themselves in their own way and they get a lot out of it. When some members first heard about an 'evaluation', they weren't too keen; it sounded like a lot of hard work (a bit 'schooly') but, once they got into it, it was great fun and one boy said how much he enjoyed seeing the record of what he'd done and was really proud of what he had achieved: 'I did all that!'

Figure 31.2 Pages of the portfolio created by members of the Afasic Youth Project. Reprinted with permission.

When we wanted young people to participate in the appointment of a new youth worker at the Project, we introduced mindmaps to 'listen' to their views on each candidate and capture them to feed into the interview process (see Figure 31.3). The mindmap really helps young people to express themselves, and helps overcome the barriers of just asking for their opinions. This way we can tease out the thoughts and ideas that our members would otherwise find difficult to express. I find mindmaps are always good in helping to draw out ideas and links.

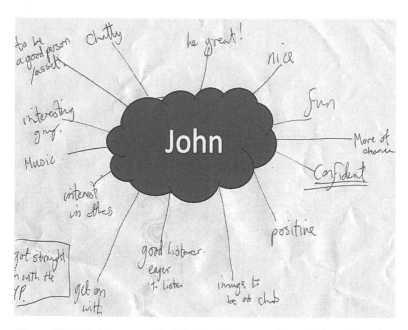

Figure 31.3 Mindmap created while listening to members of Afasic about the appointment of a new youth worker.

Another favourite tool of mine is Post-it® notes. They are very good: nice and manageable, with bright colours, different shapes. Not only are they attractive and eye-catching, but they make everything more approachable – not so intimidating; not as daunting as a load of text.

To sum up my feelings about listening to young people: it is often the *attitude* of people that gets in the way of communication and understanding. For example, being patronizing – impatient – putting you down – and just repeating the same thing, in exactly the same way, if someone says they don't understand!

Some of the things that help understanding are a positive, non-judgemental attitude – so that you feel valued and that you're being listened to and, what really helps is when people are open-minded and are prepared to try alternative ways to help the communication.

On a personal note, the way I cope with my speech and language difficulties is very specific to me. So it is not a case of 'one size fits all' – it's important to find out what works with the individual. We all have different ways of coping and using the things that work best for us. Also, trying new things and different approaches helps to adapt to the individual and their different ways of learning – sometimes things don't work out – so you try something different.

Because we need to gain confidence about what we can do, it needs a lot of encouragement, with a good positive attitude from other people. It's really important to encourage others to look at the person as a whole (especially their strengths) – and not just focus on their disability.

Reflection on issues and evaluation

A youth/leisure setting has key features that set it apart from formal education settings – not least in attendance being voluntary and its ethos recreational. Staff and members alike are freed from narrow constraints of an academic curriculum, so young people can talk about whatever interests them or ask whatever they want. Workers bring diverse talents and experience, but selection can prioritize commitment to listening and two-way communication over subject expertise. Opportunity to incorporate the personal experience of young adults like Abigail in *running* provision gives invaluable insights for all staff and volunteers.

In 2006, a small research project was undertaken in the Youth Project by a team from City University that provided an external opportunity to listen to members' views both about the Project and other aspects of their lives. The young people's comments about the Project frequently emphasized freedom to 'be themselves' and they suggested that they found confidence in being with others 'like us', as the original boys had requested. The implied value of a specialist provision challenges prevailing interpretations of inclusion but, as Abigail's account shows, the confidence to find a voice is a vital plank in helping young people with speech, language and communication needs to feel truly included.

References to this project

Afasic (no date). *Youth project evaluation*. Retrieved March 2011 from http://www. afasicengland.org.uk/young-people/youth-project-evaluation/

Davies-Jones, C., with Myers, L., Botting, N., Chiat, S. & Joffe, V. (2007) Teenagers deserve to have fun! A report of a research project undertaken by City University on the Afasic Youth Project in N.E. London. *Afasic News* (Autumn), 10–12.

Myers, L., DAvies-Jones, C., Chiat, S. Joffe, V. & Botting, N. (2011) 'A place where I can be me': A role for social and leisure provision to support young people with language impairment. *International Journal of Language and Communication Disorders, 46*:6, 739–750.

32 Making a Film as a Means of Listening to Young People

Sue Roulstone, Clodagh Miskelly and Robbie Simons

Robbie's report

My name is Robbie Simons. I am a full-time student currently studying BTEC Extended Diploma in Health and Social Care, as I am keen to become a nurse and work in a caring environment which I believe I will enjoy because I will be using complex communication skills. Communication is a factor that I have struggled to perform because of my condition which affects how I interact with others (I have Asperger's Syndrome).

I have recently taken part in a research project where I worked with a group of researchers relating to the mind of a young individual with speech and language difficulties. The research workshops took place over four years (2006–2010) where I got involved in meeting members of the research team and meeting other people who have similar difficulties. The head of the research team was Professor Sue Roulstone who was assisted by Doctor Clodagh Miskelly, Tom Dalton and Lesley Hemmings as well as all the members from the film production team called Brook Lapping. I developed strong friendships with the four other boys who were also participants in the research project and we all produced our own ideas. I became involved in the speech and language research project because my schoolteachers and my parents suggested I should, and I wanted to meet new people and wanted to know about what it was really like to be a teenager with speech and language problems.

The first speech and language therapy research workshops took place at Southville Centre near Bristol where we got involved in describing our hobbies, what we enjoy doing and what things we feel uncomfortable about performing. We had group discussions, created posters and produced our own videos describing what we like to do as well as creating our own acting scenes (dressed up as a hooligan) which we all really enjoyed.

We created our own puppets by drawing fictional or made up characters where they were then designed into puppets by BAFTA winning animator Kevin Griffiths and where we soon met him at the UWE (University of the West of England in June 2008) Frenchay Campus and created short films using our puppets which we presented to the research team. We also produced a group video using all the puppets that we created which was filmed by Tom Dalton.

(Continued overleaf)

(All of the films were very enjoyable.) We were asked by the research team whether we would like to have our short films shown to other teenagers with speech and language difficulties and I felt very comfortable in doing so. I was sent a letter about a possible production of a film showing our puppet films and all of our research into what it's like to be a teenager with speech and language difficulties. We were posted individual message recorders where we described ourselves about how we felt about living with speech and language difficulties and what we did in our daily lives which we passed on to Faye Smith (a member of the Research Unit). A few months afterwards, Tom Dalton came to visit our homes where we were filmed describing our hobbies and the events what we find difficult about communicating (unfortunately I was unable to be filmed due to a family bereavement). Professor Roulstone also came round to my house and asked me questions regarding the production of the film which I found very interesting.

The production of the film took quite a while and fifteen months after we all got together, we met in Bristol (November 2009) to see the production of the film and we also had discussions about our opinions on the film discussing what we enjoyed and what could have been improved, overall I really enjoyed it. At the beginning of the year (2010) I was sent a letter from Professor Roulstone about a premiere for the film which was shown at the UWE Frenchay Campus. I was really excited and on the evening we also received awards for our contributions to the production of the film (I was awarded for best script). Our own special talents helped to make the film a real success and I hope that other young people with speech and language difficulties find it interesting.

Taking part in a speech and language therapy research project is an exciting opportunity that can appeal to other young people like myself as it influences their ability to communicate with one another and develop positive interaction. I was a little anxious when I first took part in the research project but I started to settle in and became more involved when we all started to know each other and produced our ground rules. Feeling a little uneasy may be an inevitable feeling that young people with speech and language difficulties may experience when getting involved in group projects but people like myself would see it as a challenge. I have been used to relying on persuasive language in order to motivate me to get involved in group projects and situations that I am not used to. We learn from experiencing situations that we are not used to but I believe my involvement in the project has improved my ability to communicate with people and I feel more comfortable in group work and starting a conversation. There were no things that I didn't enjoy about the project and I am happy that we all had the chance to contribute to the production of the film. If other individuals with speech and language difficulties are invited to take part in similar projects, I would recommend becoming involved, the experience will be memorable.

Getting involved in the research project has really influenced me as I have become more confident and it has also improved my speech and communication which I am very grateful for. I send my thanks to all the team for such a wonderful opportunity for me to get involved in society.

Purpose of the project

This project was a participatory project with a group of teenage boys. In keeping with our aims of foregrounding and valuing the boys' perspectives this chapter began in the box above, with the perspective of one of our participants, who has written his report especially for this publication.[1]

This project aimed to explore the views of young people with speech, language and communication needs (SLCN) about what it is like to be a teenager with speech and language difficulties and to make a film that would share their perspectives with teachers, therapists, psychologists and other people working with young people. Research has shown that, for a high proportion of children who present with a range of speech, language and communication impairments in the early years, these difficulties persist into adolescence and adulthood (Johnson, Beitchman, Young, Escobar, Atkinson, Wilson et al., 1999; Snowling, Adams, Bishop & Stothard, 2001; Stothard, Snowling, Bishop, Chipchase & Kaplan, 1998). Difficulties with literacy, processing phonological and other language material, social behaviour and mental health have all been demonstrated through assessment tasks, surveys, observations and other experimental tasks. However, there has been little report of the perspectives of the young people themselves.

The young people

The project was open to teenagers in mainstream secondary school aged between 11 and 16 with primary speech and language impairment. The participants were recruited at an activity day organized by Afasic[2] in Bristol. After an introduction to the research, six young people and their parents expressed an interest and six boys attended the first workshop. After hearing more about the project and going through the consent process, five boys decided to continue. No girls came forward to be part of the project. As it was our prime intention to value the perspectives of the participants, we did not undertake formal assessment of the young people, nor did we seek confirmation of a diagnosis from medical or educational sources. Our intention was that participants

---

1   Editorial control of Robbie's contribution has been similar to all other authors – with corrections for occasional typos and minimal suggestions for rewording.

2   A UK national organization for parents and families of children and young people with speech, language and communication impairments (www.afasicengland.org.uk).

themselves would describe their difficulties to us. Since the parents were the prime initiators of participation in the project in the first instance, the inclusion of any individual boy is based on the parents' perception that their child has a speech and language impairment. This led to the inclusion of a broad range of speech, language and communication difficulties, beyond the usual definition of primary speech and language difficulties.

Investigators

Sue Roulstone is a professor and qualified speech and language therapist with experience of working with a range of children and young people with speech, language and communication needs. Clodagh Miskelly is a researcher and workshop facilitator who specializes in participatory research and participatory media methods. These two researchers were supported by a speech and language therapist who was experienced at working with teenagers and by various members of the film company – in particular, Tom Dalton who joined the project after the first 18 months to run the filmmaking component. Further information about who was involved in the project is given by Robbie, one of the participating teenagers, who provides his version of the process in the box above.

Method and procedures

Our approach was qualitative and participatory; that is, we used approaches aimed at ensuring that the participants had some degree of control over the process and its outcomes for both the research and the film. This was intended to enable young people to answer the research question from their own perspective and in their own way.

The project had two parts. First we held five half-day and three full-day participatory research workshops with a group of teenagers to explore their perceptions and views. The design and facilitation was intended to enable the participants to shape the process and outcomes of the research. Next, the young people and researchers worked with a film company, Brook Lapping, to produce a film.

The project took place in Bristol over an extended period, the workshops continuing over two years and the filmmaking process for a further 18 months. A range of activities were used to encourage the participants to reflect on and communicate about their experience as young people with speech, language and communication needs. The box below gives some examples of the activities that were used in the workshops. The workshops gradually led toward the filmmaking phase of the project as we worked with the boys to come up with ideas for the content and form of the film. This led into a one-day animation and puppetry masterclass and a two-day workshop where the participants produced animations and filmed shadow-puppet scenes.

Workshop activities

'Big Brother' diary room
- The boys made short videos of interviews. They built a set, designed the questions, operated the camera and directed the action and the lighting.

A typical day
- On large sheets of paper, the boys set out their typical day, using writing, drawings and stickers. They talked to the researchers about the ups and downs of the day and put stickers on to show how they felt about the different aspects of their day.

Storyboards
- Each participant was encouraged to make their own storyboard about something of interest to them or about an event that had happened to them. They presented these to each other and videoed their presentations.

Camera missions
- The boys were given a disposable camera and given a mission to accomplish. These included capturing: a day in your life/a tour of your bedroom/what makes you happy, sad, angry, laugh.

Following this, each boy was visited at home by filmmaker Tom Dalton. Material shot during the workshops by the boys, materials they produced in the workshops and their animations and footage shot by Tom in their homes was edited into a 25-minute film. This was viewed by the boys with their parents. The participants suggested some amendments to the film, which were carried out. The boys were very happy with the result and happy for the film to be shown to a wide range of people, including other young people.

The boys and their parents consented to being involved, with an understanding that they could opt out the project at any time and that their identities would be protected within the film. The boys expressed ideas for disguise and alternative identities for themselves, to be used within the film (see Figure 32.1). For example, one boy selected a Spike Milligan face, another selected the image of a soldier and another of a head full of fire, and yet another chose to have a cricket match as his identity. The producer then created 'masks' that were used periodically within the film. These have a dual function within the film, in that they conceal the boy's faces but also tell us something about their perceptions of their own identities.

Within the workshops, the boys understood that they could opt out of any activity or decline to answer questions. One boy always brought a book to read during activities. He would sometimes opt out in the first instance and read his book, but then join a discussion from the side of the room whilst still reading his book. Additionally the participants collectively agreed a set of ground rules for conduct in the workshops, including rules about behaviour, confidentiality and respecting each other's views.

Data included video footage, the boys' pictures, photos and writings. This was first organized by workshop. Videos from the half-day workshops were examined for examples of explicit communications from the boys about themselves, their language and communication. It would have been possible to make observations on the basis of their behaviours; however, children and young people with speech, language and communication needs are frequently the subject of observation by professionals, who then draw diagnostic conclusions about the nature of that person's impairments. In an attempt to ensure that we captured the boys' perspectives, rather than that of the researchers, we therefore focused on those communications from the boys which explicitly revealed their views about themselves.

Findings and outcomes

Through workshops we came to understand the young people's comfort zones

– the practices, contexts and topics with which they felt most comfortable and able or willing to participate, and in particular how they preferred to communicate or participate using different mediating technologies (e.g. video, mobile phone) or practices (e.g. improvisation) that they used. This had an impact on the filmmaking, because what the boys produced and how we worked with them helped shape the film and ensured that it was a film made *with* them (with researchers and filmmakers), rather than about them.

Reflection on issues

Throughout the process the young people did not directly address the question 'What's it like to be a teenager with communication difficulties?' There are many reasons for this, including their possible difficulties with metacognitive skills (see Dockrell & Lindsay, 2011, Chapter 17 in this volume, for discussion of these and related factors) or a possible lack of researcher skill in posing questions and activities that allowed participants to explore this question. However, over time, it became clear that the boys were puzzled by our focus and preferred to talk about themselves in more general terms and to focus on their hobbies and interests. Clearly, at the time, their own speech, language and communication was not of interest. The research question therefore shifted from its original focus on 'What's it like to be a teenager with speech language and communication needs?' to 'What it's like to be me?' The film became a collage of images that had emerged as an important aspect of their identities, showing five very different teenage boys who by making a film about themselves, rather than what we perceive as their difficulties, challenge us to see them differently.

Acknowledgements

We are very grateful to the five boys who participated in this project and gave up a number of Saturday mornings to work with us. Thanks also to Lesley Hemmings, who supported the workshops and gave valuable input into the planning of activities and subsequent interpretation of data. We would also like to thank the boys' families for bringing the boys to all the activities and for their interest in the project. Our thanks also go to Afasic for helping us to recruit the boys to the project.

References to this project

Speech & Language Therapy Research Unit (2010) *The Bristol project* [DVD]. Bristol: Author. Available from http://www.speech-therapy.btck.co.uk/News/Film Further details are available from info@speech-therapy.org.uk

References

Dockrell, J.E. & Lindsay, G. (2011) Cognitive and linguistic factors in the interview process. In S. Roulstone & S. McLeod (Eds), *Listening to children and young people with speech, language and communication needs.* London, UK: J&R Press.

Johnson, C.J., Beitchman, J.H., Young, A., Escobar, M., Atkinson, L., Wilson, B. et al. (1999) Fourteen-year follow-up of children with and without speech/language impairments: Speech/language stability and outcomes. *Journal of Speech, Language, and Hearing Research, 42,* 744–760.

Snowling, M., Adams, J., Bishop, D. & Stothard, S. (2001) Educational attainments of school leavers with a preschool history of speech-language impairments. *International Journal of Language and Communication Disorders, 36,* 173–183.

Stothard, S., Snowling, M., Bishop, D., Chipchase, B. & Kaplan, C. (1998) Language impaired preschoolers: A follow up into adolescence. *Journal of Speech, Language, and Hearing Research, 41,* 407–418.

Figure 32.1 Alternative identities for the participants.

33 Listening to Siblings of Children with Speech, Language and Communication Needs

Jacqueline Barr

Purpose of the project

The purpose of this investigation was to explore the experience of being a school-aged sibling of a child with a disability using sibling voices.

Children and young people

School-aged siblings were the participants. These siblings were children with brothers and sisters with a range of disabilities, including intellectual impairment, Down's syndrome, Asperger's syndrome, autism, cerebral palsy, Attention Deficit Hyperactivity Disorder (ADHD), cystic fibrosis, epilepsy, muscular dystrophy, spina bifida, physical impairment and anorexia nervosa.

Investigator

The investigator is a trained primary school teacher who is now working in the disability sector. Her qualitative PhD examines the experiences of siblings of children with disabilities in primary school settings. She also brings to her research personal experience of being a sibling of someone with both a disability and a chronic illness.

Method

In order to listen to siblings of children with speech, language and communication needs, one of the innovative methods used in this investigation was to use internet responses from an Australian-based sibling support forum as its data source. Responses came from child and adolescent siblings regarding their experiences of being a sibling of a child with a disability. The rationale for using this site was threefold. First, the administrating organization's focus on disability is broad, meaning that it was possible to gather data from siblings of children with a variety of disabilities. Second, the site is freely accessible to the public. Third, the site contained an extensive number of postings from siblings that comprehensively expressed the sibling experience.

Procedures

Every contribution made to the sibling support site over a 20-month period was downloaded. In total, 676 contributions were sourced. Contributions ranged in length from one sentence to four pages and detailed a number of different sibling experiences. Siblings composed their responses as comments, stories and poems and responses to questions presented by the site administrator. Typically, contributions were anonymous; however, some included first names or pseudonyms. Consequently, the contributions were de-identified before analysis.

Each contribution was assigned a number (i.e. from 1 to 676). Within this chapter, (#) indicates the number assigned to each quote. Errors, such as non- or incorrect capitalization and non- or incorrect usage of punctuation marks have been unchanged, giving a true representation of the contributors' thoughts, feelings and experiences. Simple spelling/typographical errors were corrected (e.g. 'form' instead of 'from') for ease of reading. Since it was not always possible to distinguish the sex of the contributor, all contributors are referred to as female.

Findings and outcomes

Two elements of the sibling experience emerged from a thematic analysis of the data: 1) Interactions with others and 2) Emotions. Deeper analysis of these elements revealed a number of themes and subthemes (Table 33.1) and a brief explanation of each is given below.

Strangers
Siblings indicated they felt sometimes embarrassed when their brother or sister's physical appearance or behaviour drew the attention of strangers.

Table 33.1 Themes outlining the sibling experience. Interactions with others.

Theme	Subtheme
Interactions with others	
Strangers	a) stare and I feel embarrassed b) have a negative attitude towards people with disabilities
Peers	a) don't understand what it's like to be me b) use certain words that upset me c) say nasty things about my brother/sister d) tease me about my brother/sister
My family	a) doesn't have a lot of time for me b) plans are often disrupted and I miss out on things c) give me a lot of responsibility and I worry that I'm not helping enough
Emotions	
Love	a) companionship b) unconditional love
Loss	a) sadness and guilt b) resentment
Gratitude	a) identity formation b) enhanced sibling bond
Collision of feelings	

One day my Mum, my brother and I went to the Zoo. Heaps of people were there and my brother was screaming and saying 'Ahhhhhhhhhhhhhhhhhhhhhhh, boggy, boggy' and 'dagdagdag'. Everyone looked at him while I took a few steps away from my brother to show that he was not my brother. I felt I should not have been in that family. (#184)

Siblings also indicated that people treated their brother or sister 'like a baby'. The question 'One thing that annoys me about the way my sib [sibling] is treated is...' was answered:

That my brother is treated like some sort of baby and people think that he can't understand things, but he can when he has enough time to take in the sentences. (#435)

Peers

Interactions with peers were another facet of the sibling experience where the contributors indicated difficulties, particularly with respect to feeling different:

[You] feel different from your friends because you have grown up faster and can't relate to them as well as you did, can't talk to friends about it because they don't understand or don't want to listen, even though you really need to talk about it, everyone always says 'how is your Sib [sibling] and mum and dad, gosh it must be so hard for them,' but they never see how hard it is to be the sibling. (#663)

Further, hearing unfavourable comments about their brother or sister were hurtful to siblings:

[Other children] say cruel hurtful things that no one deserves to hear. My brother is not retarded or a waste of space!!!!!!!!!! (#228)

My family

Many contributors indicated they felt they received less attention from their parents than their brother or sister:

> You feel like your parents care more for your brother or sister and it's like you're all left out. I feel like that sometimes (#662).

Siblings also spoke of the responsibilities that they undertook:

> My friends didn't go home to perhaps give their sister a bath, or feed her dinner (#48).

Feelings of grief for their parents were also apparent:

> I know many people have the same feelings of sadness mixed with a longing to not have it so for their parents. I often find it quite hard to deal with (#122).

Emotions

Love

Siblings typically viewed the relationship with their brother or sister as not impacted by the disability. Siblings' accounts of activities that they enjoyed participating in with their brother or sister were typical, and reference to the child's disability was not made.

> [We] play football in the backyard and [go] to the park together (#423).

Feelings of love for their brother or sister with a disability were evident in a number of contributions. Rather than focusing upon the limitations the disability brought, siblings described how the disability helped to make their brother or sister who they were:

> I love my brother for who he is and no one can change that (#175).

Loss

Siblings explained feelings of loss for the brother or sister that they could have had, coupled with loss caused by the disability's implications:

> I've always cried at the thought that my brother would never be normal. I always think that 'Why him? Why does it have to be him?' (#156).

Guilt was also described by siblings when explaining the limitations the disability placed on their sibling relationship:

> [When] my sister is trying to tell me something but I can't understand what she is saying, which upsets her and makes me feel guilty (#523).

Gratitude

Siblings' contributions also revealed the gratitude they felt because of their brother or sister's disability positively influencing siblings' identities.

> I have been shaped by my sister, and there are many other ways she's changed my life, but I wouldn't have it any other way! (#600)

Explanations of the enhanced bond that siblings felt with their brother or sister were also evident in contributions. One sibling stated:

> Life would be so boring not being one [a sibling]. You don't take anything for granted, you get so many more cuddles, it's the whole life experience that is great and rewarding (#591).

Collision of feelings

Siblings' collision of feelings was apparent when viewing explanations of their love and gratitude concurrently with their feelings of loss. One contributor explained the somewhat confusing experience of being a sibling:

> You see things about life that other people don't see and have to put up with things that other people don't have to put up with. You see the way that just because a person looks or acts differently does not mean that they are bad or weird, and simultaneously you have to put up with things like your sibling being in hospital for extended lengths of time

or knowing that you always have to be on guard against them choking and things like that (#598).

Implications for practice

Implications of this study are relevant to those working within the family-centred model. Health and education professionals need to be aware of siblings' interaction with others and the diversity of emotions siblings experience in relation to being the sibling of a child with a disability and the confusion this can cause. As trusted adults in children's lives, health and education professionals, as well as parents, can provide siblings with the opportunity to discuss their experiences. Educators should be well versed in the counselling options available to students in their schools and assist children in seeking advice from the school counsellor if needed. Similarly, health professionals can advocate to parents the need to listen to siblings' emotions.

Reflection on issues

The internet eliminates barriers of space and place and provides an emotionally safe environment allowing participants to disclose their experiences anonymously. When using the internet as a source of data, researchers must adhere to the ethical principles of research involving human participants. Gaining informed consent when using internet data may pose difficulties for researchers. The concept of *public space* can assist researchers in assessing whether the informed consent of individuals is required (cf. Keski-Rahkonen, 2005; Robinson, 2001). For this investigation, permission to download and analyze the responses was granted from the website administrator. The website is not named due to the ethical agreement between the author and the website administrator. Ethical clearance was also granted from the university ethics committee. Due to the public nature of the website, this investigation was considered exempt from requiring informed consent from individual contributors.

There are a number of cautions when using data sourced from the internet. First, there is no way to authenticate the sibling status of the contributors. Issues of reliability of this form of data can be overcome by researchers 'remaining true to the philosophical stance of the qualitative approach selected' (Strickland, Moloney, Dietrich, Stuart, Cotsonis & Johnson, 2003, p. 246). It is acknowledged that contributions used in this investigation may have been made by people who were not siblings of children with disabilities.

Acknowledgements

The author wishes to acknowledge the input of her supervisors, Professor Sharynne McLeod and Dr Graham Daniel.

References to other reports and write-ups of this project

Barr, J. (2006) Cavalry on the hill: The experience of siblings of children with communication impairments. Unpublished Honours dissertation, Charles Sturt University, Bathurst.

Barr, J. (in process) 'I'm not like most other kids': Sibling experiences of disability and implications for education. Unpublished PhD thesis. Charles Sturt University, Bathurst.

Barr, J. & McLeod, S. (2010) They never see how hard it is to be me: Siblings' observations of strangers, peers and family. *International Journal of Speech-Language Pathology, 12:2,* 162–171.

Barr, J., McLeod, S. & Daniel, G. (2008) Siblings of children with speech impairments: Cavalry on the hill. *Language, Speech, and Hearing Services in Schools, 39,* 21–32.

References

Keski-Rahkonen, A. (2005) The process of recovery in eating disorder sufferers' own words: An Internet-based study. *International Journal of Eating Disorders, 37,* 80–86.

Robinson, K.M. (2001) Unsolicited narratives from the Internet: A rich source of qualitative data. *Qualitative Health Research, 11:5,* 706–714.

Strickland, O.L., Moloney, M.F., Dietrich, A.S., Stuart, M., Cotsonis, G.A. & Johnson, R.V. (2003) Measurement issues related to data collection on the World Wide Web. *Advances in Nursing Science, 26:4,* 246–256.

34 Listening to Improve Services for Children and Young People with Speech, Language and Communication Needs

Sue Roulstone and Sharynne McLeod

Why listen?

Writings on the participation of children in decision-making and the need to take account of their views in all aspects of their care have proliferated over the last decade and a half. Many have written about the motivation for listening to children and indeed many of those arguments are rehearsed in earlier chapters of this book. Sinclair and Franklin (2000) summarized the arguments in eight reasons for involving children:

- to uphold their rights
- to fulfil our legal responsibilities
- to improve services
- to improve decision-making
- to enhance democratic processes
- to promote children's protection
- to enhance children's skills
- to empower and enhance the self-esteem of the children.

Many of the contributions in this volume have emphasized the political, legal and philosophical reasons for listening to children and young people. Sinclair (2004, p. 115) comments that 'children's participation is a value- or rights-based principle much like democracy, not something that has to be justified by evidence or which needs to "prove" that it works'. Within a culture of evidence-based practice, one might legitimately also ask about the impact that such involvement has on services. As Sinclair also notes, in the spirit of learning and improving participatory practices, one might at least want to know what works well and how one might improve practice. However, when Kirby and Bryson (2000) reviewed the evidence on the impact of children and young people's participation in public policy development and decision-making, they found little evidence for impact on strategic decision-making, although there were reported benefits to children and young people who participated, such as increases in confidence and skills attainment, having fun and making friends. Oldfield and Fowler (2004) found high levels of participation activity in their investigation of a wide range of voluntary and statutory agencies. However, they noted that this was mainly confined to young people in the 14- to 19-year age group with little engagement of children under the age of 8 years. Their respondents believed that children and young people had influenced policy and new developments particularly in the area of policies and services generally, with less influence about service delivery, monitoring and evaluation. In the time since then, there has been surprisingly little research of how children's participation impacts upon policy or service development, particularly in terms of children and young people with speech, language and communication needs, although there is more research on the process of children's participation. Percy-Smith (2009) reported, in an evaluation of children and young people's participation in two health trusts, that it was difficult to identify any direct impact of the young people through the formal decision-making channels, although there was a range of evidence that the young people's views were taken into account in decision-making and that the young people had effectively influenced decisions through their own initiated actions and lobbying. As with other participatory projects, the young people reported a range of personal benefits, particularly the increase of confidence and widening their own horizons and opportunities. These kinds of outcomes are also evident in Robbie's report (see Roulstone, Miskelly & Simons, 2011, Chapter 32 in this volume), where he comments on his increased confidence and improved communication. Such positive outcomes for participants are to be welcomed; the enhancement of their skills is clearly seen as a benefit of participation. However, Tisdall (2008) reminds us that 'participation is not therapy... and is meant to have some impact on decision-making'. So, whilst the enhancement of the children and young people's skills is an attractive advantage of their participation, it cannot be viewed as the prime purpose of the participatory process. As Tisdall also notes, the evidence suggests that children and young people are frustrated by participatory projects that are tokenistic and do not bring about real change in services or care. Percy-Smith (2011, Chapter 8 in this volume) commences his chapter with a quote that illustrates a young person's frustration with tokenistic listening: 'At the meeting we were told what was proposed and we put our views across about it. No one wanted the merger... But they did it anyway. They were just ticking boxes, because it looks like they are just listening to us even if they are not.'

The process of listening to the voices of children and young people has only recently begun to permeate the speech and language therapy literature. There has therefore been little debate of why we should be listening and encouraging their participation in decision-making. This book has brought together some of the key writers in the field of speech, language and communication needs and together they have covered most of the reasons set out by Sinclair and Franklin (2000) shown above.

In the context of services for children with speech, language and communication needs, there are perhaps two key aims to the process of listening to the perspectives of children and young people: to better understand the nature of the impairments that children and young people experience; and second, as a result of our improved understanding, to improve and/or (re) design services so that they are relevant to the needs of the children, young people and their families.

Understanding the impairment

Most of the literature to date concerning the nature of speech, language and communication impairments has focused on the skills and abilities of the children and young people as assessed by a variety of tests, experimental activities and standardized assessments. There are relatively few reports that provide the perspectives of the children themselves regarding the nature and impact of their speech, language and communication impairments, if indeed they perceive themselves to be impaired in these skills. Understanding the impairment from the perspective of the child or young person can indeed produce surprises (e.g. 'chocolate... makes you autism', Kelly, 2005, p. 261) and new insights into the nature of the impairment and therefore, possibly, in terms of ways to intervene.

At an individual child level, it is good practice to target those areas of functioning that are perceived by the child to be problematic. Such functional goals are considered to be crucial in motivating the child to achieve within the therapy process (e.g. Frost & Bondy, 2002) and are routinely considered when working with individual children. However, currently our theoretical models of speech, language and communication impairments do not include theories built from the perspectives of the children themselves. Once again, the authors in this book show themselves to be at the forefront of research in this area, providing new conceptualizations of speech problems that start from the child's perspective (for examples, see each chapter in Part III). When we listen to children's perspectives, for instance, we find that a speech impairment is a shared problem which includes a problem with the adult's listening as well as the child's speech (McCormack, McLeod, McAllister & Harrison, 2010).

The absence of the children's perspective in how we view the nature of these impairments is also apparent in intervention evaluation studies where outcome reports largely focus on the linguistic and cognitive skills of the children rather than on the broader impact of intervention, although this, too, is beginning to change. For example, in 1998, when Law, Boyle, Harris, Harkness and Nye first wrote their systematic review of interventions, they remarked that none of the studies reported outcomes in terms of the World Health Organization framework. In their latest update of the systematic review (Law, Garrett & Nye, 2003/2010), they report that there is evidence of an impact of intervention on children's socialization and behaviour, as well as parental stress and self-esteem, although they continue to remark on the need to address what they term as 'these second order effects'. Nonetheless, measurement of intervention outcomes tends to be carried out by the adult researcher rather than take account of children's perspectives on their own progress. The notion of 'patient reported outcomes' has been highlighted as a desirable method of evaluating the impact of services in a recent UK government White Paper (Department of Health, 2010), but the mechanisms for doing this have not yet been established as legitimate within our research field. Many of the authors in the present volume have provided insights into child-relevant outcomes (e.g. quality of life – Markham, 2011, Chapter 28 in this volume) and continued research and policy initiatives may see mechanisms for incorporating these into everyday practice.

Designing relevant services

In a qualitative evaluation of a participatory project, Percy-Smith (2007) identified three types of benefits to services that were perceived by the professionals engaged in their participatory project with young people. First, they felt that clear messages from the young people informed service planning: the adults commented that listening to the young people helped to inform planning so that services were relevant and acceptable to young people. Second, participation was felt to be supportive to the process of implementing national policy at a local level. Third, the service leaders felt that the young people brought directness to discussions that influenced the direction of policy to the needs of the young people.

Children and young people's perspectives then can provide information that can impact at a number of different levels when planning services. For example, in *The Bercow report: A review of services for children and young people (0–19) with speech, language and communication needs* (Bercow, 2008), teenagers showed some ambivalence to the delivery mechanisms of speech and language therapy in schools: 'And the SLT [speech and language therapist] came into school and that was embarrassing as well and one of my teachers was doing it with us as well' (A aged 15 years, in Roulstone & Ayre, 2008, p. 17).

Such children may appear to be lacking in motivation or unwilling to attend therapy sessions; understanding their perspective and giving them a voice in planning, not only their own particular intervention regime, but facilitating their contribution to more general planning and design processes may well improve the relevance of the intervention services for the whole age group.

How and when to listen

The wider literature contains a plethora of guidance for those undertaking projects that aim to engage children and young people and we have referenced some of these key websites and reports at the end of this chapter. However, within these reports there is no particular attention give to the particular issues and challenges of working with those who have speech, language and communication needs. Throughout the current volume, and particularly in Part III, our contributing authors have shared their expertise and reported on the techniques they have used in a number of different research and community-based projects. These reports provide illustrations of how we can listen to children and young people of different ages. In applying these techniques to practice contexts, it is possible to consider a child's individual therapy context or a service level context. For example, the *Speech Participation and Activity Assessment of Children* (SPAA-C, McLeod, 2004) described here in Chapters 21, 22 and 23 can not only be used as a research tool but also as a tool to support discussion between a therapist and individual children. This has some similarity in principle with the notion of the 'structured conversations', an idea that has been being evaluated in the UK in schools as a way of conducting discussions with individual children and parents about their learning needs and goals (Humphrey & Squires, 2011). Through a better understanding of the child's perspective, mutually agreed goals can be identified which focus interventions on those aspects of the child's problem of most value or importance to the individual. It can be all too easy to make assumptions about a child's needs, and the use of such tools within a culture of listening can aid the explicit discussion of children's perspectives.

In considering a whole service, the perspectives of children and young people can inform service improvements in three ways: in (re)designing services or aspects of a service, in solving problems and in the monitoring and evaluation of services. Following an exploration of user involvement in cancer services, Tritter, Daykin, Evans and Sanidas (2004) concluded that user involvement should not be a one-off activity but something that is integrated into the way that services are organized and delivered. So it is important to analyze the various components of our services to identify ways in which children and young people can contribute. The next section sets out a series of steps, adapted from Tritter et al. (2004), that can help to identify how to involve children and young people in service level issues.

Which children and young people use the service?

First, it is useful to consider the range of children who access a service, their ages, in which contexts they are seen (for example, children's centres, hospitals, home) and their presenting impairment or disability. By itemizing the range of children and young people that we come into contact with, we can ensure that at some point the perspectives of all are listened to. It is also important to reflect on those children who are missing, where we suspect (from the known prevalence and demographics of our area) that they are not accessing services. Finding ways to access these children and their families can be challenging and it may be necessary to identify contexts and activities that those children or their families already access, such as sports facilities or other childcare contexts, in order to meet up with them at all. Listening to the experiences of children who do not typically access services can help us to address aspects that are viewed as inaccessible.

Identifying the purpose

Having identified the range of children and young people associated with our services, we need to be clear about the purposes of listening. Being clear about this ensures that the listening is not a tokenistic process but has real meaning and carries with it the possibility that the children and young people can make an impact on services. Examples of the reasons for a listening project are shown in Table 34.1. Once a group of children and young people has been identified, then an initial step might be to work with them to develop a consensus statement about the purposes and the remit of their involvement.

Table 34.1 Purposes of listening to children and young people to improve health, education and social services.

Exploring children's experiences of services	It is important to give children and young people the opportunity to tell us what they think of our services; the good and the bad stories can help us to shape our future services.
Developing ideas for improving services	Children's experiences of service can help us to shape services, but they may also have direct ideas for ways to improve a service.
Problem-solving in tackling difficult service issues	If there are controversial or knotty problems to be solved, children and young people may have innovative solutions. They also may have a view on any solutions that professionals suggest before they are implemented and before planning is taken too far.
Monitoring standards	One way of auditing how well a service maintains standards is to ask the views of the children and young people who access those services – they may also have a view on the standards themselves. For example, if one of the standards is about maintaining a waiting list of no more than three months, it is useful to discuss that standard with the children to find out if that length of time is acceptable and meaningful.
Evaluating results and assessing the impact of services	In the UK, services are increasingly required to demonstrate their service users' views on the impact. It is no longer enough to demonstrate linguistic and communication outcomes; it is necessary to show how those outcomes make an impact on the lives of the children and young people themselves.

At what points in the system do we need to listen to children and young people?

The next step is to identify the children's journey through the service and the points at which we particularly need to listen and understand their perspectives. We may decide that we need the perspectives of children and young people about our referral processes, or about the mechanisms of assessments, or about the venues where we see them, and so on. Finally, following this analysis, one can then design the listening activity. In Table 34.2, we show some examples of how this analysis might work along with some related listening activities.

Table 34.2 Listening to children and young people at different times in their lives.

Children and young people	Purpose/question	Aspect of the system
Teenagers with primary language impairments in mainstream schools	Do teenagers prefer: to be seen in-class or in withdrawal; to have support from speech and language therapists or learning support assistants?	Providing intervention in schools
Possible activities A series of workshops in a number of secondary schools for a range of the teenagers, both with and without speech, language and communication needs, to explore views about receiving help. Ask the young people to design information that should be given to all children in the school about receiving help.		
Considerations Further defining the age group of young people that are the focus of this activity might be helpful in order to establish groups that can work together. Having someone else who knows the teenagers but who is not involved in the delivery of specialist interventions will enable the children to talk more freely.		
Children and young people	Purpose/question	Aspect of the system
Children in their last year in the infant classes of a special school and about to move into a mainstream school	What sort of support do children need and value as they move into a new school, move into mainstream schools?	Transition to new school and to a different aspect of a service

Possible activities
Invite children who made this kind of move in the preceding year to join in a workshop. Ask them what they would tell the children like them as they prepare to move school. Explore their experiences of moving school through pictures, looking at before and after the move.
Considerations
Providing children with a digital camera to capture places that are happy, sad, safe, fun, scary, boring, etc. can facilitate conversations about aspects of their new and old schools that should be maintained or changed.

Children and young people	Purpose/question	Aspect of the system
Children with speech impairment	To observe children's perspective on their progress	Impact of intervention over time

Possible activities
At agreed points in interventions that target children with speech impairments, children are asked to 'draw yourself talking to someone'. The speech and language therapists annotate the pictures with any comments that the children make about their pictures, and at the end of the intervention provide a summary of any themes that emerged (see McLeod, McCormack, McAllister, Harrison & Holliday, 2011, Chapter 21 in this volume, for further descriptions of this task).
Considerations
Children like to keep their pictures, so it is sometimes better to keep a photo of the picture, with the child's permission.

Conclusions

It is now an expectation that, as professionals, we will take account of the views of the children and young people who access our services. Despite this acknowledgement, reports have indicated that professionals demonstrate a reliance on the views of parents or other adults rather than seeking the views of the child directly (Franklin & Osbourne, 2009) and that children with speech, language and communication needs are not routinely involved in decision-making about their own care (Franklin & Sloper, 2006). Authors in this volume leave us in no doubt that launching into this kind of activity without careful planning is not to be recommended and can lead to a tokenistic approach that might be frustrating for the children and young people. Nevertheless, there is within the volume a wealth of advice and good practice on which to draw.

Working with individuals and groups of children and young people in order to understand their points of view can be an exciting new step. We can learn from their perspectives, and their voices can help us to improve the services we offer.

Useful websites/reports on this topic

Cambridgeshire Children's Fund and Save the Children (2005) *Are you listening? A toolkit for evaluating Children's Fund services with children and young people.* Retrieved from http://www.cambridgeshire.gov.uk/NR/rdonlyres/91176010-5FF3-4708-8449-1BA2D1CABD9F/0/AreyouListening.pdf

Kirby, P., Lanyon, C., Cronin, K. & Sinclair, R. (2003) *Building a culture of participation: Involving children and young people in policy, service planning, delivery and evaluation. Handbook. Department for Education and Skills and the National Children's Bureau.* London: Crown Copyright. Retrieved from http://www.audiencescentral.co.uk/resources/?id=78

New Commission for Children and Young People (2005) *Participation: Count me in: Involving children and young people in research.* Retrieved from http://www.kids.nsw.gov.au/uploads/documents/count_me_in.pdf

Shaw, C., Brady, L. & Davey, C. (2011) *Guidelines for research with children and young people.* London: National Children's Bureau. Retrieved from http://www.participationworks.org.uk/files/webfm/files/resources/k-items/ncb/Web%20guidelines%20CYP.pdf

References

Bercow, J. (2008) *The Bercow report: A review of services for children and young people (0-19) with speech, language and communication needs.* London: Department for Children, Schools and Families.

Department of Health (2010) *Equity and excellence: Liberating the NHS.* London: The Stationery Office. Crown Copyright.

Franklin, A. & Osbourne, C. (2009) *Independent reviewing officers' communicating with children with complex communication needs. An investigation for DCSF.* London: The Children's Society.

Franklin, A. & Sloper, P. (2006) Participation of disabled children and young people in decision-making within social services departments: A survey of current and recent activities in England. *British Journal of Social Work, 36,* 723–741.

Frost, L.A. & Bondy, A.S. (2002) *The Picture Exchange Communication System training manual* (2nd ed.). Newark, DE: Pyramid Educational Products.

Humphrey, N. & Squires, G. (2011) *Achievement for all: National evaluation. Department for Education Research Report 123.* Manchester: University of Manchester.

Kelly, B. (2005) 'Chocolate… makes you autism': Impairment, disability and childhood identities *Disability and Society, 20:3*, 261–275.

Kirby, P. & Bryson, S. (2000) *Measuring the magic: Evaluating and researching young people's participation in public decision making.* London: Carnegie Young People Initiative.

Law, J., Boyle, J., Harris, F., Harkness, A. & Nye, C. (1998) Screening for speech and language delay: A systematic review of the literature. *Health Technology and Assessment, 2:9*, 1–183.

Law, J., Garrett, Z. & Nye, C. (2003/2010) *Speech and language therapy interventions for children with primary speech and language delay or disorder.* Cochrane Database of Systematic Reviews, Issue 3. Art. No: CD004110. DOI: 10.1002/14651858.CD004110.

McCormack, J., McLeod, S., McAllister, L. & Harrison, L.J. (2010) My speech problem, your listening problem, and my frustration: The experience of living with childhood speech impairment. *Language, Speech, and Hearing Services in Schools, 41:4*, 379–392.

McLeod, S. (2004) Speech pathologists' application of the ICF to children with speech impairment. *International Journal of Speech-Language Pathology, 6:1*, 75–81.

McLeod, S., McCormack, J., McAllister, L., Harrison, L.J. & Holliday, E. (2011) Listening to 4- to 5-year-old children with speech impairment using drawings, interviews and questionnaires. In S. Roulstone & S. McLeod (Eds), *Listening to children and young people with speech, language and communication needs.* London: J&R Press.

Markham, C. (2011) Designing a measure to explore the quality of life for children with speech, language and communication needs. In S. Roulstone & S. McLeod (Eds), *Listening to children and young people with speech, language and communication needs.* London: J&R Press.

Oldfield, C. & Fowler, C. (2004) *Mapping children and young people's participation in England. Research Report no. 584.* London: Department for Education and Skills.

Percy-Smith, B. (2007) *Evaluating the development of children's participation plans in two Children's Trusts. Year one report.* Leicester: National Youth Agency.

Percy-Smith, B. (2009) *Evaluating the development of young people's participation in two Children's Trusts. Year two report.* Leicester: National Youth Agency.

Percy-Smith, B. (2011) Children's voice and perspectives: The struggle for recognition, meaning and effectiveness. In S. Roulstone & S. McLeod (Eds), *Listening to children and young people with speech, language and communication needs.* London: J&R Press.

Roulstone, S. & Ayre, A. (2008) *Consultation with parents and children: Report for the Bercow Review 2008.* Retrieved from www.speech-therapy.org.uk

Roulstone, S., Miskelly, C. & Simons, R. (2011) Making a film as a means of listening to young people. In S. Roulstone & S. McLeod (Eds), *Listening to children and young people with speech, language and communication needs.* London: J&R Press.

Sinclair, R. (2004) Participation in practice: Making it meaningful, effective and sustainable. *Children in Society, 18*, 106–118.

Sinclair, R. & Franklin, A. (2000) *A quality protects research briefing: Young people's participation*. London: Department of Health.

Tisdall, K. (2008, September) Children, young people and participation. Presentation at the *Getting it right for every child: Childhood, citizenship and children's services* conference, Glasgow, Scotland. Retrieved from http://www.slideshare.net/IRISSslides/listening-to-children-taking-children-and-young-peoples-participation-forward-kay-tisdall-presentation

Tritter, J., Daykin, N., Evans, S. & Sanidas, M. (2004) *Improving cancer services through user involvement*. Oxford: Radcliffe Medical Press.